COMMON INTEREST COMMUNITIES

COMMON INTEREST COMMUNITIES:
Private Governments and the Public Interest

Stephen E. Barton
Carol J. Silverman
Editors

Institute of Governmental Studies Press
University of California, Berkeley
1994

Library of Congress Cataloging-In-Publication Data

Common interest communities : private governments and the public interest / editors,
Stephen E. Barton and Carol J. Silverman.
     p. cm.
  Includes bibliographical references.
  ISBN 0-87772-359-1
  1. Homeowners' associations—United States. 2. Community organization—United
States. 3. Local government—United States. 4. Privatization—United States. 5.
Public interest—United States. 6. Condominium associations—Israel. 7. Condomin-
ium associations—Japan. 8. Condominium associations—Netherlands. I. Barton,
Stephen E. II. Silverman, Carol Janet.
HD7287.82.U6C65 1994
643'.1'06073—dc20   94-20963
                                                        CIP

To our parents—
Louis and Roz Silverman
Allen H. and Judith S. Barton

Acknowledgements

Numerous people have helped us in the preparation of this book and in the work that lead up to it. We would like to thank the California Department of Real Estate, which funded our Common Interest Development Study, and the Institute for Urban and Regional Development at the University of California, Berkeley, which helped us implement the study. This book would not have been possible without the support of the Institute of Governmental Studies, whose Harris Trust provided funding for a conference that brought together many of the authors in this collection. Members of the Community Association's Institute (CAI) and the Executive Council of Homeowners (ECHO) graciously gave of their time and resources to help us better understand the problems of common interest developments. Finally, we would like to thank the hundreds of members of common interest development governing boards and recent homebuyers who filled out our surveys and who agreed to be interviewed at length.

Contents

Preface

I.   Introduction   1

    1. History and Structure of the Common Interest   3
        Community
        Stephen E. Barton and Carol J. Silverman

II. Private Government and the Public Interest   15

    2. The Homes Association: Will "Private Government"   19
        Serve the Public Interest? (1967)
        Stanley Scott

    3. Common Interest Communities: Private Government   31
        and the Public Interest Revisited
        Stephen E. Barton and Carol J. Silverman

III. The Public Regulation of a Private Government   41

    4. The Many Faces of Community Associations under   45
        California Law
        Curtis C. Sproul

    5. Choice, Consent, and Citizenship in Common Interest   87
        Communities
        James L. Winokur

IV. Community and Political Life in a Private Government   125

    6. Shared Premises: Community and Conflict in the   129
        Common Interest Development
        Carol J. Silverman and Stephen E. Barton

7. Conditions of "Voice": Passivity, Disappointment, and   145
Democracy in Homeowner Associations
Gregory S. Alexander

8. Managing Interdependence: The Effects of   169
Neighboring Style on Neighborhood Organization
Carol J. Silverman and Stephen E. Barton

9. Community and Direct Democracy in a   193
Limited-Equity Cooperative
Allan Heskin and Dewey Bandy

V. International Perspectives on Condominium Governance
and Management   213

10. Social Control within the Israeli Condominium   217
System
Bernard Lazerwitz and Yona Ginsberg

11. Condominium Management in Japan   247
Tsuneo Kajiura

12. Condominium Regulation and Urban Renewal in   275
Dutch Cities
Jan van Weesep

VI. Conclusion   295

13. Public Life and Private Property in the Urban   297
Community
Stephen E. Barton and Carol J. Silverman

About the Authors   315

Preface

The spread of the common interest development has created a quiet revolution in the structure of community organization, local government, land-use control, and neighbor relations. The types of development included under the term common interest development seem familiar—condominiums, planned developments, and housing cooperatives. But these terms are most often understood as referring to a type of architecture or a lifestyle rather than to the complexities of property ownership that actually define them. Their residents, owners, and officers must deal with a remarkable yet little understood form of association.

These complexities are increasingly the norm rather than the exception, particularly in recently developed parts of highly metropolitan areas. Over 30,000,000 people live in common interest developments in the United States, and over 750,000 people serve on the boards of directors of the 150,000 homeowners' associations that govern them (CAI, *Community Associations Institute Factbook*, Alexandria, Va., 1993, p. 13). Once thought to house particular groups of people, such as the elderly, young singles, and the wealthy, they now contain people from all stages in the life cycle and almost all income levels.

The common interest development is a complex form of private property ownership that creates a community of homeowners. The community is based on common property interests—there is shared as well as individual ownership and a set of community rules governing the use of both common and individually owned property within the development. Private ownership in these communities creates not only individual rights but mutual responsibilities that are expressed through a mandatory homeowners' association to which all owners of shared property interests belong.

The owners' association manages the common property, sets and enforces community rules, and levies assessments on property owners to finance its activities. With the power to provide collective services, legislate, enforce the rules, and tax its involuntary members, the common interest homeowners' association is a private organization that looks very much like a local government—whence the common reference to them as "private governments."

The common interest development is seen as many things—a form of privatization, a type of grassroots community organization, a planning tool, and a new layer of local government. It is all of these things. The contradictions between them make these communities interesting and full of ironies.

Proponents of privatization regard common interest developments as part of the movement for privatization of functions performed by local government. Yet common interest developments are often forced upon reluctant private developers by local governments exercising their regulatory powers.

Local government planners regard common interest developments as a tool for flexible planning that allows more diverse neighborhoods than traditional zoning. Yet, once formed, common interest developments are more inflexible than the most rigid local zoning ordinances.

Many developers and sales agents claim that common interest developments offer homeowners "carefree living"—an escape from the stresses of both property management and public life. Others claim that they recreate and foster a sense of community among the residents. Yet residents of common interest developments are typically described as apathetic about their association. Those who become involved often experience the conflicts and stresses of local politics within the more emotionally explosive setting of private life.

Common interest developments are extolled by some as a form of grassroots initiative and as expressions of local democracy. Yet they are mandatory—"involuntary associations"—and profoundly undemocratic, denying residents who rent the right to vote.

This volume will explore the complex nature of common interest developments and some of the practical and theoretical issues they raise for the study of local democracy and civic involvement. The literature on this subject is sparse and often inaccessible, located in aspects of scattered journal articles, in parts of books, and in government reports. We have asked many of the people who have made contributions to the study of common interest communities to write chapters that focus on their contribution to our understanding of the civic role of the common interest community association. In addition, we have asked people who have written on this subject in other countries, often in languages inaccessible to most Americans, to contribute chapters. Then we brought these contributions together in one, accessible volume. All of these chapters are original except the second, which reprints a remarkable early critique of the community association from 1967.

We begin with an introductory chapter that describes common interest developments and their historical origins. The description draws on the findings of Barton and Silverman's statewide survey of California common interest developments, previously released as a report of the California Department of Real Estate in 1987. Most available surveys of common interest developments use the membership mailing lists of the Community Associations Institute, which includes predominantly the larger associations. The California study used state incorporation records, and thus included all but the few unincorporated associations in its sampling frame.

Part Two, "Private Government and the Public Interest," begins with an article written by Stanley Scott and published in 1967 in the *Public Affairs Report*, the journal of the Institute of Governmental Studies of the University of California, as the common interest development phenomenon was starting to spread. Scott criticized the effect of large planned developments with mandatory homeowners' associations on local democracy and on the diversity of local communities. Stephen Barton and Carol Silverman respond to this article 25 years later and find that Scott's concerns were remarkably prescient in the light of subsequent developments.

Part Three, "The Public Regulation of a Private Government," examines the legal framework by which state and federal governments establish the common interest development. James Winokur draws on a previous law review article to examine the basis for the legal "servitudes," the private regulations incorporated into the definition of property ownership that are the legal basis for the common interest community. He explodes the myth that they are nothing more than an expression of consumer choice in the housing marketplace, but he finds that it is too late to go back and proposes reforms that could gradually improve the quality of life in common interest developments and improve their linkage to the rest of society. Curtis Sproul reviews judicial characterizations of common interest developments as local governments and as private businesses, updating a law review article published a decade ago. He concludes that while they have similarities to both, the problems of common interest developments are best resolved by strengthening the nonprofit mutual benefit corporation law that currently governs them. Like Winokur, he desires both to strengthen the rights of homeowners within these associations and to make them more internally democratic.

Part Four, "Community and Political Life in a Private Government," examines the internal governing process of the common interest development. Gregory Alexander reports on a previously unpublished case study in which he found apathy, avoidance, and conflict among residents of upper-income planned developments in Arizona. He suggests that these residents lack a concept of citizenship within the development that could enable them to understand their relationship with their neighbors and co-owners. Silverman and Barton present the findings of their statewide survey of California common interest developments. The study found that internal conflict is widespread. Ironically, they suggest that the effort to create homogeneous communities of private property owners intensifies conflict rather than reduces it. Silverman and Barton then present a previously unpublished comparative case study of conflict in two very different homeowners' associations that illustrates the nature of these conflicts and shows that active citizenship is possible within the common interest development. They suggest that relations among neighbors affect the residents' ability to understand the nature of their mutual association. Alan Heskin and Dewey Bandy present part of a lengthy case study of a large limited-equity cooperative and provide evidence that the lower investment interest in a limited-equity cooperative facilitates conflict resolution. The structure of property rights within common interest developments clearly has a strong affect on internal political processes.

Part Five, "International Perspectives on Condominium Government and Management," examines the predominant form of common interest development in Japan, Israel, and the Netherlands. Tsuneo Kajiura, in a comprehensive overview of the problems of Japanese condominiums, reports serious problems in reconciling individual interests and collective governance that parallel almost every aspect of the problems of common interest developments in the United States. This is all the more striking since Americans typically see Japan as virtually the opposite of the U.S., with a high degree of social solidarity and a lack of individualism. Professor Kajiura has published extensively on condominiums in Japan, and this chapter makes his work available to an English-speaking audience. Condominium apartment ownership is the predominant housing form in Israel. Bernard Lazerwitz and Yona Ginsberg draw on a study done for the Israeli government to analyze the factors that make condominiums successful and examine their ability to link new immigrants to Israeli society. Many of the behavioral issues found in U.S. common interest developments do not exist in the same way for the simple reason that Israeli condominiums do not regulate behavior but rather treat that as primarily a problem for local government. In the United States, conversion of rental housing to condominiums is identified primarily with displacement of tenants and has been severely restricted by local governments for that reason. Jan van Weesep draws on his extensive research, only part of which is available in English, to describe how condominium conversion been used by local government in the Netherlands as a redevelopment tool to generate funds to renovate and preserve rent controlled housing. As in other countries, however, conflicts between owners are frequent.

The book concludes that the problems of conflict in the common interest community are part of a broader problem of developing and sustaining a supportive relationship between private and public life that exists in any democratic society.

I. Introduction

1

History and Structure of the Common Interest Community

Stephen E. Barton
Carol J. Silverman

All common interest developments share several essential characteristics: common ownership of residential property, mandatory membership of all owners in an association that governs the use of the common property, and governing documents that provide a "constitution" by which the association and its members are governed.

Common interest developments in the United States are organized in four legal forms, depending on whether homeowners own individual units or only a right to occupy a particular unit and whether the common property is owned in undivided interests by the owners or by an association controlled by the owners. The most common forms of common interest development are the condominium and planned development subdivision. In the condominium subdivision each owner holds title to both a unit and an undivided interest in the common property, with a homeowners' association that manages the common property. In the planned development subdivision each owner also owns a unit, but the homeowners' association both owns and manages the common property.

In the two types of cooperatives, both of which are rare outside of New York City, all property is held in common and each owner holds title to an exclusive right to occupy a particular unit. In the stock cooperative the property is held by a cooperative corporation in which each owner holds a share, while in the community apartment each owner holds an undivided interest in the whole property and it is managed by the owners' cooperative association.

A statewide survey of the presidents of the governing boards of California common interest developments found 67 percent identified their common interest development as condominiums, 26 percent as planned developments, one percent as cooperatives, and six percent were unsure of their legal identity (Barton and Silverman 1987; hereafter referred to as the California Common Interest Development Study).

Common interest developments are as disparate as housing developments in general. They encompass single-family detached houses, townhouses with shared walls, apartments, and combinations of all of these. They range from inexpensive townhouses or small apartments to luxurious detached homes next to private golf courses or spacious apartments convenient to symphony halls. They vary in size from two units to thousands of units and have responsibility for common property ranging from only a small lawn or some easements to the residential buildings to miles of private roads, water and sewer lines, elaborate recreational facilities, and private security systems. Some provide no services beyond necessary building and grounds maintenance while others provide security guards, garbage disposal, and even entertainment. See Table 1.1.

Historically, most apartment common interest developments in the United States have been organized as condominiums and most single-family detached common interest developments as planned developments, with townhouses divided between the two. There is no necessary relationship between legal type and physical structure, however. Despite the popular stereotype of condominiums as apartments the California common interest development study found that the majority were townhouses, single-family homes with shared side walls, and some developments of detached homes with common property are legally organized in condominium ownership. (See Table 1.2.) In some other countries, such as England, individual apartment ownership uses the legal structure of the planned development.

The median size of common interest developments in California is 43 units, with a mean of 88 units, according to the Common Interest Development Study. One quarter have 16 units or less and one quarter have 100 units or more. The trend is toward smaller associations, with the median size of associations formed prior to 1976 at 72 units and the median for subsequent associations at only 34 units.

Table 1.1. *Facilities Provided by California Common Interest Developments*

Open space or lawns	92%
Lawncare or gardening	87%
Park or playground	84%
Meeting place	72%
Garbage disposal	65%
Parking lot or structure	62%
Swimming facility	58%
Roads	43%
Water or sewer lines	42%
Other recreational facilities	21%
Entry guard or security patrol	15%

Source: California Common Interest Development Study, 1987.

Table 1.2. *Legal Type and Physical Structure of California Common Interest Developments*

	Condos	PDs	Coops	Unknown	Total
Detached Houses	4%	11%	0%	3%	18%
Townhouses	34%	11%	*	2%	48%
Apartments	24%	1%	1%	*	26%
Mixed	5%	3%	*	*	8%
Total	67%	26%	1%	6%	100%

*=less than half of one percent
N=573

Source: California Common Interest Development Study, 1987.

Common interest development services are paid for by monthly assessments on each unit, although some funds are raised through direct charges for use of particular services. Assessments are usually the same for all units, although some associations set them proportional to square footage or the number of bedrooms. In the California Common Interest Development Study the range of assessments reported ran from $1 to $1,500 monthly, but 80 percent charged between $40 and $175, with a median of $95. In addition, one quarter of the associations reported a special assessment averaging $200 for the previous year. While the sums involved are modest, they add up to a budget of about two billion dollars a year for all California common interest developments.

For both individual owners and for the association the consequences of nonpayment can be severe. Associations can place a lien on the property of an owner who fails to pay and even foreclose and take over ownership. The financial interdependence of the owners can also create hardships for those who pay their assessments. In declining developments where many owners fall into default, even walk away from their property, the remaining owners are burdened with all the costs of maintenance.

In the United States, common interest developments invariably have more or less elaborate systems of rules incorporated into the property. These conditions, covenants, and restrictions (CC&Rs) set out restrictions on what the owners can and cannot do with their own and the common property. They may restrict "nuisances" in very general terms, or may lay out detailed requirements for noise-dampening floor coverings, the allowable size, number, and species of pets, and what kinds of plants may be placed on decks or balconies. They often set detailed rules covering the outward appearance of dwellings, covering the color of drapes and blinds and the color and style of screen doors.

CC&Rs typically govern changes in dwelling units, even if the units themselves are individually owned, restricting additions, the installation of skylights, and the placement of antennas and basketball hoops. And they govern the use of common property, including the walls, floors, and ceilings of units where the homeowner owns only the airspace on an individual basis. The rules govern everything from parking to use of a swimming pool. Not all the details may be in the CC&Rs. Some will be set by the homeowners association using the authority granted by the CC&Rs. But CC&Rs tend to be set up to give the association very little flexibility.

The CC&Rs also set out the governing procedures for the homeowners' association. The governing board of the homeowners' association is usually chosen in elections with one vote per unit owned. Traditionally the powers of the governing board are closely circumscribed. In the California Common Interest Development Study over 60 percent of associations reported that a supermajority of more than 50 percent plus one was required to approve a special assessment. The majority vote typically required to raise monthly assessments is usually based on the total number of potential votes, rather than the number who actually chose the vote, so that failure to vote counts as a negative vote on any proposed increase.

Modern common interest developments have their historical origins in eighteenth century London, where exclusive residences were built around private parks, held in trust for the exclusive use of the surrounding owners. Small developments based on the English model were built in the United States in the middle of the nineteenth century; New York's Gramercy Park in 1831, Boston's Louisburg Square in 1844, and San Francisco's South Park in 1852. These developments not only provided private parks and streets closed off from the rest of the city by gates, but also were protected by covenants restricting the use of the land to residential purposes and specifying the acceptable race, religion, and even drinking habits of the occupants (Urban Land Institute 1964; Weiss and Watts 1989; Shumate 1988).

A variety of means was used to handle ownership of the common property. The park and streets in Gramercy Park were owned by a trust, with a board of trustees that was elected by the 60 homeowners. Louisburg Square's 28 homeowners formed what may have been the first actual homeowners' association through the agreement of all owners after the individual lots had already been sold. The original developers had recorded covenants in the county land records that established architectural and land-use controls. The new owners added provisions for regular assessments to pay for the upkeep and improvement of the park and streets and for election of the "Committee of the Proprietors of Louisburg Square" by a majority vote of those attending the annual meeting.

South Park was planned for 69 homes on Rincon Hill in the South of Market area of San Francisco, but only half was completed as planned. Its residents were unsuccessful in efforts to stop a street widening project, the Second Street cut, which removed a large part of Rincon Hill, opened the area to commerce, and destroyed the area as a haven for the wealthy. After the cut was completed in 1869 apartment houses were built on some of the remaining lots, homes converted to apartments or commercial uses, and the park was eventually sold to the city.

Around 1900 planned developments entered a new phase. With a greatly expanded upper-middle-class market, large developers were able to plan entire neighborhoods with a thousand homes, rather than under a hundred. These neighborhoods provided private parks and infrastructure, which was not yet available from city governments in outlying suburban neighborhoods. Initially deed restrictions lasted only five to 15 years but were gradually extended until they became permanent. Developers also learned to establish homeowners' associations to manage the common property and enforce restrictions and began to grapple with the difficulties of the transition from developer to homeowner control.

In 1891 the Roland Park Company began a series of four neighboring developments in Baltimore with from 700 to 1,200 homes in each. Construction was not completed until the 1930s. The developments had common parks and streets, and the deeds to each home had covenants that restricted land uses but did not establish mandatory homeowners' associations before the lots were sold. As a result, in two neighborhoods it took 18 and 26 years to pass control over to homeowners' associations, while in one neighborhood disagreement among neighbors lead to creation of two voluntary homeowners' associations, with the Roland Park Company remaining in charge of enforcing covenants and managing the common property. In the 1930s one homeowners' association sued the company to stop construction of garden apartments nearby and finally bought the land for a park.

Another successful early association was St. Francis Wood, with 500 homes, built in 1912 in San Francisco. Like the Roland Park developments it was designed by Frederick Law Olmstead and equipped with private streets, parks and tennis courts, and covenants establishing detailed architectural and use controls, racial restrictions, and a mandatory homeowners' association. The association ran into difficulties because covenants set assessments at a fixed level that was gradually overtaken by inflation. Voluntary assessments paid by most members enabled the association to continue (Barton 1985; Weiss and Watts 1989).

As municipal service capabilities improved in the 1920s and 1930s, St. Francis Wood and many other associations gave their streets and some parks to the city government to maintain. By the 1980s, in a time of fiscal retrenchment for local governments, private streets were once again being proposed as a means to upgrade neighborhoods (Newman 1981; Oakerson 1989)

Radburn, begun in 1929 in New Jersey, was one of the few planned developments without express racial restrictions, and even Radburn apparently discriminated in practice. Radburn was the product of the efforts of the visionary Regional Plan Association of America to create a model garden city, which they hoped would inspire the reconstruction of American metropolitan areas. They intended that Radburn would be a vehicle for local democracy and, as soon as the first residents moved in, established the Radburn Citizens Association, which conducted a wide range of social and cultural activities for residents. Meanwhile the Radburn Association, formed before residents moved in, held ownership of and took care of the common property such as park land and roads. While the Citizens Association was run by the residents, who oversaw the activities of a paid recreation director, the majority of the governing board of the Radburn Association were not homeowners until 1938, nine years after the first homes were sold (Ascher 1953; Schaffer 1982).

Unlike most political associations, the "constitution" of the common interest development homeowners' association is not created by its first members, but rather by the subdivision developer, who often maintains influence for some years after the first residents move in. While the residents' difficulties in reaching agreement after they move in suggest that this is a sensible practice, even today the issue remains of how best to prevent abuse by the developer, both in the rules and procedures established and in the transition to homeowner control.

Mandatory homeowners' associations did not only exist where there was common property to maintain. Restrictive covenants were a well-known tool for exercising control over a community, and as early as the 1850s developments with restrictive covenants against alcoholic beverages were established by temperance societies (Schwartz 1976). Zoning proved to be a better tool for most purposes, since it enabled the local government to shoulder the expense of enforcement and could be passed by a majority rather than requiring unanimous consent or prior creation by a developer. Developments with deed restrictions were still favored in upper-income neighborhoods, where they allowed a degree of detailed architectural control only recently achieved by some local governments with design review ordinances.

When the U.S. Supreme Court held racial zoning unconstitutional in 1916, neighborhoods had to rely on private agreements to uphold racial segregation. During the 1920s the mandatory homeowners' association spread into thousands of neighborhoods as a means of enforcing racially restrictive covenants. This was an effort to hold back the spread of urban black communities, which gained population when industrial employment opened up to African-Americans during World War One. These single-purpose associations faded out rapidly after 1948 when the U.S. Supreme Court held that government enforcement of racially restrictive covenants was also unconstitutional. Mandatory homeowners' associations without common property remained influential only in a few areas such as Houston, where mortgage lenders required their use because the city has no zoning ordinance. (Long and Johnson 1947; Vose 1967).

In 1960 the mandatory homeowners' association was a familiar concept, but there were still less than 500 homeowners' associations with common property in the United States, mostly in upper-middle-class planned developments (Urban Land Institute 1964). This was soon to change.

A more urban form of common interest development, the housing cooperative, got its start under the auspices of labor unions in New York City during the 1920s. Influenced by European thinking about ways to provide better housing affordable to workers, the cooperative also spread to provide a form of homeownership for middle- and upper-income residents in areas dominated by apartment buildings. Cooperative ownership never gained broad market appeal outside New York City, however.

To deal with consumer dislike for the shared rather than individual ownership in cooperatives, developers adopted a new approach—what one treatise called "Condominium: The New Look in Co-ops" (Ramsey 1961, cited in van Weesep 1987). Condominium ownership combines individual ownership of apartments with shared ownership of the building and other common property. The new condominium homeowners' associations were then modeled on existing planned development homeowners' associations, with the same detailed restrictions on what owners could do with their individual units and in the common areas.

In 1961 the federal mortgage insurance system revised its rules to include condominiums and cooperatives and model state enabling legislation for condominium subdivisions was passed by all 50 states beginning with Hawaii in 1961 and ending with Vermont in 1969 (van Weesep 1987). By 1970 between condominiums, planned developments, and cooperatives there were as many as 10,000 common interest developments and their homeowners' associations. By 1990 Community Associations Institute estimates of the number of common interest developments had reached 150,000.

The exponential growth of common interest developments was a response to nationwide demographic, economic, and fiscal changes. Families were smaller, with fewer children. Dramatic increases in housing costs compared to income culminated in the 1980s in the first decline in homeownership rates since the Depression of the 1930s. In response developers greatly increased production of smaller and less expensive townhouses and low-rise apartments (Dingemans 1975).

Economic stagnation, reductions in federal transfers to local governments, and property tax limitation movements also made it harder for local governments to pay for the infrastructure and services new developments required. Many local governments responded by requiring the developer to provide such infrastructure as streets, street lighting, water and sewer lines, parks, playgrounds, and parking areas. Making these facilities remain privately owned, with a mandatory homeowners' association that is responsible for the maintenance further reduces costs to local government (Longhini and Mosena 1979; Dowden 1980). Thus, for example, the Bay Area city of Fremont (best known perhaps as the home of Olympic skating gold medalists Brian Boitano and Kristi Yamaguchi), once provided a recreation center and swimming pool in each neighborhood. After the passage in 1977 of Proposition 13, which limited property taxes, Fremont began to require that a common interest homeowners' association provide these amenities in new developments.

Finally, expanding downtown financial and service districts in some cities lured higher-income people to central city neighborhoods with easy access to work and cultural facilities. The new residents' desire for homeownership was met by conversion of tens of thousands of apartments from rental to condominium ownership. In turn, the desire to protect tenants from eviction and prevent the loss of more affordable rental housing lead hundreds of local governments to pass laws restricting condominium conversion.

Somewhat to the surprise of their critics, a substantial minority of condominium apartments continued to be rented (HUD 1980). While this preserved rental opportunities, it created new problems for homeowners' associations who now had to deal with having resident tenants who were not eligible to be members of the association and landlord owner-members who were not residents and were unlikely to participate in the affairs of the association. Whatever their relationship to the larger society, the early planned developments were associations of equals and cooperatives normally forbid any but temporary rentals. With the spread of condominiums a fundamental inequality became an important part of association life.

The numbers of common interest developments continue to grow at a rapid pace, especially since about half of U.S. population growth during the 1980s took place in three states, California, Florida, and Texas, where common interest developments are a familiar part of new housing development. At least 1,000 new common interest developments are created each year in California. In Orange County over 80 percent of all new housing was in common interest developments, while about 60 percent were in common interest developments in San Diego County and most of the Bay Area, including the counties of Alameda, Contra Costa, San Francisco, San Mateo, and Santa Clara. Overall, 40 percent of all new ownership housing built in California in the late 1980s was in a common interest development (Construction Industry Research Board 1989).

During the 1970s and 1980s the common interest development, a once minor form of local organization, became part of the lives of millions of people. Estimates of the number of common interest developments in the United States range up to 150,000 nationwide, with at least 15,000 in Florida and 20,000 in California. This is more than three times the number of local government bodies, including everything from counties, cities, and towns to school, water, and mosquito abatement districts. With an average size in the neighborhood of 80 units, this implies that there are about 12 million units of housing that are part of common interest developments, with as many as 30 million residents. There are 1.8 million units in California alone, with about four million residents. With a typical governing board of five people, there are as many as 750,000 people nationwide and about 100,000 Californians serving as elected officials in these associations.

There are many aspects of the common interest development that have not yet been adequately explored, perhaps because of the apparent familiarity of their constituent parts—private property, homeownership, homeowners' associations. But under this familiar guise, the common interest development blends institutions in very unfamiliar ways. It uses private ownership to create not only individual rights but mutual responsibilities. These responsibilities are expressed through the mandatory homeowners' association, an organization that can be characterized paradoxically as either an involuntary association or a private government. An examination of the experience of residents and owners as they grapple with this form of community allows us to better understand such basic American institutions as homeownership, private property, and local democracy.

REFERENCES

Ascher, Charles S. 1953. "Private Covenants in Urban Redevelopment." In *Urban Redevelopment: Problems and Practices*, ed. Coleman Woodbury. Chicago: University of Chicago Press.

Barton, Stephen. 1985. "The Neighborhood Movement in San Francisco." *Berkeley Planning Journal*, Vol. 2, No. 1-2: 85-105.

_____, and Carol J. Silverman. 1987. *Common Interest Homeowners' Associations Management Study*. Sacramento: California Department of Real Estate.

Construction Industry Research Board. 1989. "Average Price and Distribution of New Home Sales by Type of Ownership: California and Selected Counties." Pasadena.

Dingemans, Dennis J. 1975. "The Urbanization of Suburbia: The Renaissance of the Row House." *Landscape*, Vol. 20, No. 1: 20-31.

Dowden, James C. 1980. *Community Associations: A Guide for Public Officials*. Washington, D.C.: Urban Land Institute and Community Associations Institute.

Long, Herman H., and Charles S. Johnson. 1947. *People Versus Property: Race Restrictive Covenants in Housing*. Nashville: Fisk University Press.

Longhini, Gregory, and David Mosena. 1979. *Homeowners' Associations: Problems and Remedies*. American Planning Association Advisory Service Report #337, Chicago.

Newman, Oscar. 1981. *Communities of Interest*. New York: Doubleday.

Oakerson, Ronald J. 1989. "Private Street Associations in St. Louis County: Subdivisions as Service Providers." In *Residential Community Associations: Private Governments in the Intergovernmental System?* Washington, D.C.: Advisory Commission on Intergovernmental Relations, May.

Schaffer, Daniel. 1982. *Garden Cities for America: The Radburn Experience*. Philadelphia: Temple University Press.

Schwartz, Joel. 1976. "Evolution of the Suburbs." In *Suburbia: The American Dream and Dilemma*, ed. Phillip C. Dolce. Garden City, N.Y.: Anchor Books.

Shumate, Albert. 1988. *Rincon Hill and South Park: San Francisco's Early Fashionable Neighborhood*. Sausalito: Windgate Press.

United States Department of Housing and Urban Development Office of Policy Development and Research. 1980. *The Conversion of Rental*

Housing to Condominiums and Cooperatives: A National Study of Scope, Causes, and Impacts. U.S. Government Printing Office, Washington, D.C.

Urban Land Institute. 1964. *The Homes Association Handbook.* Washington, D.C.

Van Weesep, Jan. 1987. "The Creation of a New Housing Sector: Condominiums in the United States." *Housing Studies*, Vol. 2, No. 2: 122-33.

Vose, Clement E. 1967. *Caucasians Only: The Supreme Court, the NAACP and the Restrictive Covenants Cases.* Berkeley: University of California Press.

Weiss, Mark A., and John W. Watts. 1989. "Community Builders and Community Associations: The Role of Real Estate Developers in Private Residential Governance." In *Residential Community Associations: Private Governments in the Intergovernmental System?* Advisory Commission on Intergovernmental Relations, Washington, D.C.

II. Private Government and the Public Interest

Editors' Note

In February 1967 Stanley Scott published his pioneering critique, "The Homes Association: Will 'Private Government' Serve the Public Interest?" Scott raised doubts about the increasing use of mandatory homeowners' associations in the development of new housing and called for efforts to develop more desirable alternatives. In Scott's view, large homeowners' associations that provided important community facilities weakened citizens' connection with their local government; their exclusivity encouraged economic and racial segregation, thus weakening the civic fabric of American society; and the central role of the private developer and the requirement of property ownership for membership in the association weakened local democracy.

Scott's point of view was simply ignored in the ensuing 20 years, while the use of common interest homeowners' associations grew from a few hundred planned developments and condominium subdivisions to an estimated 150,000 such developments. Only in 1983 did a similar critique emerge in Richard Louv's *America II*, a scathing commentary on the major emerging trends in American society. Louv proclaimed common interest communities to be a "shelter revolution" that would permanently change American notions of private property, privacy, local government, and the single-family home.

Stephen E. Barton and Carol J. Silverman, using a study of common interest homeowners' associations in California, revisit Scott's critique 25 years later and find that it holds up very well. Democracy within the associations was often incomplete, with developer influence on the associations lingering even after most of the homes have been sold and a substantial proportion of disenfranchised renters in most common interest developments. Few links were in evidence between mandatory homeowners' associations and local government. In addition, the professionalization of maintenance seemed to discourage the self-help activities traditional for many homeowners and risked creating financial difficulties among working-class and first-time homebuyers. And the use of perpetual private covenants, rather than zoning, to control land use risks freezing development patterns in place when they are no longer appropriate.

Today it is unrealistic to think that the use of some form of common interest development can be avoided. Every year the routine practices of local governments, developers, planners, and architects add several thousand new common interest developments nationwide. Developers use them to provide common areas and facilities that no single owner could afford and to make homeownership affordable in areas where high land costs mean only densely constructed housing is economically practical. Cities require them as a means to pass the cost of maintaining certain public facilities over to a private association of homeowners. Architects and planners promote them because these features also promote creativity and environmental sensitivity in design and land use. It is all the more essential, then, that we understand the difficulties created by the associations that govern these developments and develop better designs for the associations as well as the land and buildings.

2

The Homes Association: Will "Private Government" Serve the Public Interest?

Stanley Scott

In 1964 the Federal Housing Administration (FHA) outlined a new policy on planned-unit housing developments. This represented a major change in attitude, permitting much-needed flexibility in community design and encouraging experimentation with new patterns of cluster housing and imaginative use of open space, parks, recreational facilities, and other amenities in FHA-supported developments. In an effort to ensure that the additional flexibility would not also allow future down-grading of the communities through subdivision or other undesirable use of the reserved open space, FHA's new policy was accompanied by a forceful endorsement of *automatic homes associations*[1] to own the open space and other common properties. If not modified, this policy will

---

This report is based in part on work done for the Center for Planning and Development Research, in the Institute of Urban and Regional Development, University of California, Berkeley. Views expressed are the author's own, and do not necessarily reflect those of John W. Dyckman, Chair of the Center, or William L. C. Wheaton, Director of the Institute.

[1] An automatic homes association is a nonprofit corporation operating under recorded land agreements, which owns and controls common neighborhood properties. Each lot owner is a member, and each lot is subject to a charge for its proportionate share of expenditures necessary to maintain the common properties.

probably result in establishment of long-lived homes associations in much of the best large-scale urban residential development to be built with FHA financing.

This is a disquieting thought, for reasons discussed below. Doubts were first raised by FHA's publication on planned-unit development.[2] They were not allayed by the subsequent appearance of a meticulously researched and well-edited but distinctly partisan Urban Land Institute (ULI) report on whose background research FHA had based its home association policy.[3] These documents have now been followed by a market-acceptance survey that confirms earlier misgivings.[4]

SUMMARY OF CRITICISMS

Basic criticisms of the FHA-ULI homes association policy are summarized in the following paragraphs. First, the assignment to homes associations of open space, parks, and other important community facilities *bypasses the local governments* that could appropriately be designated as custodians of such property. Second, the associations have been and presumably will continue to be employed primarily in upper-middle and high-income residential areas. Any significant inclusion of multiple dwellings appears to be discouraged by FHA policies, and the lower-income brackets are viewed as a likely source of special problems. Policies of *exclusiveness* are only thinly veiled as efforts to "maintain high standards," or "insure property values," or provide a "private community."

Third, the automatic homes association and its binding covenant would be designed and *established by the developer* before a single house had been sold—that is why they are called "automatic." Yet anything so important as the life of a community as control of open space or management of other shared facilities is sufficiently affected with the public interest to justify a strong public role during the formative period, when the community-to-be is without residents.

---

[2]U.S. Federal Housing Administration, *Planned-Unit Development with a Homes Association* (Land Planning Bulletin No. 6, Rev. 1964).

[3]Urban Land Institute, *The Homes Association Handbook* (Technical Bulletin 50, October 1964).

[4]Urban Land Institute, *Open Space Communities in the Market Place . . . A Survey of Public Acceptance* (Technical Bulletin 57, December 1966).

Fourth, for the protection of his own interests, FHA-ULI urge the *developer to retain control* of each homes association during the initial period of community growth. He is expected to exercise a strong benevolent paternalism in determining the composition of the association's leadership and influencing its early policies. But this puts too much power in the developer's hands. Surely alternative methods can be found for a more publicly responsible stewardship during the formative period. Fifth, despite its generally glowing account of the virtues of home associations, the 1964 ULI report recognizes some real difficulties in making these *"private governments"* work effectively and responsibly.

Sixth, recommendations against mixing owners of single-family homes and renters of multiple-family dwellings in the same association encourage "institutionalization" of *segregated* housing patterns. Seventh, association *voting is based on ownership*; consequently renters would have no voice in the governance of common facilities affecting their daily lives and supported by their rent payments. Eighth, the legitimate desire for maximum financial stability and security of the housing developments —*viewed as investments*—appears to be given such overriding importance that it may obscure other equally important goals. Ninth, despite their drawbacks, homes associations are now being widely promoted, partly because there has been *a failure to invent* more desirable alternatives.

LOCAL GOVERNMENT DISMISSED

The possibility of using local government instead of homes associations to own and manage open space and other common properties is dismissed rather summarily:

Although this study focused on development with private organizations of home owners, there were some subdivisions reported which have followed the public route for common area maintenance. This means that a local public body accepts ownership and/or responsibility for operation and maintenance of common areas within the development. The desirability of such an arrangement is questionable, particularly in cluster developments and others with common facilities directly related to the homes, since the use of general tax funds for maintenance of facilities requires availability of such facilities to the general public. The special district may be able to avoid this problem by taxing only the residents of the specific area affected. The suitability of private operation of common areas closely related to groups of private properties remains doubtful.[5]

"PRIVATE" COMMUNITIES AND EXCLUSIVENESS

Emphasis on the importance of private control is elaborated subsequently, when the undertone of exclusiveness is made explicit:

A PRIVATE COMMUNITY TO COMPLEMENT HOME PRIVACY. . . . In addition to the private home, the resident has a *private community*, that is the homes association's common properties and the members using them. . . .[6]   [Emphasis supplied]

Size is important in judging the desirability of "private" control over common properties as well as the concept of a "private" community. It would be difficult to find fault with an association as small and intimate as the one serving Greenwood Common in Berkeley, with its 12 lots and "postage stamp" open space that is closely related to the homes. But the developments envisioned by ULI are typically very much larger than this and the common properties of more general ability. Approximately half of the automatic homes associations surveyed by ULI contained between 200 and 999 living units. The report speculates on even higher population potentials when discussing the large new communities:

Large central common areas and community-wide facilities will be brought into existence in new satellite communities, new towns, and other very large developments. The needs here are best met by creating not only an association for each cluster of several hundred homes, but also an association for the larger area embracing numerous smaller associations. The large association provides those facilities and services used on a broad scale to serve the larger community area. . . .[7]

Under this policy the common properties in communities containing many *thousands* of inhabitants would be controlled by homes associations. While any maximum figure must be chosen rather arbitrarily, a strong case can be made that properties and facilities suitable for public

---

[5]Urban Land Institute, *The Homes Association Handbook* (1964), 12.
[6]*Ibid.*, 143.
[7]*Ibid.*, 220.

use,[8] and serving populations of several hundred persons, are of such importance to the community that local governmental ownership should be given serious consideration. When the numbers served reach into the thousands, a blanket policy calling for government by private associations becomes highly questionable. For different reasons the 1964 ULI report recognizes size as a consideration in the employment of homes associations.[9]

"BENEVOLENT" PATERNALISM: CONTROL BY DEVELOPER

Whatever its size, the association would be established by the developer before any lots were sold and would be controlled by him for an extended period, probably until the community is half to three-fourth complete:

The developer should incorporate the association before selling any lots. . . .[10]

. . . the developer must retain strong control over the association in its early stages to prevent a premature transfer of title and premature assessments by the association, and to coach the association to a good start.[11]

The ULI Report of December 1966 is, if possible, even more emphatic in urging outright manipulation by the developer.

It is a serious error for a developer to give up control of the association during the early years . . . he should control the directors and officers as well as have voting control for at least two or three years, or until he has finished most of his program.

---

[8]Community facilities that may be assigned to homes associations include open space, golf courses, parks, playgrounds and recreation centers, stables, riding and walking trails, swimming pools, lakes and beaches in waterfront communities, social and cultural centers, and so on.

[9]For example: "Size Makes a Difference . . . Small Associations Can Be Informal . . . " (p. 249). "Very Large Associations Can Be Unwieldy . . ." (p. 249). ". . . since homes associations have fewer functions than town governments, there is even less reason for residents to attend large unwieldy meetings. Therefore, large homes associations should adopt the representative form of meeting" (p. 272).

[10]Urban Land Institute, *The Homes Association Handbook* (1964), 208.

[11]*Ibid.*, 233.

John Fisher, of Fisher and Frichtel of St. Louis, operates a highly successful association. . . . His basic advice about associations is, "Rule 'em with an iron hand."[12]

Such arrangements obviously do not ensure adequate consideration of the residents' legitimate interests, should they conflict with those of the developer. And the 1966 ULI report plainly states: "Homeowners' interests may be just the opposite of the developer's."[13] Perhaps local government should play a role from the beginning, looking after the residents' interests and mediating possible developer-resident disputes.

The 1964 ULI report is disarmingly frank, however, in suggesting practical strategies and techniques to maintain effective developer control, hopefully without the new homeowners being fully aware of what is going on:

> The developer starts an association with officers and a board of directors of his own choosing. For a considerable period, he needs to retain control over the association, *preferably without displaying or directly exercising it.* [Emphasis supplied]
>
> Developers may use several methods of choosing board members. A developer may appoint only employees or friends. Of course, he may then be accused of stacking the deck in his own favor. He may appoint reputable community leaders to serve as directors or trustees. Although such directors usually enjoy the confidence of the residents, they may lack the necessarily familiarity with the development and its problems. This may be especially true when the development is in the lower-income bracket and the directors come from the higher economic strata. In this bracket, however, the success of the association may require the presence of some outside source of guidance on a continuing basis.[14]

PATTERN OF SEGREGATION "INSTITUTIONALIZED"

The reference to the "lower-income bracket" brings up other themes that lie just beneath the surface of the reports. The reader gets a distinct impression that the authors do not wish to contemplate—and do not

---

[12]Urban Land Institute, *Open Space Communities in the Market Place...* (1966), 71.

[13]*Ibid.*, 72.

[14]Urban Land Institute, *The Homes Association Handbook* (1964), 242.

anticipate—any significant inclusion of multiple dwellings or low-income residents in the planned communities:

> Developments with multifamily structures pose a special problem in terms of membership and voting rights. . . . These problems are absent where the number of multifamily living units in the development is no greater than a relatively minor percentage of the entire number of living units.[15]

> Current interest in townhouses and other high density residential development should not divert attention from the fact that most association developments to date are land subdivisions of single-family detached homes. . . . The homes association concept should be widely used to produce better neighborhoods of detached homes. . . .[16] (It should also be noted that most of the associations studied were composed of medium-high to high-priced residences.)

Furthermore, to the extent that multiple dwellings and renters *would* be involved, the 1966 ULI report urges separate associations for each group, to avoid mixing single-family homeowners and multiple-dwelling renters in the same organization. Again, this emphasizes the "institutionalizing" of segregated housing patterns that the homes association policy would encourage:

> In a large development where there are several different areas of single-family houses, townhouses, and garden or other apartments, there is need for separate associations for each group. Normally, *renters and home owners have different interests* and do not mix well in an association.[17]

RENTERS ARE DISENFRANCHISED

Developer-manipulated associations do not adequately protect homeowners' interests. Nevertheless, owners would be a good deal better off than the disenfranchised renters:

---

[15]*Ibid.*, 209.

[16]*Ibid.*, 144.

[17]Urban Land Institute, *Open Space Communities in the Market Place...* (1966), 72.

. . . the dues for renters are paid for by the developer or apartment house owner, which usually means *the renters do not get voting rights.*[18] [Emphasis supplied]

Presumably the expense of maintaining the common properties would ultimately be paid by the renters. For this reason, as well as for the sake of simple fairness and equity in a democratic society, residents of multiple dwellings ought to have a say regarding the conditions of the communities in which they live. Yet the homes association device would deprive them of any effective voice. Disenfranchisement would be obviated if the common properties were entrusted to a responsible local government.

THE OVERRIDING GOAL: FINANCIAL SECURITY

Another underlying theme is the need to protect the mortgage-holder's investment and the government's mortgage guarantee. The goal of financial soundness is stressed so much that one fears it may obscure other desirable goals for urban communities. This comes out rather clearly in a comment on lower-income developments:

Greatly needed, especially in lower-income developments, will be a director or directors representing local financial institutions, especially mortgage-lending organizations. We recommend a by-law provision for nomination of candidates by local banking or lending organizations holding mortgages in the development.[19]

Financial stability is obviously important and should not be sacrificed. Neither should other desirable goals for the future of urban communities be sacrificed to the single overriding end of maximizing investment security. This is particularly true when FHA financing is involved and the public is the ultimate insurer.

OTHER GOALS

This critique of the new FHA policy and Urban Land Institute reports should not be taken to suggest that many of the goals being sought are not good ones, or that the methods outlined will not accomplish the ends desired. Obviously some of the very best housing developments in the

---

[18]*Loc. cit.*

[19]Urban Land Institute, *The Homes Association Handbook* (1964), 243.

country are made up of high-priced, single-family structures in exclusive neighborhoods where there are neither low-income groups nor multiple dwellings. Many of these neighborhoods have retained their character over long periods of time partly (sometimes in large part) because of the restrictive covenants running with the land and the automatic homes associations that enforce the covenants and manage the properties. It is equally obvious that many of these developments have been very sound investments that seldom, if ever, gave their mortgage holders a sleepless night.

Yet our society has important goals other than the creation of high-quality, upper-class, single-family, amenity-filled neighborhoods whose property values are secure and whose homeowners never fail to meet a mortgage installment—laudable as some of the latter objectives may be. In the next two or three decades, residential patterns will be established or rearranged and many other features of existing and future urban communities determined. The policies under which this is done will influence fundamentally the quality and nature of future urban life. Decisions made during this period will also influence the role, strength, effectiveness, and perhaps even the survival of our institutions of *public* local self-government.

The FHA-ULI reports outline what appear to be blanket policies that would help to freeze neighborhood patterns under long-term restrictive covenants and entrust major open space, parks, recreation, and other community facilities to private "governments." These would be established by the developers and presided over by private, pseudo-legislative bodies subject to deliberate manipulation. Uniform and national application of such policies to all FHA-supported new communities built in the foreseeable future—during the crucial era of urban restructuring that lies ahead—could be most unfortunate, desirable as some of their immediate and concrete results may be in specific situations.

As was suggested earlier, some of the shortcomings of the policy stem from its adoption for two limited and related aims: first, to ensure the maintenance of property values, and second, to stabilize residential patterns for relatively long periods. The restrictive covenant and the homes association appear to have been seized upon because their legal basis is well established, they are easy to utilize, and they favor the interests of the developer and lender in almost every way.

ASSOCIATIONS NOT THE FINAL ANSWER

We should not be satisfied—as FHA and the Urban Land Institute appear to have been—with the assumption that the home association provides a final answer. The association looks more like a stop-gap alternative that should be employed cautiously until better arrangements can be worked out.

The fact that associations are recommended *at all* for large-scale development is strong evidence that existing local machinery does not provide adequately for the interim period of community building. Answers to questions raised by the homes association device will lie partly in further work on prototypes for new public mechanisms to deal effectively with the problems of large communities, particularly during their period of development.

Several possibilities occur. The special taxing district controlled by a city or county is one likely approach. The city of Los Angeles, for example, has adopted an "Open Space Maintenance Districts Ordinance."[20] In unincorporated areas, variations on California's "County Service Area" concept could be tried, tailored to fit the individual state's pattern of local institutions.

Despite the criticisms presented here, it should be frankly recognized that the developer-controlled association may have advantages during the early stages because the existence of attractive and well-managed community facilities encourage sales. In the initial marketing phases of a project, the prudent developer will perceive his self-interest in getting a good job done.

But public ownership possesses other long-range advantages. First, the larger community interest can be safeguarded from the start. Second, the superior fundraising capabilities of local government will probably

---

[20]City of Los Angeles Ordinance No. 129.015: "The purpose of this ordinance is to form districts within the city within which property may be assessed to pay the costs and expenses of improving and maintaining open spaces belonging to the city. . . . The Board of Public Works of the City of Los Angeles shall have complete charge, supervision and control of all open areas maintained or improved pursuant to the provisions of this ordinance. . . . The Mayor, subject to confirmation by the council, may appoint an Advisory Board composed of five property owners within a district, which Advisory Board may make recommendations to the Board of Public Works with respect to the work and operation of the open areas."

prove more helpful in later years when the costs of maintaining, replacing, or enlarging the common facilities may soar. Third, early public dedication would make the common properties tax free from the start. Fourth, appreciation in the value of the properties would accrue to the community.

But the developer's interest in well-managed facilities suggests another possible approach: an initial period of joint public-developer stewardship. The developer could be required to dedicate the open space and other facilities to the appropriate local government at the beginning, but under contractual terms giving him a voice in their management during the marketing period.

Obviously further thought and experimentation with new forms of community facility management are essential. The state and national associations of municipalities and countries would be well advised to place the topic high on their agenda of unresolved "new community" issues. Perhaps the Advisory Commission on Intergovernmental Relations should examine the problems, as well as state-level bodies like California's Intergovernmental Council on Urban Growth.

Whatever is done, it should be done soon. Meanwhile FHA and the developers, for lack of a superior prototype, are methodically seeding many of the best new urban communities with long-lasting automatic home associations.

3

Common Interest Communities: Private Government and the Public Interest Revisited

Stephen E. Barton
Carol J. Silverman

Twenty-five years ago, Stanley Scott asked of the common interest homeowners' association—"Will 'Private Government' Serve the Public Interest?" (1967). Scott argued that large developments with mandatory homeowners' associations might pose certain dangers to a democratic society. They would be socially divisive, increasing segregation by income and housing status. They would be undemocratic, allowing real estate developers undue influence over the community and disenfranchising renters. And they would give priority to private interests, cut the connection between residents and local government, and reduce concern with broader public interests. He called for a slow-down in the use of this means of development while better alternatives were developed.

At the time Scott wrote, there were only a few hundred such associations. Today there are an estimated 150,000. It is undoubtedly too late to slow down the creation of these communities, but surely we have enough experience to evaluate his warning and to discuss potential reforms in the structure and use of the common interest homeowners association. In doing so we will draw particularly on the California Common Interest Development Study (Barton and Silverman 1987).

DO COMMON INTEREST DEVELOPMENTS LEAD TO A
MORE RIGID AND DIVIDED SOCIETY?

Scott's first set of concerns were with the effect of the common interest development on the structure of society. The developments he focused on were large, encompassing entire neighborhoods, and were sold to middle- and upper-income homeowners. They typically provided extensive private infrastructure and services, such as guarded entrances, which enhanced their exclusivity.

There is certainly reason to remain concerned about creation of such separate societies. Particularly with the cutbacks in local government's fiscal capacity over the past decade, large new upper-income developments may provide their residents with services, including roads, street lighting, parks, and playgrounds that are simply not available to the residents of the older sections of a developing county. In recent hearings before the California legislature, concern was expressed over the development of a "two-tier" society in growing rural counties.

But while creation of large-scale new communities continues, the trend is toward greater numbers of smaller common interest developments. The 1987 California Common Interest Development Study reported a median size of 34 units for developments built in the 1980s, compared to a median of 72 units for those built prior to 1976. The typical common interest development in California today is composed of 34 townhouses occupying all or part of a block in an already developed suburban setting. Its common facilities are typically a small amount of shared green space, a private driveway and guest parking area, and perhaps a pool. The median resale price was $125,000 in 1987, close to the median home price for the state of California at that time. Residents of these developments reflect the racial diversity of the neighborhood in which they live and typically include a minority of renters with lower incomes than those of the resident owners.

While most common interest developments are not large and exclusive, they can contribute to exclusion in another way. The land uses in these developments are set not only by local government general plans and zoning ordinances, but by conditions, covenants, and restrictions that are incorporated into the definition of the property of each homeowner. Where large numbers of low-density, single-family developments have such CC&Rs, this has the potential effect of freezing land uses in place in perpetuity and inhibiting the future growth and development of urban areas.

As the economy and population of a metropolitan area develops, densities gradually increase. People add second units to their homes, and detached homes are replaced by low-rise apartment buildings. This is typically considered a form of urban blight by real estate analysts, whose predecessors developed the early common interest communities precisely to prevent neighborhood change and avoid such a fate. But one person's blight may be another person's home.

The effect of large areas filled with covenanted developments is likely to be quite different from the effect of a mere handful of protected neighborhoods. Such a form of development, in suburban areas with increasing amounts of employment, can prevent increases in housing supply near jobs. As a result, housing prices and rents will increase due to a shortage of housing affordable to ordinary workers. The result can be substantial hardships for renters and new home buyers, although there are financial rewards for the older homeowners whose property increases in value.

The normal political power of homeowners is sufficient to greatly slow development that changes the character of existing neighborhoods. This is entirely appropriate, since rapid change can be psychologically very difficult for people to deal with. Nonetheless, the political system should be able to balance the human costs of in-fill development and the environmental costs of growth pressures that are redirected to the urban fringe and be able to change land uses to higher densities that make efficient use of massive public investments in rail transit. The result of widespread use of private covenants may be to make it impossible to adapt. States may find that they need to override certain covenants legislatively in the public interest.

Finally, even the lower-priced, higher-density developments that are affordable to working class and lower-middle-income buyers bring new problems for those buyers. Traditionally, many such homeowners make substantial use of their own labor and skills in fixing up their homes as well as in adding to their home as children are added to the family. Such flexibility and use of "sweat equity" are not permissible in many common interest developments.

To start with, owners can not change their houses at will—the association has architectural controls and in most townhouse and apartment developments the building structure is common property, requiring permission from all owners in order to make changes. Moreover, the association decides when to make repairs, hires contractors to make them, and decides how they will be paid for. Volunteer labor is sometimes used for unskilled tasks such as road repair, play area construction, and painting, but the association board of directors is legally responsible to all the owners for the quality of the work done.

Traditional homeownership allows the owner whose income is reduced or expenses increased by illness, unemployment, new children, or retirement to defer maintenance and improvements. A major purpose of common interest homeowners' associations is precisely to ensure a uniform standard of maintenance. This may benefit the majority by helping keep up property values in the neighborhood, but at the cost of hardship to homeowners in difficulty. The effect is worsened by the reduced scope for do-it-yourself work by the homeowner.

The governing board of directors of a typical small association manages an annual budget of over $50,000, negotiates with a variety of contractors, and enforces detailed regulations concerning the use of common and individual property without the assistance of a paid professional manager. Thus the association substitutes management for maintenance as the type of skill needed among the homeowners. All of this suggests that the idea of privatizing public housing will prove far more difficult than the simple slogans of homeownership for low-income people might suggest.

ARE COMMON INTEREST DEVELOPMENTS UNDEMOCRATIC?

In the early stages of a common interest development the most powerful influence is the developer. The developer decides on and attaches the conditions, covenants, and restrictions to the property. These covenants establish the association and provide its "constitution." The association normally remains under developer control until 75 percent of the homes are sold.

Even after control has formally passed to the owners the developer may continue to exercise disproportionate influence. In a system with one vote for each home, the developer will hold a block of votes until all units are sold. In addition, developer control may be supported by employees or professionals whose services were compensated with ownership of a unit, rather than entirely in cash. And developers may vote the proxies of investor owners who buy units to rent out and then retain the developer to provide management services. In some cases the developer has remained in control of or been represented on an association's board for many years.

Developers of course have a major interest in protecting their investment in the new development while they are selling it, but may also wish to maintain influence in the association in order to keep ongoing costs and monthly assessments low while they sell their remaining units and to prevent litigation over construction defects. Homeowners' associations report widespread problems with construction defects and with monthly assessments that were initially set too low to maintain the property in order to make units more attractive to new buyers. In the California Common Interest Development Study, 24 percent of board presidents reported litigation or threats of litigation over construction defects. Associations with a developer on the board of directors, however, were less likely to have a preventive maintenance plan or to have studied reserve needs, were less likely to report construction defects or excessively low assessments, and were far less likely to have taken legal action against the developer.

Typically the association's constitution makes it very difficult to change rules established while the association is under developer control. Rule changes will typically require agreement of more than a majority, often two-thirds or three-quarters of the property owners. Thus even the failure to vote counts as opposition to any proposed action, making it particularly difficult to make changes in associations with absentee owners as well as those with developer-owned units.

With voting rights in the association based on property ownership, residents who rent are disenfranchised. Only 21 percent of California common interest developments reported being entirely owner-occupied. The median association reported 20 percent of the units occupied by renters, while in 14 percent of associations a majority of the units are rented (Barton and Silverman 1987). As a result, homeowners who expected an association of their peers may find a peculiar situation, in which residents who rent are not members of the association and cannot vote, while owners who do not live in the development are members of the association and can vote. Investors who own more than one unit have more than one vote.

With renters kept outside the association they are less likely to follow its rules. Indeed, renters are generally not directly responsible for rule violations, rather the property owner is responsible to the association and the renter is responsible to the property owner. The absentee owners are typically less interested in the association than resident owners and are less likely to participate in it or even to vote. The upshot is a serious loss of human resources for the association.

Most industry professionals and government officials we interviewed felt that it was entirely appropriate that developers exercised control over the "constitution" of the association and that voting was based on property ownership. In their view owners in common interest developments are partners and investors in a business that owns and manages real property. These investors have freely chosen to buy in such developments and should take responsibility for their choice.

Each of these views is only a partial truth. In order to have a genuine choice people must also understand what they are choosing. Yet even real estate agents who sell this kind of property often have a poor grasp of the special nature of the common interest development and its owners' association. A survey of homebuyers found that misinformation and lack of understanding were widespread among buyers in common interest developments (Silverman, Barton, Hillmer, and Ramos 1989). Moreover, in some areas very little is available that is not in such a development.

Resident homeowners have both investment interests and use interests in their homes and in the development, while when units are rented these interests are split, with the owner having only an investment interest and the tenant having the interest in the actual use of the home. As a result, absentee owners are likely to oppose changes that increase the quality of life but that cost more than the corresponding increase in the value of the property.

An appropriate recognition of the dual nature of the interests in the common interest development would be to give two votes to each unit, one for the residents and one for the owner, with both being voted by resident owners. An alternative approach used by some associations is to forbid or limit renting out homes in the development. This approach diminishes the pool of rental housing at a time when fewer people are able to buy and is dangerous to the investment value of the home purchase because it forces people to sell if they have to move, even if the market for homes is currently weak.

Finally, common interest homeowners' associations have rule enforcement powers that are commonly exercised in ways that are offensive to normal conceptions of due process of law and the separation of powers. The association board of directors passes rules, prosecutes violators, and then judges the guilt or innocence of the people involved. A few associations use the more appropriate means of employing third-party arbitrators to hold hearings on rule violations. Government assistance is needed to establish such an arbitration system, since few arbitrators are familiar with the specialized problems of common interest developments.

DO COMMON INTEREST HOMEOWNERS ASSOCIATIONS STRENGTHEN OR WEAKEN CIVIC INVOLVEMENT?

On the surface, common interest homeowners' associations represent a flowering of local participation. With 150,000 associations nationwide and an average board of directors of five people, there are 750,000 volunteers serving on the governing boards of these associations and a total membership of as many as 20,000,000 people. There are about 100,000 board members in 20,000 associations in the state of California alone. At least one political scientist has argued that such associations are more durable, better at mobilizing resources and thus preferable to voluntary neighborhood associations (Rich 1980).

But the nature of involvement in an "involuntary association" is different from that of the voluntary association in important ways. To start with, the associations' governing board exists to maintain the association and provide services to the homeowners. It is an inward-looking form of organization, unlike the voluntary association, which is primarily concerned with mobilizing neighbors to influence the local government that is the primary provider of local services. The associations we have studied generally avoided taking stands on electoral issues outside the development on the grounds that this was the prerogative of the individual member. They feared that conflict over outside issues would weaken the association. Government affairs committees were rare, usually composed of a single individual who wanted to be involved in local issues. Association activism was limited to zoning and permit issues with immediate impact on the development itself. Mandatory membership seems to depoliticize the association.

In certain areas, however, entire cities or unincorporated areas are composed of common interest developments. This is particularly true in certain parts of southern California, with cities such as Irvine. In such cities, local government usually has regular and formal ties with the homeowners' associations. In addition, common interest homeowners' associations in unincorporated areas have taken the lead in working to incorporate as cities, in order to gain control over public services and land-use decisions in neighboring areas. Most of the small number of elected officials who come out of common interest homeowners' associations in California come from cities in which virtually every neighborhood is a common interest development (Boyer-Stewart 1991).

Some have argued that homeowners' associations do encourage participation, but only of a sort that builds on their inward-turning and exclusionary nature. Mike Davis, in his history of Los Angeles, has argued that homeowners' associations played an important role in exclusionary use of environmentalism to prevent construction of rental housing, to try to keep out minorities, and to lower taxes (Davis 1990).

Scott was concerned that common interest developments that provided their own services would break the connection between citizens and local government. Especially with limits on local property tax revenues, common interest developments have been used by local governments as a way to require residents of new developments to pay for some of their own services while still paying local taxes. Residents in such developments have an incentive to oppose taxation that supports public services that they already provide and pay for themselves, however.

"Double taxation" is a frequent concern within publications aimed at common interest homeowners' associations and their managers, and in New England a large number of associations did begin a campaign to get tax credits for the services they provided. We know that mandatory homeowners' associations played an important role in the antitax movement that helped pass Proposition 13, the California property tax limit, in 1977 (Lo 1990). Unfortunately, public opinion surveys do not ask about membership in mandatory homeowners' associations, so we have no clear evidence about the influence that membership in such associations actually has on voting on tax and bond issues.

Finally, the transfer of responsibilities from local government to the homeowners' association creates important problems for the membership. The processes of representative democracy insulate neighbors from many direct conflicts. In most cities, neighbors who disagree with each other on a proposed second story addition or the necessity of street repair confront a third party such as a planning commission or a city council. In common interest developments these neighbors confront other neighbors. The board of directors is seen not as trustees of the public interest, but as neighbors with unfair powers over others, and the mixture of political and personal conflict can poison neighbor relations.

Similarly, in local government the use of a professional police force and a staff of inspectors to enforce building, health, and fire codes helps insulate neighbors from direct confrontation over local regulations. But in many common interest developments the board of directors of the association takes on the task of enforcing association rules. People whose cars are ticketed or towed for parking in the wrong place sometimes react with great hostility, including threats of violence, against what they see as the abuse of power by a neighbor rather than as the necessary enforcement of association rules.

Social scientists commonly argue that skills in participation, knowledge of the democratic process, and concern for the public interest are learned in America's many types of association memberships. One must wonder what is actually learned in an association based on property ownership rather than residence or citizenship. They are, however, one of the most widespread and rapidly growing types of associations in the United States and an integral part of the housing available to its citizens.

CONCLUSIONS

Common interest developments are intricately intertwined with local, state, and larger quasi-governmental bodies. As we have said above, many associations would not have been formed, save for local government requirements. Local communities require developers to use the common interest form since it permits the infrastructure to be privately owned and maintained and thus reduces municipal costs. Associations' legal status and quasi-governmental powers are established and increasingly regulated by state government. Finally, secondary mortgage market lending restrictions affect the ability of people to sell their units and the subsequent quality of life in the association.

The growth in common interest developments is transforming the urban and suburban landscape, not just physically but also politically, yet the consequences have not been sufficiently recognized. When these larger issues are considered, as was the case in special state assembly hearings in California in 1989, the dominant impulse is to write such developments off as private—and not properly a subject for government concern. Yet, as we have argued, the common interest development is shaped by local governments through their land-use powers, and the state that regulates their governing structures. Inattention now has long-term consequences in the future as common interest developments comprise ever increasing percentages of residences in the United States.

REFERENCES

Barton, Stephen E., and Carol J. Silverman. 1987. *Common Interest Homeowners' Associations Management Study.* California Department of Real Estate, Sacramento, October.

Davis, Mike. 1990. *City of Quartz: Excavating the Future in Los Angeles.* New York: Verso.

Lo, Clarence. 1990. *Small Property, Big Government: The Property Tax Revolt.* Berkeley: University of California Press.

Rich, Richard C. 1980. "A Political-Economy Approach to the Study of Neighborhood Organizations." *American Journal of Political Science*, Vol. 24, No. 4: 559-92.

Scott, Stanley. 1967. "The Homes Association: Will 'Private Government' Serve the Public Interest?" *Public Affairs Report: Bulletin of the Institute of Governmental Studies*, Berkeley: University of California, Vol. 8, No. 1, February.

Silverman, Carol J., Stephen E. Barton, Jens Hillmer, and Patricia Ramos. 1989. *The Effects of California's Residential Real Estate Disclosure Requirements.* California Department of Real Estate, Sacramento, October.

Stewart, Robin Boyer. 1991. "Homeowner Associations Sally Forth into the Political Wars." *California Journal* (April): 268-72.

III. The Public Regulation of a Private Government

Editors' Note

Like all forms of private property, the common interest subdivision is a creation of government. The rights and obligations of property ownership are defined by laws that are fought over and amended in local, state, and federal legislative bodies, interpreted by judges, and enforced by police and sheriffs. Yet government creates private property for the purpose of giving legal, governmental protection to a domain of private action that is, within its limits, free from restraint by government as well as by private persons. Some would then argue that having established private property rights, government's only role is to defend them. But it is no obvious matter to determine the content and extent of the rights that government should defend.

The mutual rights and obligations of the owners in a common interest subdivision are established as covenants or deed restrictions—what legal scholars call "servitudes"—that are incorporated into the definition of the property that is owned. There are extensive and centuries old legal debates over the appropriate limits to servitude restrictions. Some argue that they are accepted by the free choice of the buyer and should not be altered or limited by government, while others, like James Winokur, argue that much more is involved.

In "Choice, Consent, and Citizenship in Common Interest Communities" Winokur argues that many homebuyers in common interest developments have exercised only the appearance of choice where servitudes are concerned. Looking for a home in a desired neighborhood most buyers understand little about the accompanying servitude restrictions or the homeowners' association, the "servitude regime," that governs the development. He suggests reforms that place more emphasis on the association as a democratic body and on allowing the flexibility necessary to develop among the residents a sense of being citizens in a community.

The characterization of the common interest community as a "private government" contains an implicit reform agenda. In a democratic country we expect all governments to be democratic. This would imply, most strikingly, that each adult resident have one vote, including tenants. The role of tenants in these communities, and any rights they should have to participate in decision making within the association, however, have yet to become part of any active political agenda.

Where government endorses the exercise of private power over members of a group, it often sets standards for the exercise of that power. Thus the Securities and Exchange Commission protects stockholders in corporations from the most flagrant abuses by corporate management and boards of directors. The National Labor Relations Board protects workers' rights against both management and against the unions that represent them. Florida has established a Bureau of Condominiums, with an owners' "Bill of Rights," and in California legislation has been proposed that would create a similar Department of Common Interest Developments.

Another approach to protection of the public comes in the decision over the appropriate body of law that the courts should apply to common interest developments. In "The Many Faces of Community Associations under California Law," Curtis Sproul argues that common interest homeowners' associations are a complex phenomenon involving aspects of a real estate business and aspects of a local government, but that the legal standards these models imply cannot be fully applied without doing violence to some of the character of these associations. Instead, dealing specifically with California but with broader applications for the principles involved, he proposes to require that all community associations incorporate as nonprofit mutual benefit corporations, as most of them are already. He then proposes to amend mutual benefit corporation law to strengthen the rights of homeowners to participate in and control their association and to encourage the use of mediation to resolve disputes.

4

The Many Faces of Community Associations under California Law

Curtis C. Sproul

INTRODUCTION

Four phenomena of modern society—the high cost of residential property, the property tax revolt of the late 1970s, the shrinking availability of attractive development sites, and the public's desire to own affordable residences with both low maintenance requirements and rights in greenbelt and recreation amenities—have created a surge in the number of homes located within common interest residential communities. In California, the three most common forms of common ownership living are condominiums, cooperatives, and planned developments.

Common interest developments[1] offer their residents a comfortable living environment, often including central recreation facilities and greenbelts or parks, as well as the benefit of collective maintenance of the common facilities and residence exteriors. To assure that the project developer's original development plan is preserved, the residential lots or

---

[1]The term "common interest development" is defined in California Civil Code §1351 to include any community apartment project, condominium project, planned development, or stock cooperative. Each of these forms of real property ownership involve a combination of individually owned lots or units coupled with rights in common area parcels or spaces that are either owned by an association whose members are the individual unit/lot owners or by the owners as tenants in common.

units within the project, as well as the common areas, are subjected to a recorded Declaration of Covenants, Conditions, and Restrictions (referred to in this chapter as the "Declaration" or "CC&Rs").[2] The Declaration typically describes all easements within the development, imposes a system of architectural or design review, imposes private restrictions on the use and enjoyment of property and sets forth a regulatory scheme to ensure that the restrictions are observed by future owners.

Community maintenance functions within common interest developments are generally discharged by a property owners' association comprised of the lot or unit owners within the common interest development.[3] The community association is normally formed as a nonprofit corporation with membership in the association and attendant assessment obligations being mandatory for all owners.

Under the California Nonprofit Corporation Law,[4] these property

---

[2] In most common interest developments there is a single Declaration recorded against all separate interests and common areas. However, in larger developments that take on the characteristics of small communities the principal developer may record a Master Declaration, which presents the equitable servitudes essential to implementing the essential features of the master plan. That Master Declaration then contemplates and permits the recordation of separate "sub-Declarations" applicable only to a particular tract or phase of development within the overall project.

[3] In fact, all California common interest developments are required to have a community association for purposes of repairing, replacing, and maintaining the common areas and any other portions of the development that the Declaration directs the association to maintain. See Cal. Civ. Cd. sections 1363 and 1364.

[4] Cal. Corp. Cd. 5000-9928 (West Supp. 1984). California's Nonprofit Corporation Law creates three classifications of nonprofit corporations: mutual benefit corporations, public benefit corporations and religious corporations. Cal. Corp. Cd. 5000-9928 (West Supp. 1984). If the corporation is formed primarily for religious purposes it is regulated by the provisions pertaining to religious corporations. Id. 9110-9690. If the corporation is not a religious organization but is tax exempt or otherwise has its assets irrevocably dedicated to charitable or public purposes it is regulated by the provisions pertaining to public benefit corporations. Ia. 5110-6010. If the nonprofit corporation is neither a religious nor public benefit organization and permits a distribution of its assets to its members upon dissolution, it is classified as a mutual benefit corporation under California law. As the term suggests, most "mutual benefit" corporations are formed to facilitate pursuit by the corporation's members of a common interest or activity. Community associations fit squarely within this category. Id.

owners' associations are classified as mutual benefit corporations. California community associations are also subject to Department of Real Estate (DRE) regulations during the period of developer control[5] and by the Davis-Stirling Common Interest Development Act.[6] However, as to matters relating to the internal governance of the association, both the DRE regulations and the Davis-Stirling Act generally follow the Mutual Benefit Corporation Law. Accordingly, nonprofit law, traditionally confined to charitable organizations and private interest groups, is being utilized as the basic structure for local governance in many modern residential communities.

Although practically all California community associations are organized as nonprofit mutual benefit corporations, several significant California cases involving common interest developments and legal commentators who have written articles on common interest developments and community associations have characterized and analyzed these associations not only as nonprofit enterprises subject to review under corporate law principles, but also as "mini-governments" or business enterprises.

This article will examine the three conceptual models most often applied to community associations. The article concludes that the legal standards that should be applied in evaluating the propriety of the official actions of community association directors and officers and the interrelationships between the association and its members are those standards imposed by California's Nonprofit Mutual Benefit Corporation Law, but it also highlights certain difficulties that are encountered in a strict application of corporate law principles to community associations.

7110-8910. See also California Continuing Education of the Bar, *Advising California Nonprofit Corporations* (1984).

[5]Business and Professions Code §11018.6 and 10 Cal. Code Regs. §§2792-2800.

[6]Cal. Civil Cd. sections 1350 *et seq.*

THE MUNICIPAL MODEL OF ASSOCIATION GOVERNANCE

Implications of Applying Municipal Jurisprudence to Community Associations

Due to the roles that community associations play in the lives of the residents of common interest developments, such associations have been described in cases and legal commentaries as "mini-governments,"[7] "quasi-governments,"[8] "volunteer legislatures,"[9] "democratic subsocieties,"[10] and "residential private governments."[11] In their seminal article on community associations, Hyatt and Rhoads go so far as to say that community associations parallel "in almost every case the powers, duties and responsibilities of a municipal government."[12]

Indeed many parallels can be drawn between the laws regulating local governments and the laws regulating nonprofit community associations. For instance, various statutory provisions applicable to government entities regulate the manner in which meetings are conducted, the notice that citizens within the municipality are entitled to receive, conflict of interest transactions involving members of the governmental unit, and the manner in which citizens participate in the voting process. Finally, elected officials are subject to strict prohibitions against self-dealing and conflict of interest transactions of any kind, and they must comply with comprehensive financial disclosure laws. Each of these provisions finds

---

[7]Community Associations Institute and Urban Land Institute, *Managing a Successful Community Association* 2 (1974).

[8]*Cohen v. Kite Hill Community Assn.*, 142 Cal. App. 3d 642, 650-51. 191 Cal. Rptr. 209, 214 (1983).

[9]Hyatt and Rhoads, "Concepts of Liability in the Development and Administration of Condominium and Home Owners Associations," 12 *Wake Forest L. Rev.* 915, 931 (1976).

[10]*Hidden Harbor Estates, Inc., v. Norman*, 309 So. 2d 180, 192 (Fla. Dist. Ct. App. 1975).

[11]Reichman, *Residential Private Governments: An Introductory Survey.* 43 *U. Chi. L. Rev.*, 253, 257-59 (1976), where the author traces the origin of community associations to England in the 1700s. Nevertheless Reichman acknowledges that changes in consumer preferences and in the building industry during the 1960s accelerated the popularity in community associations. Comment, "Democracy in the New Towns: The Limits of Private Government." 36 *U. Chi. L. Rev.* 379 (1969).

[12]Hyatt and Rhoads, *supra* note 5, at 918.

a counterpart in the context of corporate governance under the California Corporation Code.

If community associations are merely another form of local governmental entity, it follows that such associations should be managed and operated in accordance with the laws and regulations governing the affairs of municipalities, rather than by the laws regulating nonprofit corporations under California's Nonprofit Mutual Benefit Corporation Law. However, all the implications of that conclusion need to be carefully explored and evaluated. The appropriateness of applying the municipal governance model to small associations whose functions do not parallel those of towns and cities must also be carefully considered. Although both are community associations, the scope of the association's responsibilities and the residents' perception of the appropriate role, authority, and responsibilities of association management will be radically different in a community of 6,000 homes than in a 20-unit condominium project.

One common practice of community associations that would be brought into question by their characterization as local governments is that of allocating votes other than on a one-person/one-vote basis. The one-person/one-vote concept, however, is required of governments under the United States Supreme Court decision in *Reynolds v. Sims.*[13] The Reynolds Court held that apportionment of state legislative districts must be accomplished so as to avoid giving one person's vote more weight than that of another. This one-person/one-vote concept has since been applied in the context of local elections where general governmental functions are involved.[14]

If voting within the context of community associations must satisfy the strict scrutiny standard of the Fourteenth Amendment as articulated in *Reynolds,* the generally accepted allocation of voting rights on the basis of subdivision interests (number of lots or condominium interests owned) would be suspect, as would the practice, sanctioned in the DRE

---

[13]377 U.S. 533 (1964).

[14]*Hadley v. Junior College District of Metropolitan Kansas City,* 397 U.S. 50 (1970): In *Hadley* the following functions were termed "governmental": establishing tax rates, maintaining the county jail, constructing and operating hospitals, airports, and libraries, appointing county officials, and establishing a housing authority. In *Hadley* the governmental functions were more limited but did include the power to levy and collect taxes, condemn property, and issue bonds.

Regulations, of granting the real estate developer three votes for each lot, unit or parcel he or she owns, while members of the community association are allocated a single vote. The 3-to-1 voting advantage is enjoyed by developers until 75 percent of the units within the common interest development are sold.[15]

The characterization of community associations as governmental units is also creating confusion among residents within common interest communities. For example, a common complaint voiced by many community association members is that their association directors often conduct business to the exclusion of the membership and that the board should meet and reach decisions in strict compliance with the Ralph M. Brown Act,[16] which requires that government bodies conduct their business in open meetings. In contrast, most corporations are permitted to completely exclude members or shareholders from board meetings and are even permitted to conduct meetings by conference telephone. Community associations are now required by the Davis-Stirling Act[17] to permit members to attend most board meetings. However, the constraints imposed by both the Corporations Code and the Davis-Stirling Act on the manner in which community association boards conduct their business are still less restrictive than those imposed by the Brown Act.[18]

Community associations are also distinguishable from true legislative bodies in that official corporate actions of the association's directors often receive tepid acceptance and/or observance among the membership, and

---

[15]Cal. Admin. Cd., tit. 10, §2792.13 (1983). This regulation permits the developer to form the community association with this two class membership structure. The regulation establishes time limitations after which the developer memberships must be converted to regular memberships and forever cease to exist.

[16]Cal. Govt. Cd. section 54950-54961

[17]Civil Code section 1363(c).

[18]For example, while Civil Code section 1363(c) requires most meetings to be open to the members, there are no requirements under the current law that the meeting be held at or near the development. Curiously, telephone conference meetings, permitted of nonprofit corporate boards under Corporations Code § 7211(a)(6) also are not specifically prohibited. Executive sessions are permitted by the Davis-Stirling Act when the board of directors is meeting to discuss litigation, matters relating to the formation of contracts with third parties and personnel matters. The board may also meet in executive session when sitting as a disciplinary body if the member who is being disciplined requests a closed session.

the board's efforts to enforce the development's property-use restrictions are often resented. Community associations are, in practically every instance, the lowest rung on the legislative hierarchy, possessing a very limited jurisdiction over the most mundane aspects of residential living. Enforcement of land-use restrictions and similar decisions by community associations often seem at odds with the time-honored concept that a man's home is his castle—a private haven, free of governmental intrusion.[19] Accordingly, community association enforcement efforts are generally afforded less deference upon subsequent review by the courts than even the decisions of an arbitrator in a civil dispute.

Curiously, although the web of regulatory jurisdiction established in the governing documents of a common interest community (particularly the Declaration) often affects the private property rights of residents, community associations typically encounter high levels of member and resident apathy concerning the activities, affairs, and management of the association. Because large numbers of residents chose to remain uninvolved, the dominance and power of individuals and factions who actively participate in association management can be disproportionately great[20] and if that power is exercised irresponsibly or capriciously, a "tyranny of the petty" can result.

Although Hyatt and Rhoads argue that regulations adopted by community associations should be considered in their "real capacity as municipal ordinances," rather than as restrictive covenants in accordance with property law, Hyatt and Rhoads support the inference that such regulations are not legislative acts by asserting that the "clear test of the validity of a rule [adopted by a community association] is 'reasonableness,'"[21] including affording members the opportunity to be heard prior to the effective date of the rule. Traditionally the decisions of true legislative bodies have been protected by a higher standard that places the

---

[19]This notion has its roots in the fundamental right of privacy in family life. See *Halet v. Wend Investment Co.* 672 F2d 1305 (9th Cir., 1982).

[20]The dominance and control of interested member factions is even greater when the governing documents sanction the use of cumulative and proxy voting, as authorized by both the Corporations Code and the DRE regulations.

[21]See *Johnson v. Keith*, 368 Mass. 316, 331, 331 N.E. 2d 879, 882 (1975) ("Because restrictions in the master deed and in the bylaws may be amended by the unit owners they resemble municipal laws more than deed restrictions"); Hyatt and Rhoads, *supra* note 5, at 932, 934, 947.

burden on the challenger to establish that the legislative action is clearly arbitrary or unreasonable.[22]

Of course, conclusory designations of community associations as governmental or legislative bodies beg the question of whether the governmental characterization is accurate and should be applied to the affairs of community associations in lieu of the corporate law rules and standards by which the actions of other mutual benefit corporations are measured. In support of their contention that community associations are "essentially performing a governmental function," Hyatt and Rhoads cite the community services the association often renders to its members such as utility services, road maintenance, street and common area lighting, refuse removal, security services, the dissemination of internal organs of communication (i.e., newsletters), association assessment powers, and the mandatory nature of association membership.[23] Upon examination, there is nothing inherent in any of the principal functions, powers, or characteristics of community associations that compels the conclusion that community associations are essentially governmental entities.

The Purposes of Community Associations Cannot be Equated with Those of Municipalities

The Maintenance Responsibility

The maintenance responsibilities that are typically imposed on community associations with respect to common areas and the roof and exterior surfaces of attached residences are a natural outgrowth of the typical design features of common interest communities (i.e., high-density housing, uniform appearance and construction of residences, and open spaces set aside for the common enjoyment of all owners). In many forms of common interest development, such as most condominium projects, the association owns the common areas and is obligated to maintain, repair, and replace its properties and assets for the benefit of its members to the same extent as any corporation. Even when title to the common areas is held by all owners as tenants in common, collective discharge of these maintenance responsibilities through a central association is the only practical alternative. In fact, if the Davis-Stirling

---

[22]*Village of Euclid v. Ambler Realty Co.* 272 U.S. 365 (1926).
[23]Hyatt and Rhoads, *supra* note 5, at 926.

Act did not require common interest developments to be managed by community associations,[24] it is likely that owners of property within such developments would promptly conclude, on their own, that the benefits and economies of cooperative maintenance outweigh the time-honored notion that a man's home is his castle.

As a result of the sustained decline in California's real estate market, the trend of most residential developers is to limit their development risk by creating smaller development projects or phasing a larger development in order to provide flexibility to alter or abandon the master development plan if marketing projections do not materialize. In smaller developments, the maintenance obligations of community associations are often quite limited and certainly have little in common with the range of duties and responsibilities imposed on local governments. In fact, the association's maintenance and repair obligations are often confined to the roof repairs and the maintenance of exterior building surfaces, limited green-belt areas and privately owned parking cul-de-sacs. Such limited responsibilities more closely resemble the sharing of maintenance obligations among owners of a common road easement than they do any formal governmental process.

In 1976, when Hyatt and Rhoads published their *Wake Forest Law Review* article,[25] "jumbo" real estate projects, characterized by extensive common area recreation facilities, miles of private roads, private security patrols, shopping malls, and the like had reached a zenith of popularity and were on the wane. The adverse impact of Proposition 13 on the availability of public funds for infrastructure, tightening banking regulations on development loans, the poor economy, and a substantial increase in residential construction defect litigation cases have all combined to sap the enthusiasm of residential developers to undertake the risk of complex jumbo developments. Developers also learned that when construction quality took a back seat to the pursuit of short-term profits, the common interest development template also spawned an effective plaintiff's litigation vehicle, namely the community association and its ability to fund the cost of litigation through member assessments.

Although the obligations of community associations in very large projects are much more akin to governmental functions, the fact that a limited number of community associations provided services with

---

[24]See Civil Cd. §1363(a).
[25]Hyatt and Rhoads, *supra* note 5.

attributes of police powers does not merit a general characterization of all such associations as governmental entities. Furthermore, many of the more extensive planned developments that were conceived in the 1960s subsequently converted to true municipalities or created community service districts, county service areas, and landscape and lighting districts in order to finance local improvements and services typical of true governmental entities.[26] In any event, practically all jumbo projects discharge actual police power functions, such as law enforcement (beyond the services typical of private security personnel), fire protection, water service, and waste water management by means of local governmental districts and municipal/county law enforcement agencies, not by means of the development's community association.

To avoid the future litigation threat presented by a community association with a broad assessment funding base, most developers of large projects make every effort to place all major infrastructure components in the hands of true governmental entities, while confining the role of community associations to the discharge of limited maintenance responsibilities within discrete phases of the development containing commonly owned components.

The Assessment Power

Legal commentators[27] and the courts[28] have also drawn an analogy between the assessment authority of community associations and the

---

[26]The California Government, Public Utilities, Water and Health and Safety Codes contain provisions for the formation of a long list of special purpose local districts to finance the building, operation, and maintenance of a myriad of local community improvements and services. The form of local district that is empowered to provide the broadest range of services is a Community Services District (Cal. Govt. Cd. sections 61000, *et seq*.; "CSDs"). CSDs can provide water, garbage and fire protection services, recreation and parks construction and programs, police protection, street maintenance and lighting, libraries, transportation services and ambulance services (See Govt. Cd. section 61600). In addition, with special statutory approval, CSDs can take on additional responsibilities and a number of common interest developments have used this authority to transfer CC&R enforcement and architectural regulation to a CSD having boundaries coextensive with those of the common interest development. (See Govt. Cd. section 61600.10 and 60400-60917).

[27]*E.g.*, Hyatt and Rhoads, *supra* note 5, at 918.

[28]See *Cohen*, 142 Cal. App. 3d at 651. 191 Cal. Rptr. at 214.

taxing power of municipalities in concluding that community associations are in fact local government instrumentalities. This argument, focusing on the association's funding source, is so closely tied to the services the association is obligated to perform that it must stand or fall with the "municipal function" argument for governmental characterization. The bylaws of practically every nonprofit corporation contain provisions for dues or assessments to fund the corporation's activities, coupled with enforcement mechanisms in the event that dues are not timely paid. Usually those disciplinary measures include the suspension or termination of membership rights in the event of nonpayment. Such corporations are not characterized as governmental entities even though dues enforcement can involve the deprivation of property rights, particularly when the membership rights include proprietary interests in real property owned by the corporation (for instance, a percentage interest in golf course real property owned by a private country club).[29]

The Mandatory Aspect of Association Membership

The final characteristic that the courts and commentators often cite as an indicia of the municipal qualities of community associations is the mandatory quality of the association membership.[30] Just as an individual must accede to the laws of the local community where he desires to reside, so must persons who acquire residences in common interest communities accept membership in a local community association and the responsibility to honor the private covenants imposed by the development's CC&Rs as obligations appurtenant to their property interest.

---

[29]See Cal. Admin. Code tit. 10, R. 2792.25 (1980). This DRE regulation permits the governing instruments of California community associations to impose monetary penalties, temporary suspensions of an owner's rights as a member of the association or other similar discipline for failure to comply with the governing instruments provided the alleged offender is afforded notice and an opportunity to be heard in accordance with the minimum requirements of section 7341 of the California Corporations Code. State law and the DRE regulations also permit community associations to enforce delinquent assessments through the initiation of foreclosure proceedings against the defaulting owner and his subdivision interest. See Cal. Bus. & Prof. Code 11003.2: Cal. Civ. Code 1356; Cal. Admin. Code tit. 10.R. 2792.16 (1984).

[30]See *Cohen,* 142 Cal. App. 3d at 651.191 Cal. Rptr. at 214; Hyatt and Rhoads, *supra* note 5 at 924.

While it is certainly true that a person residing within a particular municipality cannot elect to secede from the jurisdiction of the local government so long as he resides there, persons have a much broader range of individual choice with respect to the specific residence in which they reside. That home may be an apartment, a conventional residence in an established community without private covenants, or a common interest residential unit. If the common interest option is selected, the perception of residential units within the development as fungible commodities is not far off the mark. Most common interest communities exist within larger metropolitan areas and the unique qualities of any particular common interest subdivision often exist more in the mind of the developer's marketing consultant than in the actual features of the project.

With the vast range of housing choices commonly available to home buyers, it is difficult to perceive the purchaser of a unit in a particular planned community as being any more compelled to buy into that community and its private association than a person who elects to join a particular charity, golf club, or other nonprofit corporation. Of course, once having made the election, the new member must agree to abide by the rules and regulations of the nonprofit enterprise, but the requirement of mandatory compliance as a condition to membership in the entity is a common characteristic of many nonprofit associations and thus should not, in itself, convert the community association into a municipality. If the buyer subsequently discovers that the development's rules (or the association's particular administration of those rules) is not for him, the buyer can choose to leave. The frequency with which most people move within a locality suggests that there are few constraints on the exercise of this option.

THE BUSINESS MODEL OF ASSOCIATION GOVERNANCE

The Business Enterprise Characterization

The clearest articulation of the business model of community associations is found in the California Supreme Court case of *O'Connor v. Village Green Owners Association.*[31] In that case the Court invalidated an "adults only" age restriction contained in the recorded declaration of

---

[31]33 Cal. 3d 790.662 P.2d 427.191 Cal. Rptr. 320 (1983).

covenants, conditions and restrictions of the Village Greens condominiums. The Supreme Court ruled that such restrictions violate California's Unruh Civil Rights Act that prohibits arbitrary and invidious discrimination by business establishments.[32]

Although the text of the Unruh Act makes no reference to "age" as an impermissible basis for discrimination (while listing "sex, race, religion" and a number of other personal characteristics), in earlier decisions the California Supreme Court ruled that the bases of discrimination specifically referenced in the Unruh Act were intended to be illustrative rather than restrictive. On this basis the court held that the Unruh Act barred any type of arbitrary discrimination in business establishments including discrimination based on age. Finally, the court responded to the Unruh Act's exclusive focus on discrimination by "business establishments" by finding that the Village Green Owner Association was, indeed, a business:

> Contrary to the association's attempt to characterize itself as but an organization that "mows lawns" for owners, the association in reality has a far broader and more businesslike purpose. The association, through a board of directors, is charged with employing a professional property management firm, with obtaining insurance for the benefit of all owners and with maintaining and repairing all common areas and facilities of the 629-unit project. It is also charged with establishing and collecting assessments from all owners to pay for its undertakings and with adopting and enforcing rules and regulations for the common good. In brief, the association performs all the customary business functions which in the traditional landlord-tenant relationship rest on the landlord's shoulders.[33]

It is interesting to note that practically the same laundry list of functions used to support the characterization of community associations

---

[32]The Unruh Civil Rights Act provides, in relevant part: "All persons within the jurisdiction of this state are free and equal, and no matter what their sex, race, color, religion, ancestry, or national origin are entitled to full and equal accommodations, advantages, facilities, privileges or services in all business establishments of every kind whatsoever." Cal. Civ. Code 51 (West 1982).

[33]*O'Connor v. Village Green Owners Assn.*, 33 Cal. 3d at 796 n. 56, 662 P.2d at 431 n.56, 191 Cal. Rptr. at 324 n. 56.

as municipalities was used in *O'Connor* to rule that such associations are business establishments.[34]

The *O'Connor* decision relied heavily on *Marina Point, Ltd. v. Wolfson*,[35] which found a similar apartment complex age restriction, violative of the Unruh Act. When the *Marina Point* business establishment analysis is applied to a common interest community, rather than to an apartment project, the analysis fails for at least two reasons. First, an examination of community association activities does not support the conclusion that these entities are business establishments.[36]

Although the majority in *O'Connor* refused to characterize a community association as an organization that merely mows lawns and performs other routine home maintenance tasks, in practice the principal functions of most community associations focus upon routine property maintenance and the enforcement of rules affecting ordinary aspects of private residential living that are clearly nonbusiness in their orientation.

---

[34]Hyatt and Rhoads engage in a similar sort of academic alchemy although they are more careful to draw on other association functions in noting the "business aspects" of associations such as preparing budgets and managing finances, asset and property management, taxation, insurance and employee relations. Hyatt and Rhoads, *supra* note 5, at 919.

[35]30 Cal. 3d at 721, 640 P.2d at 115, 180 Cal. Rptr. at 496.

[36]In his dissent in *O'Connor v. Village Green Owners Assn.*, Justice Stanley Mosk strongly utilized the majority's conclusion that community associations are in the business of being landlords:

An association of homeowners . . . cannot by any stretch of the imagination be held to be a business . . . a homeowners association, the principal function of which is to perform or arrange for the services of an owner of a single family dwelling would normally perform or arrange—such as mowing lawns, fixing defective plumbing, repairing roofs, cutting trees and watering gardens—does not come within the definition of the term "business establishment" as it is used throughout the decision in *Marina Point*. The association has no patrons, tenants or customers, only dues-paying members: it is in no way entrepreneurial in nature; and it is not open for public patronage. To consider the association a "business enterprise" under the Unruh Act would require the ludicrous holding that the owner-resident of a single family dwelling is engaged in a "business enterprise" when he or she hires a gardener or a plumber. 33 Cal. 3d 790 at 800, 803.

Given these considerations, the characterization of community associations as business enterprises appears strained.

The second analytical difficulty inherent in characterizing community associations as business enterprises concerns their limited scope of authority. With the exception of certain maintenance functions, the jurisdiction of community associations generally ends at the boundaries of the project areas utilized by the owners in common with the others. In contrast, the business activity identified in the *Marina Point case* of owning, managing, and leasing units in an apartment building pervades both the owner-landlord's activities in maintaining the apartment's common grounds and exterior building surfaces, and the contractual relationship between the landlord and tenant and the tenant's rights with respect to use and occupancy of the private living space that is the subject of the landlord-tenant relationship. In fact, mere ownership of the apartment building would not be so much a business as an investment. The business aspects of the ownership are inherent in the relationship created between the building owner and the occupants of the individual residence units.

The declaration of restrictions generally confers authority on the community association to enforce the Declaration's property-use restrictions. However, that authority is not exclusive, and most property-use restrictions either seek to regulate uses of the common area or to prevent activities on the privately owned lots or parcels that constitute an unreasonable interference with the quiet enjoyment of other owners. The owners of common interest property are also given individual rights of enforcement in both the CC&Rs and by statute (i.e., Civil Code section 1354).

The Hyatt and Rhoads characterization of community associations as having "business aspects"[37] is slightly more palatable in that the authors, rather than merely asserting that community associations are businesses, focus on those features of community association management that are shared in common with business establishments. Although the Hyatt and Rhoads approach has greater analytical appeal, the "business aspects" they note, such as the association's authority to assess its members, its obligation to pay taxes and to maintain insurance, and its ability to contract for necessary labor or management services, are not confined to the business sector. Any adult must deal with such matters in the most

---

[37]Hyatt and Rhoads, *supra* note 5, at 919.

private aspects of life and governmental units certainly deal with a similar list of responsibilities. Such matters are also common pursuits of almost any association of individuals formed to undertake a common purpose, whether that undertaking is oriented toward business, pleasure or the promotion of charitable or other nonprofit objectives.

The preceding arguments are not intended to suggest that community associations never perform business functions. Rather they suggest that the duties and responsibilities of community associations do not offer a compelling justification for their classification as businesses, particularly with respect to premises liability issues. In larger developments community associations may have a full-time management staff and substantial common facilities to operate and maintain. However, the trend is away from such "jumbo" projects, and the smaller developments are generally self-managed by the community association's board of directors that is, in the words of Justice Mosk, formed primarily "to perform or arrange for the services an owner of a single family dwelling would normally perform or arrange—such as mowing lawns, fixing defective plumbing, repairing roofs, cutting trees, and watering gardens."[38]

Landlord Characterization

The expansive legal implications of the *O'Connor* business establishment characterization of community associations has already become apparent—literally in the O'Connor's backyard. *Troy v. Village Green Condominium Project*,[39] a 1983 decision involving the same condominium project, relied heavily on *O'Connor* in applying a landlord-tenant analysis in ruling on the liability of a community association to its members who suffer bodily injury as the result of the criminal acts of a third party.[40] The plaintiff in the *Troy* case was a unit owner who fell victim to an intruder who entered her condominium unit, molested, raped, and robbed her. The plaintiff alleged that the board of directors of the Village Green Owners Association were on notice of the crimes occurring within the

---

[38]*O'Connor*, 33 Cal. 3d at 803 n. 56, 662 P.2d at 435. 191 Cal. Rptr. at 328. (Mosk, J. dissenting). Justice Mosk further noted that community associations are in no sense entrepreneurial in that they have no patrons, tenants, or customers —only dues paying members.

[39]149 Cal. App. 3d 135, 196 Cal. Rptr. 680 (1983).

[40]*Id.* at 139-40, 196 Cal. Rptr. at 682-84.

project and knew that additional lighting would deter crime, but nonetheless "negligently and carelessly failed to reasonably carry [the lighting] investigation forward and to propose to the members of the Association what alternatives were available, at what costs, to improve the project's lighting conditions." The Village Green Board did, in fact, know that the project had experienced a crime wave, and prior to the assault, the board recommended that its members leave lights on within their units in order to deter crime. The association was also investigating methods of improving lighting within the common areas, but extra lighting installed by the plaintiff in the common area near her unit was disconnected at the request of the association's architectural control committee for failure to conform to the committee's architectural guidelines and approval procedures. The record also disclosed that although the plaintiff, on several occasions following an earlier burglary of her unit, had submitted written requests to the board for improved lighting, the requests had not been acknowledged.

> Respondents contend that it would be unfair to impose upon them a duty to provide "expensive security measures" when they are not landlords in the traditional sense, but [rather] members of a homeowners association which has limited funds and cannot significantly increase its budget without the approval of a majority of the Association members. However, respondents are, for all practical purposes, the Project's "landlords." . . . [T]his issue was . . . resolved contrary to the respondents' point of view in *O'Connor v. Village Green Owners Assn.*[41]

Although the California Supreme Court correctly concluded that Ms. Troy's case had stated a valid cause of action for damages due to negligence on the part of the association board, the court's landlord-tenant analysis, conceived in *O'Connor*, was not the way to get there. The line of landlord-tenant cases cited in *Troy* involves landlords owning commercial/business property or lessors who are in the business of renting residential premises (such as multiple-unit apartment buildings). The strong public policy considerations that underlie such landlord-tenant relationships are resulting in tort decisions establishing expansive concepts of strict liability in evaluating the responsibilities of landlords with respect to tenants and other persons injured on the premises.

---

[41]28 *Troy v. Village Green Owners Assn.* 149 Cal. App. 3d at 143-44. 196 Cal. Rptr. at 685-86.

When *Troy,* with its seemingly innocuous reliance on landlord-tenant analysis, converges with the true commercial tenancy decisions that it cites, heading community associations down the road towards the concept of strict liability, the implications are alarming. On the one hand, courts are characterizing community associations as mini-governments, but on the other hand courts are showing little interest in extending to these "governments" any of the immunities enjoyed by true governmental entities.

The public policy that supports the doctrine of strict liability is based on allocating the risk of loss of certain business ventures involving foreseeable risk to those who stand to gain most from the enterprise, rather than on the unsuspecting consumer. In the context of common interest communities, the essential ingredients of implied warranties, disproportionate access to essential information, and special relationships involving the opportunity for great economic gain to one party are lacking. Individuals residing outside of common interest communities cannot expect an absolute indemnity from their neighbors against the common risks of urban life, and there is no reason why a different result should obtain within such communities.[42]

THE NONPROFIT MODEL OF ASSOCIATION GOVERNANCE

The debate over which body of law provides the most appropriate regulatory scheme for community associations centers on the two principal functions of such associations; namely (1) administration and enforcement of property-use restrictions among neighboring property owners; and (2) prudent management of the association's financial resources, including the investment, application, and collection of homeowner assessments. There is nothing inherent in either of these functions that suggests that the interests of members can receive adequate

---

[42]It is also worth noting that governmental entities have fared better than community associations in cases similar to *Francis T. v. Village Green Owners Association.* For example, in *Denton v. city of Fullerton* (1991) 233 CA 3d 1636, 285 CR 297) and *M.B. v. City of San Diego* (1991) 233 CA 3d 699, 284 CR 555, the courts of appeal held that the defendant cities could not be held liable for injuries sustained in criminal assaults under a negligence theory because no special relationship existed between the plaintiffs and the police, which created a duty to protect or warn the plaintiffs of impending dangers.

protection from abuses by the governing body only through application of government law concepts.

Community associations originated in the context of private relation- ships (private residential real estate development) and are given a structure of governance, generally under the corporate laws of the state in which the project is located, that provides a well-defined system of private law regulation and control. The two principal functions of community associations certainly are not strangers to effective regulation within that private law context.

California's present Nonprofit Corporation Law provides a compre- hensive guide for the formation and operation of community associations as incorporated entities. Even when an association is formed as an unincorporated entity (usually because the project consists of a very small number of units), Civil Code section 1363 (a) provides that the associa- tion shall have all the powers granted to a nonprofit mutual benefit corporation under the California Corporations Code. This well-defined corporate structure is useful to community associations whose boards of directors are often comprised of volunteer residents with little prior experience in real estate or financial management. In contrast to the elected officials with whom they are likened, directors of community associations are often pressed into service, rather than affirmatively seeking office as a desired career opportunity. After all, few would aspire to a volunteer office, requiring countless hours of commitment to the performance of tasks that are often unappreciated by the volunteer official's constituents.

The regulatory structure provided to community association directors by the California Nonprofit Mutual Benefit Corporation Law includes a comprehensive set of defined terms[43] and detailed provisions regarding such matters as: the manner and timing of notice to members, member- ship meetings, inspection rights, voting rights, quorums, selection and removal of directors, the standard of conduct that directors must observe, and the discipline of members. The Mutual Benefit Corporation Law also contains specific provisions designed to accommodate the unique needs of community associations. For instance, Corporations Code section 7312(d) carves out an exception to the general rule that no person may hold more than one membership in a nonprofit mutual benefit corpora- tion. Section 7312(d) states that community association articles or

---

[43]Cal. Corp. Cd. 5002-5080 (West Supp. 1984).

bylaws may permit a person who owns an interest or who has a right of exclusive occupancy in more than one parcel or unit to hold a separate membership in the owners association for each such parcel or unit. Moreover, whereas any member of a nonprofit corporation can generally avoid the obligation for levies, dues, or assessments imposed by the corporation by promptly resigning, this rule does not apply when the obligation arises as a condition to the ownership of real property. Finally, section 8724 of the Corporations Code imposes stringent restrictions on the right of a community association to transfer all or substantially all of its assets or to dissolve its holdings.

In addition to the specific provisions of the Mutual Benefit Corporation Law for community associations, the DRE regulations impose further requirements with respect to the content of community association governing documents (i.e., the articles of incorporation and bylaws of the corporation and the Declaration of CC&Rs). These DRE regulatory requirements are generally designed to ensure that members receive proper notice of both membership and board meetings, that members are accorded minimum due process in disciplinary proceedings and that the association is managed openly. For example, the regulations require that membership meetings be held at least once a year at a location either within the subdivision or as close thereto as possible. In the case of director meetings, notice of the meeting must be posted prominently within the common area, the meetings must be open to all members, and the board may only meet in executive session to discuss and vote on personnel matters, litigation in which the association is or may become involved and similar business. Section 2792.26 of the Commissioner's Regulations requires observance of the procedures for notice and hearing set forth in section 7341 of the California Corporations Code and prohibits enforcement of most monetary penalties by means of foreclosure.

Because community associations are not currently required to incorporate and because the jurisdiction of the Department of Real Estate over the content of common interest development governing documents ceases when the developer no longer controls more than 25 percent of the association membership votes, the California legislature has used the Davis-Stirling Common Interest Development Act as a vehicle for imposing restrictions on the largely unfettered management discretion enjoyed by corporate directors under the Mutual Benefit Corporation Law (see below).[44] To temper the potential for breaches of fiduciary duty and other abuses of power that could occur in an environment of unsupervised managerial discretion, the Davis-Stirling Act has imposed a number of specific member disclosure and approval requirements that are designed to increase the awareness of, and participation by members in, the formation and execution of community association policies.

The list of Davis-Stirling Act controls that must be observed by management include the following:

1. *Obligation to Conduct Most Meetings in Open Session.* The Davis-Stirling Act has imposed Brown Act-style open meeting requirements on community association boards by affirming the right of members to attend board meetings and, conversely, by limiting the of boards to adjourn into executive session.[45] Community association directors are only authorized to meet in executive session to discuss litigation, matters relating to the formation of contracts with third parties, and personnel matters. The board of directors must also meet in executive session when sitting as a disciplinary body if the member who is the subject of the hearing so requests.[46]

2. *Assessments.* While the governing documents of any community association confer power on the association to assess its members, the Davis-Stirling Act now mandates that community association boards "levy regular and special assessments sufficient to perform the association's obligations under the governing documents." This mandate was imposed in recognition that many volunteer boards often avoided the imposition of needed assessment increases for fear of incurring the wrath of their neighbors.

Note, however, that the Davis-Stirling Act imposes a counterbalancing protective measure for the interests of the general membership by directing that annual assessment needs be accurately established by

---

[44]One would think that once the period of developer control has ended and the permanent residents are given control of an association that has as its purpose maintenance of the common properties and preservation of the plan of development there would be an identity of interest that would serve as an effective check and balance on the authority of the association's directors. However, high levels of apathy undermine the effectiveness of member oversight.

[45]Civil Code section 1363(c).

[46]These open meeting requirements, and the scope of permitted exceptions, are quite similar to the Ralph M. Brown Act open meeting rules applicable to public agencies. See Cal. Govt. Cd. §§54956.8-54957.

data developed by the board through the preparation of capital replacement reserve studies every three years and by mandating the content of the association's annual budget disclosures.[47] (See Paragraphs 3 and 4, below). Members are given the right to vote on substantial increases in the association's regular assessments or any special assessment in excess of 5 percent of the association's budgeted gross expenses for the year in which the assessment is levied.[48]

3. *Three-Year Reserve Study.* At least once every three years the board of directors must make a study of the reserve account requirements of the development. This study must also be reviewed by the board on an annual basis and adjusted at one-year intervals as required.[49]

4. *Annual Budgets and Financial Disclosures.* On an annual basis (and within maximum and minimum time periods) the board must prepare and distribute detailed budgets and annual financial reports to the members. [50] If the board fails to distribute the budget within the period that is not less than 45 days nor more than 60 days prior to the beginning of the association's fiscal year, assessments for the coming year cannot increase over the previous year's assessment without member approval.[51]

5. *Quarterly Financial Review.* On a quarterly basis the board must review a reconciliation of the association's actual financial performance to the performance forecasted in the budget.[52]

6. *Maintenance of Common Areas, Etc.* The association, acting through its board of directors, is obligated to repair, maintain, and replace the common areas and those portions (if any) of the separately owned lots or units that the Declaration directs the Association to repair, maintain, and/or replace.[53]

7. *CC&R Enforcement.* Although the board has discretion in selecting which violations of the Declaration of Restrictions merit enforcement, the board has a general duty to enforce the covenants and restrictions for the benefit of all owners and residents. [54] In discharging this enforcement responsibility several cases have stressed the obligation

---

[47]Civil Code section 1366.
[48]Civil Code section 1366.
[49]Civil Code section 1365.5(d).
[50]Civil Code section 1365.
[51]Civil Code section 1366(a).
[52]Civil Code section 1365.5.
[53]Civil Code section 1364.
[54]Civil Code section 1354.

of community associations to provide their members with reasonable notice and fair enforcement procedures, consistent with concepts of procedural due process. [55] See below.

8. *New Buyer Disclosures.* The association, acting through its board and managerial personnel, is obligated to furnish selling owners with copies of the governing documents and specified financial information so that the seller can provide this information to prospective purchasers.[56]

9. *Collection and Fine Policies.* The association, acting through its board, must deliver to the members, on an annual basis, a statement describing the association's policies and practices in enforcing lien rights and other legal remedies to collect delinquent assessments.[57] In addition, if the association has adopted a policy of imposing fines or other monetary penalties for violations of the governing documents, the board must distribute to each member a schedule of fines "in accordance with authorization for member discipline contained in the governing documents." [58]

10. *Notification of Right to Receive Minutes.* Under section 8333 of the Corporations Code, members of nonprofit mutual benefit corporations have the right to inspect the accounting books and records of their corporation and the minutes of any board or committee meetings. The Davis-Stirling Act is unique in requiring community associations to notify their members "at the time the *pro forma* budget is distributed or at the time of any general mailing to the entire membership" of their right to receive copies of the minutes of meetings of the board of directors and how and where those minutes may be obtained.[59]

11. *Notification Regarding Assessment Increases.* The association, acting through its board, must send each owner notice, by first-class mail, of any increase in the regular or special assessments not less than 30 nor more than 60 days prior to the date the assessment is due.[60]

---

[55]See *Ironwood Owners Assn. v. Solomon* (1986) 178 CA 3d 766; *Cohen v. Kite Hill Community Assn.* (1983) 142 CA 3d 642; see also, Cal. Corp. Cd. §7341; Merritt and Siino "Architectural Control Committees and the Search For Due Process" 15 *CEB Real Property Law Rptr.* 117 (April 1992).

[56]See Civil Code section 1368.

[57]See Civil Code section 1365(d).

[58]Cal. Civil Code section 1363(i).

[59]See Civil Code section 1363(d).

[60]See Civil Code section 1366 (c).

Essentially, the California legislature has used the Davis-Stirling Act as a vehicle for creating a special category of nonprofit entities that are unique among nonprofit corporations generally in their obligation to operate consistent with a host of member accountability and disclosure provisions that can be traced, in many instances, to legal concepts that have evolved in the context of law relating to municipal governance. While legal scholars may question the wisdom of *de facto* amendments to the Corporations Code, creating a special subclass of corporate entities, through amendments to the California Civil Code, the Davis-Stirling requirements do improve the structure of governance and accountability of corporate management in the performance of responsibilities that many courts and commentators view as quasi-governmental in nature.

CALIFORNIA'S COMMUNITY ASSOCIATION REGULATORY SCHEME AS APPLIED TO COVENANT ENFORCEMENT AND MANAGERIAL DISCRETION

Applications of Corporate Due Process Procedures in the Resolution of Community Association Land-Use Disputes.

As previously noted, one of the principal functions of community associations is to preserve the common plan (the "plan") and scheme originally envisaged by the project developer and embodied in the recorded Declaration of Covenants, Conditions, and Restrictions (the Declaration). Normally the plan consists not only of a particular uniform architectural design for residences, but also of a series of property-use restrictions designed to prevent undesirable property uses and activities within the subdivision. The plan is preserved through the enforcement of property-use restrictions contained in the Declaration and by requiring architectural review of any new construction or alteration in existing improvements. Generally, the declaration provides that enforcement of its provisions may be undertaken by any individual lot owner or by the association on behalf of all lot owners, but as a practical matter owners generally expect the association to enforce the Declaration.

The association's enforcement role is most often cited in support of the claim that community associations are performing legislative functions. The property restriction enforcement is also the greatest source of dispute between owners and their community association. The question arises whether the California laws governing community associations (primarily the Mutual Benefit Corporation Law and the

Davis-Stirling Act) provide appropriate standards and procedures for the resolution of such disputes.

The trend of both the cases and commentators is in favor of a system whereby land-use disputes are resolved through negotiation and mediation, rather than through a legislative or quasi-judicial decision-making body. The new revisions to Civil Code section 1354 (effective January 1, 1994) require community associations to offer their members the opportunity to resolve most CC&R enforcement disputes through the use of alternative dispute resolution procedures.[61] Civil Code section 1354, as revised by AB 55, requires any party seeking to enforce the governing documents through injunctive and/or declaratory relief (including such actions that include allegations of damages up to $5,000) to first offer the opposing party the opportunity to participate in a form of binding or nonbinding alternative dispute resolution selected by the parties. Only if ADR is refused or nonbinding ADR fails to resolve the dispute can a court action be filed to enforce the governing documents.

One issue that remains unclear under the new Civil Code ADR provision is whether the Declaration of CC&Rs can mandate a particular form of ADR, administered by a panel of volunteers from the community appointed by the association's board of directors. Most modern Declarations state that before any monetary fines or penalties can be imposed or member privileges suspended, a member accused of violating the governing documents must be given prior notice and an opportunity to be heard in a procedural framework that complies with the minimum requirements of Corporations Code section 7341.[62] In the opinion of

---

[61]AB 55, which added Stats 1993, Ch 303, amending Civil Code section 1354 to add subparagraphs (b) through (j).

[62]Although the Corporations Code provisions focus on disciplinary action and speak in terms of "expulsion, termination and suspension" of membership rights, the DRE regulations have extended the due process requirements of Corporations Code section 7341 to encompass any disciplinary or enforcement action initiated by a community association against its members. Although the DRE regulations on disciplinary procedures are not specifically applicable to the actions of the community association's architectural control committee, there is always the possibility that any decision of the architectural committee will later require enforcement action by the association or result in a dispute with the applicant or neighboring owners, and for that reason the architectural review process should be administered in accordance with procedural due process. Otherwise, when the community association seeks judicial assistance in enforcing property use

this author, a governing document provision directing a particular mode of extra-judicial dispute resolution is consistent with AB 55; resort to professional arbitration or mediation service providers should not be required under the new Davis-Stirling ADR rules unless the development is so small that it is impractical or impossible for the association to convene a disinterested ADR hearing panel.[63]

The two principal qualities that must be inherent in any alternative dispute resolution model are fairness and due consideration of competing claims. Providing a structure that promotes fairness and due process in disputes among members of nonprofit corporations is an important feature of California's Nonprofit Mutual Benefit Corporation Law. Although the bylaws of a mutual benefit corporation may specify the procedures for suspending, disciplining, or expelling members, those provisions must be drafted consistent with the procedural due process requirements reflected in section 7341 of the California Corporations Code. Disciplinary measures that do not comply with those requirements are void.[64] As an additional safeguard against inequities in the discipline of members, California Nonprofit Corporation Law states that not only must the procedures used in disciplinary proceedings be consistent with procedural due process, but also the corporation's enforcement action must be based on substantive grounds that do not violate contractual or other rights of a member. The substantive grounds for enforcement are generally those obligations and restrictions set forth in the recorded Declaration of CC&Rs and to the extent that those restrictions are violative of law (for instance, age restrictions on the ownership of units) observance of due process requirements will not validate the association's enforcement action. Similarly, any attempt to permanently expel a person from membership in the community association for a Declaration violation would also be without effect since such expulsion would violate the regulations of the DRE.

With respect to due process requirements, the Mutual Benefit Corporation Law expressly requires that the procedures used in disciplining members be administered in good faith and in a fair and reasonable

---

restrictions and decisions of its architectural committee, there is a strong likelihood that the court will determine that the procedures used by the committee were unfair and thus of no effect.

[63]See *Ironwood Owners Association v. Solomon* (1986) 178 CA 3d 766, 224 CR 18.

[64]See Civil Code section 7341(a).

manner.[65] Although the community association is free to establish its own procedures, the statute also provides a "safe harbor" procedure deemed to be fair and reasonable. That procedure requires 15 days' prior notice, an opportunity to be heard, orally and in writing, at least 5 days prior to the imposition of discipline, and communication in writing of the procedures that the association will apply to the disciplinary action.[66] Any notice required by the statute may be given by any method reasonably calculated to provide actual notice. If notice is given by mail, first class or registered mail must be used, and the notice must be sent to the latest address of the member shown on the association's records.

Should a community association violate the requirements of section 7341 in its enforcement of CC&R property-use restrictions or other member disciplinary actions, the code makes specific reference to a member's right to seek judicial review of the association's actions.[67] In an action filed under section 7341(e), the court may order any relief it finds equitable under the circumstances. Case law decided under similar circumstances (but prior to the effective date of the Mutual Benefit Corporation Law) indicates that a writ of mandamus can be granted, ordering the corporation to hold a fair hearing or to reinstate the member. The court may also award monetary damages if the member has suffered financial loss as a result of improper action.[68]

---

[65]Corp. Cd. section 7341(b).

[66]Corp. Cd. section 7341(c).

[67]Cal. Corp. Cd. section 7341(e). These sanctions are now reinforced by the Davis-Stirling Act alternative dispute resolution rules (Civil Code §1354(b)-(j), effective January 1, 1994; see footnote 62 and accompanying text), which provides that if a person seeking to enforce the governing documents of a community association fails to observe Civil Code §1354's ADR provisions and proceeds immediately with the filing of a complaint, the complaint may be subjected to a demurrer or a motion to strike.

[68]See *Westlake Community Hospital v. Superior Court,* 17 Cal. 3d 465, 551 P 2d 410 (1976); *Cason v. Glass Bottle Blower's Assn.* 37 Cal. 2d 134, 231 P. 2d 6 (1951).

**Fiduciary Responsibilities of Community Association Management
Under the California Nonprofit Mutual Benefit Corporation Law**

Allocation of Authority within Community Associations

Although the directors of nonprofit community associations are elected to office by the corporation's members, the structure of corporate governance fashioned by the California Corporations Code is essentially a "top down," oligarchical structure. Unless either California statutory law or the corporation's governing documents reserve a particular issue or action for approval by the members, the Corporations Code provides that the "activities and affairs of a corporation shall be conducted and *all corporate powers shall be exercised* by or under the direction of the board of directors" (emphasis added).[69] Thus, unless member approval is specifically required either by some statute or by the association's governing documents, members who are not directors or officers have little or no role to play in the day-to-day management of their development. Although the same can be said of the daily functions and responsibilities of municipal governments, the jurisdiction of community associations is more intrusive of private property interests (often extending to such personal issues as exterior maintenance of each resident's home, the type and number of pets a resident can own and whether garage doors must remain closed when not in use). When the authority of community association management over such mundane aspects of daily life is superimposed over the residents' absence of any meaningful opportunity to participate in the course and direction of their association, the result is often an unwelcome, if not resented, surprise for many new purchasers of common interest residential property.

The friction between the community's regulatory interests under the Declaration and private rights is increased whenever the association's managers administer their trust in a haphazard or inconsistent fashion.[70]

---

[69]See Cal. Corp. Code § 7210.

[70]Frequent causes of disagreement that create friction and distrust between community association boards of directors and their members include: (i) claims by members that the Ralph M. Brown Act (Govt. Cd. sections 54950-54962) open meeting rules should apply to board meetings (the Brown Act does not apply to community association meetings, although restrictions have now been placed on the board's ability to meet in executive session to the exclusion of members by Civil Code section 1363); (ii) demands that members be given the

High levels of member apathy concerning the activities and affairs of community associations is pervasive, and if large numbers of residents choose to remain uninvolved, the dominance and power of well-organized factions within the community is likely to increase, particularly when the project governing documents permit members to use cumulative and proxy voting.[71]

The Role of Nondirector Members in the Management of Community Associations

Perhaps the rudest awakening for first-time purchasers of separate interests in common interest developments is the rather limited role contemplated by the Corporations Code and the Davis-Stirling Act for community association members. As previously noted, the Corporations Code provides that all corporate powers are to be exercised by or under

---

right to vote on any matter affecting their association in a fashion similar to State initiative rights; (iii) the Corporations Code's tendency to favor the interests of management in the calling and conduct of board and membership meetings and the scheduling of member votes on critical issues; and (iv) restrictions and conditions imposed by the Nonprofit Corporation Law (section 8330 *et seq.*) on the rights of members to access and copy corporate records and other documentation.

[71]The author has assisted over 200 community association clients in campaigns soliciting member approvals to amend bylaws and CC&Rs. Even with a well-organized and diligent solicitation campaign it is extremely difficult to motivate more than a majority of all members to cast ballots on these important governance issues (a fact that makes the super majority approval requirements found in most CC&R amendment provisions particularly burdensome). It is fairly easy for a well organized group of members to influence the outcome of director elections, particularly if proxy and/or cumulative voting are permitted. In fact, widespread voter apathy in community associations creates the possibility for the "omnipotence of the majority" about which Alexis de Tocqueville expressed such concern in *Democracy in America* (Part One, Chapter 10). De Tocqueville was also skeptical of what he termed "mixed governments," which professed to share power among several constituencies, observing that "social power superior to all others must always be placed somewhere; but I think that liberty is endangered when this power finds no obstacle which can retard its course and give it time to moderate its own vehemence." Alexis de Tocqueville, *Democracy in America* (1835) Part One, Chapter 12.

the direction of the board of directors, *unless* a specific provision of the Corporations Code or the articles or bylaws of the corporation reserve to the members the ultimate authority to approve the action. Generally, the types of actions that are reserved for member approval under the law involve fundamental decisions affecting core policies or the very direction of the organization, such as the election or recall of directors, mergers, dissolutions, a sale of all or substantially all of the assets of the association, or substantial assessment increases.[72]

Apart from these rights conferred by statute to participate in major corporate policy decisions, community association members are given a largely passive and monitoring role under both California statutes and most common interest governing documents. In fact, prior to adoption of Civil Code section 1363(g) in 1989, an association board did not even have to permit members to attend board meetings, and there is still no requirement in the California statutes that community association boards conduct their meetings at a location within or near the development.[73] The greatest check and balance available to association members under the law is the right conferred in Corporations Code section 7510(e) for a special meeting of the members to be called for any lawful purpose by as few as 5 percent of the total membership. In short, if a group or faction within the membership does not like the way in which its association is being managed, they may call a meeting to discuss their concerns or, if need be, to vote on a recall of one or more of the directors.[74]

---

[72]See Cal. Corp. Cd. §§7220-7224; 8010-8019; 8610-8617; Cal. Civil Code §1366.

[73]This obligation is imposed by the DRE "Reasonable Arrangements" Regulations (10 Cal. Cd. Regs. § 2792.20(b)), but is only binding on associations during the period of developer control. For example, several Lake Tahoe developments represented by the author meet in San Francisco because most of the board is comprised of owners who reside in the Bay Area.

[74]Even with respect to these reactive powers vested in the members, the balance of power is subtly tipped in favor of the board. When five percent of the members demand a meeting pursuant to Corporations Code §7510(e), it is up to the board to schedule the date, time, and location for the meeting at the board's discretion and at any time not less than 35 nor more than 90 days following receipt of the members' demand (see Cal. Corp. Cd. § 7511(c)). For example, depending upon the timing of notice, the board could call for the meeting to be held at 1:00 p.m. on Super Bowl Sunday. Furthermore, if a demand is received to recall less than all of the sitting directors, cumulative

Fiduciary Responsibilities of Community Association Directors

There are several policy arguments in support of the proposition that the balance of power within community associations dictated by the Corporations Code may not be skewed unfairly to favor the interests of management at the expense of the members and residents. With the broad powers enjoyed by association directors and officers comes a strict fiduciary obligation to act in the best interests of the association the director is serving and to consider what is best for the members as a whole. The idea that a community association director's official actions and decisions must be consistent with specified minimum standards distinguishes association directors from local elected officials (see the following section). The Corporations Code standards for director conduct also subject directors to potential liabilities for their decisions and actions. The same personal liability risks are not faced by individual members or member factions who become activists in opposition to the policies of incumbent management. A member who is not serving on the board does not have a fiduciary duty to act in the best interests of the association, and he or she is free to champion narrow causes or fringe points of view.

The term "fiduciary" is derived from Roman law and, in its original context, referred to a person holding the character of a trustee. Under current legal interpretation, the term includes trustees, but also refers more generally to any person who holds a position requiring trust, confidence, and scrupulous exercise of good faith and candor. Under the traditional trustee articulation of fiduciary duties, the trustee was prohibited from dealing with the assets or property of the trust in any way that benefited the interests of the trustee (no matter how beneficial the same actions may be to the beneficiary) unless the beneficiary was fully informed and gave his or her consent in advance.[75]

Modern usage of the term "fiduciary" has expanded the concept beyond the strict trustee context to include any person who has a duty, created by a particular undertaking, to act primarily for the benefit of others in matters connected with the undertaking. The cases speak of a "special confidence reposed in one who, in equity and good conscience, is bound to act in good faith and with due regard to the interests of the person who has reposed that confidence," including corporate directors.

---

voting provisions may make it extremely difficult for the vote to succeed (see Corp. Cd. § 7222(b)(1)).

[75]See *Stern v. Lucy Webb Hayes School* (1974) 381 F Supp. 1033.

Although directors of both business and nonprofit corporations are considered as holding a fiduciary relationship with respect to their shareholders or members, it is well established that a strict trustee standard of duty, which would prohibit any self-dealing with the corporation, regardless of the benefit conferred, is generally not what is intended or required (at least not in California).[76]   In fact, there was substantial concern among the drafters of California's Nonprofit Corporation Law that, if too strict a standard was imposed on directors by the Corporations Code, it would be difficult, if not impossible, to attract qualified individuals to serve, especially in an uncompensated, voluntary capacity. There was also concern that application of the strict trustee standard would require nonprofit corporations to decline to participate in transactions in which one or more of the corporation's directors were willing to provide goods or services at below market rates.[77]

Comparison to Laws Regulating Conduct of Elected Officials

Many community association directors, particularly those serving in large common interest developments, tend to view the responsibilities of their office, and their range of discretion, as if they were governed by the same legal rules applicable to local elected officials.   Community association directors who view their position in this fashion fail to appreciate that the conduct of state and local elected officials is governed by a very different set of legal requirements.

First and foremost, elected officials are not bound to observe any minimum standard of due care towards their constituents, short of avoiding participation in clear conflicts of interest, fraud, or other corrupt practices.[78]   Elected representatives also have no obligation to consider

---

[76]"A trustee is uniformly held to a high standard of care and will be held liable for simple negligence, while a director must have committed 'gross negligence' or otherwise be guilty of more than mere mistakes in judgment." (*Stern v. Lucy Webb Hayes School* (1974) 381 F. Supp. 1033.)

[77]See H. Oleck, *Nonprofit Organizations' Problems* (1980).

[78]Laws exist that prohibit public officers from becoming financially interested in any contract made by them in their official capacity or from participating in any decision before their agency involving a transaction in which the official has a material financial interest. See Government Code section 1090 and section 81000 *et seq.* It is also a crime for a public officer to willfully fail to perform

the best interests of electors residing within the entire geographic area that their governmental unit serves. Instead, elected state and local officials are permitted to champion the interests of the specific district, area, or constituency that elected the official to office. This is in contrast to the obligation of community association directors to act in good faith and in a manner that the director believes will promote the best interests of the association and its members as a whole (see below).

Statutory Definition of the Directors' Standard of Conduct (The "Duty of Care")

The standard of conduct prescribed for directors of nonprofit community associations is the same standard that the legislature has imposed on directors of business corporations under Corporations Code Section 309. That standard, as applied to community associations and other nonprofit mutual benefit corporations, is found in Corporations Code section 7231 and is generally referred to as the directors' "duty of care." Section 7231 articulates the duty as follows:

A director shall perform the duties of a director, including duties as the member of any committee of the Board, . . . in good faith, in a manner the director believes to be in the best interests of the corporation, and with such care, including reasonable inquiry, as an ordinarily prudent person in a like position would use under similar circumstances.

Under this duty of care, a director can be held liable if the director acts negligently in the performance of his or her duties, even though the director has no interest in the transaction that is opposed to the corporation and does not receive any profit from it. In the case of *Burt v. Irvine Company* (1965) 237 Cal. App. 2d 828, the Court of Appeals explained the duty of care as follows:

The rule exempting directors and officers of corporations from liability from mere mistakes and errors of judgment does not apply where the loss is the result of failure to exercise proper care, skill and diligence. Directors are not merely bound to be honest; they must also be diligent and careful in performing the

---

any duty for which the officer is responsible (Govt. Cd. section 1222). However, there are no state laws imposing on elected officials specific fiduciary duties or standards of conduct akin to the fiduciary duties found in Corporations Code section 7231 (discussed in Paragraph 5.2).

duties they have undertaken. They cannot excuse imprudence on the grounds of their ignorance or inexperience, or the honesty of their intentions. If they commit an error of judgment through recklessness, or want or ordinary prudence and skill, the corporation may hold them responsible for the consequences.

Although the language used by the *Burt* court and in other cases to define the standard of care suggests that directors can be held liable for mere negligence or mistakes in judgment, that has rarely been the outcome in most reported decisions.[79]

Unlike trustees, nonprofit directors are specifically authorized by statute to delegate corporation management "to any person or persons, management company, or committee."[80] However, if such delegation occurs, the activities and affairs of the corporation must continue to be managed, and all corporate powers exercised under the ultimate direction of the board.[81]

The Directors' Duty of Loyalty

The admonition found in Corporations Code section 7231(a) that a director must act in a manner that the director believes to be in the best interests of the corporation has often been characterized as the "duty of loyalty." Although the statute's expression of the duty of loyalty fails to include a reference to the corporation's members (as found in § 309(a), the corresponding section of the General Corporation Law), the duty of loyalty has generally been construed as an obligation on the part of corporate directors to act in the best interests of the corporation and all

---

[79]Absent fraud or a clear conflict of interest on the part of a director, most of the cases have shown great reluctance to hold directors liable for honest mistakes in judgment, no matter how stupid or ill-advised the director's conduct may appear in hindsight. In the case of *Casey v. Woodruff* 237 Cal. App. 2d 852, however, the Court of Appeals observed that "when courts say they will not interfere in matters of business judgment, it is presumed that judgment—reasonable diligence—has, in fact, been exercised. A director cannot close his eyes to what is going on about him in the conduct of business of the corporation and have it said that he is exercising business judgment."

[80]Corp. Code § 7210.

[81]*Ibid.*

of its members, including the members of minority factions, and to administer their corporate powers for the common benefit.[82]

The great majority of cases addressing the duty of loyalty have involved situations where a director is alleged to have breached his fiduciary duty by engaging in transactions in which he has an undisclosed conflict of interest or is guilty of active fraud. However, loyalty issues are also raised, in the author's opinion, when a director champions the interests of a discrete faction of the total membership that is adamantly opposed to the policies that the board, as a body, is endeavoring to implement with support of a majority of the electorate, particularly if the director's advocacy involves the use of information that he knows to be false, misleading, or materially inaccurate, or information that he is bound to maintain on a confidential basis.

Statutory Regulation of Community Association Transactions Involving Conflicts of Interest.

California's Mutual Benefit Corporation Law takes a very liberal approach to the regulation of transactions between a corporation and one or more of its directors, in which the interested directors have a material financial interest. In fact, like the Nonprofit Law's articulation of the general standard of care that must be observed by community association directors and the statute's regulation of conflict of interest transactions is identical to that found in those portions of the Corporations Code regulating general business corporations organized for profit.[83] Although this position was resisted by the state attorney general's office, the special committee appointed by the legislature to draft the 1980 Nonprofit Corporation Law were of the opinion that if nonprofit corporations were

---

[82]In the seminal decision of *Remillard Brick Co. v. Remillard-Dandini Co.* (1952) 109 Cal. App. 2d 405, the Court of Appeals explained the duty of loyalty as follows:

It is Hornbook law that directors, while not strictly trustees, are fiduciaries and bear a fiduciary relationship to the corporation and all of its shareholders. They owe a duty to all stockholders, including the minority stockholders, and must administer their duties for the common benefit. The concept that a corporation is an entity cannot operate so as to lessen the duties owed to all of the stockholders. Directors owe a duty of highest good faith to the corporation and to its stockholders.

[83]See Cal. Corp. Cd. section 310.

prohibited entirely from participating in transactions that might directly or indirectly benefit a sitting director (at least not without approval of a high percentage of the members), mutual benefit corporations (including community associations) would often be precluded from taking advantage of services, products, or materials that various members of the corporation's board might be willing to provide at either no cost or below market rates.

For that reason, section 7233 of the Corporations Code states that contracts and other transactions between a corporation and one or more of its directors, in which the directors have a material financial interest, are neither void nor voidable because the interested directors are present at the meeting where the transaction is approved if certain disclosure and approval procedures are followed.[84]

Clearly the most prudent course of action when an association is considering a transaction involving the material financial interests of a director is to have the transaction validated by disinterested directors or

---

[84]Corporations Code §7233 provides three alternate ways of approving interested director transactions:

(a) The material facts regarding the transaction and the director's interest in it are fully disclosed to the corporation's membership and the transaction is approved by the members. The required vote of the members is a majority of a quorum of the members, unless the Articles or Bylaws specify a higher percentage for approval (see California Corporations Code §5034); or

(b) The material facts regarding the transaction and the director's interest in it are fully disclosed or known to the Board and the Board authorizes or ratifies the transaction by a vote which is sufficient without counting the vote of any interested director *and* the contract or transaction is just and reasonable to the corporation at the time it is authorized, approved or ratified; or

(c) As to transactions which are not approved by the members or the Board in either of the ways described in paragraphs (a) or (b), above, the person asserting the validity of the contract or transaction sustains the burden of proving that it was just and reasonable to the corporation at the time it was authorized, approved or ratified. This third manner in which interested director contracts or transactions can be approved was intended to apply in those situations in which there are no disinterested members or directors available to approve the transaction. This alternative was not intended to modify the rule that a director is prohibited from making decisions for the corporation he serves which benefit his own interests at the expense of the corporation and its members. See *Raven's Cove Townhomes v. Knuppe Development Co.* (1981) 114 Cal. App. 3d 783 (see Paragraph 5.4B).

by the membership. If neither method of disinterested validation is possible, the interested director may wish to petition the superior court for approval pursuant to section 7515 of the Corporations Code rather than run the risk of having the transaction challenged in a member derivative action.

California's Mutual Benefit Corporation Law never specifically uses the term "conflict of interest" or "self-dealing transaction"; instead, the code refers to transactions involving the corporation in which one or more of its directors has a *material financial interest*. Thus, in the absence of a material impact on the director's pocket book, no conflict of interest exists from a corporate law standpoint, even if the transaction benefits a class of individuals that includes the director (such as real estate brokers or contractors) or favors a relative of the director. Accordingly, some community associations adopt governing document provisions that regulate director conflicts of interest more strictly than required by the Corporations Code.

A similar scheme of prior disclosure and independent ratification is established for transactions involving loans by a corporation to one or more of its directors or the guarantee by mutual benefit corporations of obligations of any director or officer.[85] However, the Articles of Incorporation or bylaws of a mutual benefit corporation can prohibit such loans or guarantees entirely.[86]

Effect of Compliance with the Statutory Standard of Care

Absence of Personal Liability (The "Business Judgment Rule"). If a director performs his or her duties in accordance with the standard of care specified in Corporations Code section 7231, the director "shall have no liability based upon any alleged failure to discharge the person's duties as a director."[87] This exemption, which is commonly referred to as the "business judgment rule." The rule originated in the context of business corporations where shareholders often expect management to take risks in order to maximize profits, without having to fear that they will be second guessed if their business plan is unsuccessful. The justifications for the rule are less compelling for directors of nonprofit corporations since the elements of risk taking and profit seeking are

---

[85]See Corporations Code sections 7235 and 7236.
[86]*Ibid.*
[87]Corp. Cd. 7231(c).

absent, but the concept that directors' decisions should not be second guessed without a substantial basis for doing so remains relevant to nonprofit corporations.

The Exception for Tortious Conduct. In *Frances T. v. Village Green Owners Assn.* (1986) 42 Cal. 3d 490, the California Supreme Court held that the business judgment rule of Corporations Code section 7231 is not a bar to individual director liability if a director participates in tortious conduct that results in personal injury.[88] To maintain a tort claim against a director, individually, the *Frances T.* court held that the plaintiff must

---

[88]In the *Frances T.* case, the plaintiff alleged that: (i) the association directors owed a duty to her; (ii) they had specific knowledge that a hazardous condition existed which threatened her personal safety; and (iii) they failed to take action to avoid the harm she sustained. In ruling that the plaintiff had stated a cause of action against the directors *as individuals* for negligence, the Supreme Court explained why the directors could not seek protection behind the veil of the business judgment rule:

> Directors are liable to persons injured by their own tortious conduct regardless of whether they acted on behalf of the corporation and regardless of whether the corporation is also liable . . . Directors owe a duty of care, independent of the corporation's own duty, to refrain from acting in a manner which creates an unreasonable risk of personal injury to third parties . . . A distinction must [also] be made between the director's fiduciary duty to the corporation (and its beneficiaries) and the director's ordinary duty of care not to injure third parties. The former duty is defined by statute [i.e., Corporations Code Section 7231], the latter by common law tort principles. 42 Cal. 3d at pp. 503-04.

See also *Seagate Technology v. A. J. Kogyo Co.* (1990) 219 Cal. App. 3d 696, 702 and *Taylor-Rush v. Multitech Corp.* (1990) 217 Cal. App. 3d 103, 112; *Ruoff v. Harbor Creek Community Assn.* (1992) 10 Cal. App. 4th 1624. In *Ruoff,* the Court of Appeals held that in the context of a common interest development in which the common areas are owned by owners of the appurtenant separate interests as tenants in common, a person who sustains injuries in the common area has a cause of action for negligence, not only against the community association and perhaps its directors, but also against the individual unit owners.

Another helpful tip for clients serving as directors and officers of nonprofit organizations is found in the *Francis T.* case. The Supreme Court noted that a director's personal liability arises from authorizing, directing or participating in tortious conduct that causes injury to another. Thus, directors who do not vote in favor of the action that causes the injury have a valid defense to liability.

show that: (1) the director specifically authorized, directed, or participated in the tortious conduct; or (2) the director knew or should have known that a condition under the board's control was hazardous and could cause injury and yet the director negligently failed to take action to avoid the harm; and (3) an ordinarily prudent person, possessing the same knowledge as the director, would have acted differently.

The Supreme Court specifically noted that individual directors named in a personal injury suit have a defense against personal liability, namely, that their conduct was not clearly unreasonable under the circumstances or that they reasonably relied on expert advice or the decision of a subordinate who was in a better position to act. In light of the court's specific rejection of the business judgment rule as a shield from personal liability, this confirmation that directors have a defense to personal liability if they can prove that they reasonably followed expert advice or reasonably delegated decisions to a subordinate or committee seems inconsistent, yet beneficial. The Court also held that any director who did not vote in favor of the action that caused the injury would have a defense to personal liability.

A Heightened Standard May Be Applied to Developer-Appointed Directors. Another special rule may exist for those community association directors who are sitting on the board to represent the developer's interests. In *Raven's Cove Townhomes, Inc. v. Knuppe Development Co.* (1981) 114 Cal. App. 3d 783, the California Court of Appeals was faced with breach of fiduciary duty claims by the developer-controlled board of directors of the community association. The dispute focused on inadequate funding of reserves for replacement of capital assets. In holding the developer liable on a theory of strict liability for failure to supervise the association, the court of appeals noted the potential for conflicts of interest where the developer and its agents dominate the board. The court further noted the director's duty of undivided loyalty and obligation to avoid transactions that benefit the developer's interests at the expense of the association and its members.

In reaching these conclusions, the *Raven's Cove* court came very close to articulating a trustee standard of loyalty by emphasizing that the association was "in its infancy" and that "the developer [was] a fiduciary acting on behalf of unknown persons who will purchase and [later] become members of the association." The *Raven's Cove* court concluded that the fiduciary obligations of the developer-directors took on a "greater magnitude" because of the mandatory nature of association membership, because the directors were acting on behalf of members not yet identifiable, and because the internal methods of control by the membership were weak, or nonexistent.[89]

Although no reported decision involving the actions of a developer-controlled community association board has clearly stated that a higher standard of care, similar to that of a trustee, will be used in assessing a developer-director's adherence to his or her fiduciary duties, the courts do appear to examine the actions of developer-directors with much greater scrutiny. The developer's desire to maximize profits through the brisk marketing and sale of lots or units creates numerous opportunities for conflicts with the best long-term interests of future residents on such important issues as budget preparation, capital reserve analysis, architectural control, design standards, and CC&R enforcement. Judges appear cognizant of these inherent conflicts and appear willing to intervene when developer representatives participate in decisions of the community association board in a way that puts their personal interests ahead of those of the community in general.

In trying to reconcile the strong language found in these decisions with cases applying the more forgiving business judgment standard, it is also interesting to note that one of the reasons trustees have been held to such a heightened standard of fiduciary duty is that the trustee often acts in an environment where the beneficiary is incapable of effectively monitoring the trustee's conduct due to age, incapacity, or geographic separation.[90] The strict self-dealing restrictions applicable to California

---

[89]Similar language indicating the possibility of greater judicial scrutiny of developer-directors was used in *Cohen v. Kite Hill Community Association* (1983) 142 Cal. App. 3d 642 (which also involved a developer-controlled board). In the *Cohen* decision, the court observed:

> With power, of course, comes the potential for abuse. Therefore, the Association must be held to a high standard of responsibility. "The business and governmental aspects of the association and the association's relationship to its members clearly give rise to a special sense of responsibility upon the officers and directors." [T]he Association of homeowners [occupies] a particularly elevated position of trust because of the many interests it monitors and services it performs. 142 CA 3d 642, 651.

[90](See Rest. of Restitutions, §§ 190-192 (1937); Rest. 2d Trusts, § 170 (1959); Michael Hone, Position Paper prepared for Committee on Nonprofit Corporation Law, ABA Section of Corporations (1980).) Similar considerations were cited by the *Raven's Cove* court. 114 Cal. App. 3d 783, at 800.

charities does not apply to directors of community associations and other mutual benefit corporations on the theory that mutual benefit corporations have an active membership that can serve as an effective counterbalancing force and voice in protecting the corporation against abuses of fiduciary power.[91] Under such circumstances the drafters of California's Nonprofit Corporation Law determined that the appropriate focus of the law should be on full disclosure and ratification, rather than regulation and prohibition. Community associations have no well-defined and active membership during the period of developer control, however, and the developer-directors are administering the affairs of the community association in an atmosphere of clearly divided loyalties—seeking to maximize their business interests yet charged with the duty of furthering the best interests of "unknown persons who will purchase units and thereby become members of the association."[92]

Another explanation for the strict standards that the courts appear to be applying in cases involving developer-dominated community association boards is the independent fiduciary duty that the courts have long held that majority or controlling shareholders owe to their corporation and to the minority shareholders. This duty is separate and distinct from any duty they may have by virtue of serving on the board.[93]

---

[91]See Basile, "Directors' Liability Under the New California Nonprofit Corporation Law," 13 *University of San Francisco Law Review* 891 (1979) note 183, at 907.

[92]*Raven's Cove* 114 Cal. App. 3rd at 799 Cal. Rptr. at 343

[93]See *Crebs v. Uplifters Country Home* (1933) 133 Cal. App. 88; *Remillard Brick Co. v. Remillard-Dandini Co.* (1952) 109 Cal. App. 2d 405; *Efron v. Kalmanovitz* (1964) 226 Cal. App. 2d 546; *Jones v. H. F. Ahmanson & Co.* (1969) 1 Cal. 3d 93; *Fisher v. Penn. Life Co.* (1977) 69 Cal. App. 3d 506; *Kirschner Bros. Oil Co. v. The Natomas Co.* (1986) 185 Cal. App. 3d 784; *Smith v. Tele-Communication, Inc.* (1982) 134 Cal. App. 3d 338; *Trasher v. Trasher* (1972) 27 Cal. App. 3d 23.

In the case of *Jones v. H. F. Ahmanson, supra,* the California Supreme Court stated that:

[M]ajority shareholders, either singly or acting in concert to accomplish a joint purpose, have a fiduciary responsibility to the minority and to the corporation to use their ability to control the corporation in a fair, just and equitable manner. Majority shareholders may not use their power to control corporate activities to benefit themselves or in a manner detrimental to the minority. (1 Cal. 3d 108.)

Although the cases involving breaches of duty by dominant corporate shareholders all involve for-profit enterprises, it can be argued that the same legal principles should apply with equal force to nonprofit corporations under circumstances in which a community association director is claimed to have breached his or her duty to the corporation, and evidence is presented that the director was seeking to defend his or her position against hostile member factions or to protect a material financial interest possessed by the director. This exposure appears even more pronounced in situations where the nonprofit entity is affiliated in some respect with a for-profit enterprise in which a director has an interest, such as occurs when a real estate developer serves on a community association board within his or her own common interest development.

CONCLUSION

California's Nonprofit Mutual Benefit Corporation Law, as modified and supplemented by the Davis-Stirling Common Interest Development Act, generally provides an effective and comprehensive scheme for the regulation of community associations. The one substantial exception to this is that, at present, California's statutory scheme for common interest developments and their community associations provides inadequate protection for nondeveloper members against abuse during periods of developer control of the association.

Jurists in other jurisdictions have begun to construct an analytical bridge between the cases involving abuse of control positions by dominant shareholders and cases challenging the actions of directors seeking to preserve their corporate positions against hostile takeover attempts. Dissenting opinions in *Johnson v. Trueblood* (3rd Cir. 1980) 629 F. 2d 287 and *Minstar Acquiring Corp. v. AMF, Inc.* (S.D.N.Y. 1985) 621 F. Supp. 1252 have advanced the proposition that the Business Judgment Rule's presumption that a director was acting in good faith and in the best interests of the corporation he is serving should not apply once a plaintiff shareholder has established that the director's decisions/actions were motivated by the director's personal desire to retain control.

5

Choice, Consent, and Citizenship in Common Interest Communities

James L. Winokur

THE GROWTH OF COMMON INTEREST COMMUNITIES

Common interest communities (CICs) include all developments that have mandatory community associations responsible for managing common areas or assets with funds assessed by the association against individual homeowners, and enforcing use restrictions throughout the community. Thus, CICs include condominium, townhouse, free standing, single-family residence, and other planned unit developments. A novel ownership form only 25 years ago, CICs have proliferated to where they now account for a substantial portion of the entire United States housing stock. CICs currently include residences of at least 30,000,000 people and at least 12-17 percent of the U.S. population.[1] While condominium

---

[1]See *Community Associations Institute Factbook*, 7,9 (1988) [hereinafter, *CAI Factbook*], estimating 29,640,000 CIC residents some four years ago, which CAI considered to be 12.1 percent of the population. Higher estimates have been made by, e.g., Bowler and McKenzie, "Invisible Kingdoms," 5 *Cal. Law.* 55 (No. 12, Dec. 1985). A 1987 California study estimates there were then between 13,000 and 16,000 owners' associations in that state alone. S. Barton and C. Silverman, "Common Interest Homeowners' Associations Management Study: Report to the California Dept. of Real Estate" 2 (October 1987) [hereinafter "Barton and Silverman California Study"].

development may temporarily have peaked in some areas,[2] the overall number of common interest communities is expected to grow substantially again during the 1990s.[3]

As a result of the spectacular growth of CICs, more and more suburban neighborhoods are developed as either low-density subdivisions of single-family residences, or higher density, clustered housing—with all residences within a development built from one of only a few, virtually identical designs. The lots are often virtually uniform and occupied by socio-economically homogeneous residents. Uniformity is preserved within each neighborhood by a complex battery of restrictions on use, with even minor aesthetic changes typically prohibited without advance approval of a neighborhood architectural review committee. These restrictions are usually reciprocally enforceable among residence owners within a subdivision or condominium project and—more importantly—by the homeowners or condominium association.

Several factors have contributed to the recent growth of CICs. Among them is the affordability of clustered housing in which individual homes are relatively crowded, but where that crowding is somewhat offset by substantial common areas and facilities such as swimming pools—luxuries beyond homeowners' means, except where a CIC allows cost spreading. Costs saved by clustering housing include not only

---

[2]See "Apartment/Condominium Market," 27 *Nat'l. Real Estate Investor*, 53, 60 (1986).

[3]CAI estimates new common interest associations are being created at the rate of approximately 4,000-5,000 per year. In each of the 50 largest metropolitan areas throughout the U.S., well over 50 percent of all new housing has for several years now been in CIC housing. It has been estimated that up to 70 percent of all new housing built in San Diego and Los Angeles counties is subject to association administered servitude-regimes.

Regarding the growth of CICs nationally, see, e.g., Howe, "California's Homeowner Wars," *San Francisco Chronicle*, July 3, 1989, at C-1; "Homeowners' Association Task Force Report to Montgomery County Council," Rockville, Maryland (1989) at p. 12 (concluding that "virtually all subdivisions of 50 units or more are being developed as common interest communities and . . . in the near future the vast majority of our citizens will live under these quasi governments"); Barton and Silverman, "The Political Life of Mandatory Homeowners' Associations," in U.S. Advisory Commission on Intergovernmental Relations, *Residential Community Associations: Private Governments in the Intergovernmental System?* (1989) at 34, (noting servitude regimes account for over 90 percent of all new housing in San Jose, California).

decreased overall acreage for development, but also economies in construction of homes and infrastructure and in provision of public services. By definition, clustered housing developments—condominium or otherwise—require the CIC ownership format, where the homeowners share direct (condominium) or indirect (via homeowners' association) ownership of common assets. CICs have also responded to the desire of two-career families and older residents for more "carefree living" in which portions of the home traditionally owned individually—exteriors, roofing, front and rear lawns—become common assets maintained by the CIC.

An often underrated factor influencing the increase in CICs—whether with clustered or spacious single-family housing—is the preference of both local land-use regulators and residential developers for structuring their developments as planned unit developments (PUDs).[4] PUDs have allowed local governments to save themselves money by requiring that streets and other infrastructure be created by the developer and held in private rather than government ownership so that the public government avoids maintenance responsibilities.[5] Developers in turn benefit economically because infrastructure designed for *private* maintenance is often held to less exacting standards than the local governments would require for streets dedicated over to *public* ownership and care.

CIC development has thus gone hand-in-hand with privatization of a range of previously public services, including not only maintenance of facilities—streets, infrastructure, and common areas—but also services such as trash collection, snow removal, street maintenance and cleaning,[6] with community associations empowered to perform them or contract for

---

[4]*See, e.g.,* French, "Toward a Modern Law of Servitudes: Reweaving the Ancient Strands," 55 *So. Cal. L. Rev.* 1261, 1263 (1982) [hereinafter, French, "Reweaving the Ancient Strands"].

[5]*See, e.g.,* Dowden, *Community Associations: A Guide for Public Officials,* 7-13 (1980) [hereinafter, Dowden]; *Brentwood Subdivision Road Assoc. v. Cooper,* 461 N.W. 2d 340 (1990); 61 Ops. Cal. Atty. Gen. 466 (1978); Kenney, "Dictators of Taste," *Eastside Week,* October 2, 1991 (Seattle) [hereinafter, Kenney].

[6]*See New Jersey State League of Municipalities et al. v. State of New Jersey,* Docket No. BUR-L-790-90 (November 5, 1990), recognizing such services as essentially public services, for which CIC residents are, in effect, double taxed, but holding the New Jersey statute mandating reimbursement unconstitutional for failing to equally protect tenant victims of similar double taxation.

their performance. Owners' associations thus manage, and perform services for which public governments often want no responsibility. To assure the associations a reliable source of income with which to perform their quasi-public services, covenants are imposed by the original development documents to bind residents to association membership and financial support.[7] Once associations are created and servitudes imposed to manage common areas and facilities, association-administered use restrictions are often added to the association responsibilities.[8]

EVALUATING COMMON INTEREST COMMUNITIES

"Multitasking" with Mixed Success

Common interest communities have two related but distinct sides: (1) the ownership vehicle through which individual homeowners share ownership and responsibility to maintain common assets, and (2) the mutually enforceable use restrictions designed to preserve neighborhood character and uniformity. Both these features are supported by covenants that obligate all owners obey use restrictions and to contribute financially to the association that is, in turn, charged with common asset maintenance and restriction enforcement.

CICs serve the worthy economic functions of reducing housing and related costs to housing providers and consumers, and to local governments.[9] In their use restrictions, CICs often help maintain desirable

---

[7]For discussion of CIC financial responsibilities and analysis of CIC legal remedies in collecting unpaid assessments, *see generally* Winokur, "Meaner Lienor Community Associations: The Super Priority Lien and Related Reforms Under the Uniform Common Interest Ownership Act," 27 *Wake Forest Law Review* 353 (1992).

[8]*See generally, e.g.,* Dowden, *supra* note 5, 7-13 (1980). For extensive review of the emergence of restrictive promissory servitudes as a judicially favored legal device, *see generally* Winokur, "The Mixed Blessings of Promissory Servitudes: Toward Optimizing Economic Utility, Individual Liberty and Personal Identity," 1989 *Wisconsin L. Rev.* 1 [hereinafter, Winokur, "Mixed Blessings"].

[9]For argument that the shifting of maintenance responsibilities for traditionally public-type infrastructure benefits the developer and the seller from whom developer acquired the development site, see Perlstein, CAI President's Column, We CAIr (Conn. Ch. CAI newsletter), at 2, 10.

character and quality in many residential areas. They support neighbor-hood characteristics important to many residents—such as quiet, privacy, and status.[10] Consistency of aesthetic design throughout a neighborhood can sometimes produce residential areas of striking beauty.

But CIC operations often generate troublesome burdens. Performance of association maintenance obligations is often compromised by amateur management unsophisticated in financial planning and business operations and sometimes insensitive to ethical issues.[11] With many CICs created in the past 25 years just now beginning to age, many associations are coming face to face with their "history of deferred maintenance and failure to plan for future capital expenditures under amateur resident management."[12]

---

[10]CICs support a suburban lifestyle which, for example, relies on car transportation more than walking or public transit and focuses on supermarkets and shopping center department stores over ethnic or esoteric neighborhood shops. *See, e.g.,* H. Gans, *People and Plans: Essays on Urban Problems and Solutions* 29-30 (1968) [hereinafter Gans].

[11]*See, e.g.,* C. Norcross, *Townhouses & Condominiums: Residents' Likes and Dislikes* at 80, 83-85 (Urban Land Institute, 1973) [hereinafter Norcross]. *See also,* Reichman, "Residential Private Governments: An Introductory Survey," 43 *U. Chi. L. Rev.* 253, 290 (1976) [hereinafter "Residential Private Governments"] (noting resident dissatisfaction with failure of developers to train association boards).

The "Barton and Silverman California Study," *supra* note 1, not only reports the inability of associations to even fill vacant board seats, but also portrays many board members as "not thoroughly knowledgeable about their own associations," and "mistaken as to the contents of their association documents." *Id.* at 12. Barton and Silverman give examples of a board member mistakenly believing a controversial city parking rule to be an association-administered rule, and an association committee chairman unaware of the committee's task. *Id.* See also S. Williamson and R. Adams, "Dispute Resolution in Condominiums: An Exploratory Study of Condominium Owners in the State of Florida" 68 (Human Resources Mgt. Center, College of Business. Administration, University of North Florida, 1987) at 68 [hereinafter "Williamson & Adams Florida Study"], reporting 61.7 percent of responding condominium residents either "strongly agreeing" or "agreeing" that "[m]ost condominium officers lack the technical training to be effective managers."

[12]*Id.* at 21. Although most associations believed their reserves were adequate to avoid large special assessments, Barton and Silverman report that a third of all associations had no completed study of their reserve needs on which to base

CIC use restrictions often exclude not only all nonresidential uses,[13] but also residential uses varying from the servitude-imposed norm in density, cost, or caliber of improvements. CIC servitude restrictions can effectively segregate social classes, isolating residents of one neighborhood from outsiders who neither live, shop, nor work with residents of exclusive districts.[14]   With exceptions, many CICs have become aesthetically undifferentiated and culturally desolate.[15] Servitude-regimes have generated growing resident dissatisfaction with "straight jacket" restrictions that invade aspects of home life previously left to personal choice.[16] Litigation between servitude-regime residents and their owners

---

their optimism. *Id.* Indeed, only 28 percent of the associations whose responses included reserve figures reported reserves at least equaling the 75 percent of annual expenses recommended by some industry experts. *Id.* 30 percent of all associations had called for special assessments within the past two years. *Id.* at 20.

[13]Budd, "Home Is Where The Businesses Are," *Common Ground* 24 (September/October 1991) [hereinafter, Budd]. For discussion of recent tensions surrounding in-home uses some consider residential while others consider commercial, see Liebmann, "Suburban Zoning, Two Modest Proposals," 25 *Real Prop. Prob. & Tr. J.* 1 (1990).

[14]*See* J. Jacobs, *The Death and Life of Great American Cities* (1961) [hereinafter Jacobs]; at 115; K. Lynch, *A Theory of Good City Form* 250, 267 (1981). *See also* R. Sennett, *The Uses of Disorder* 70-73 (1970) [hereinafter Sennett]. E. Blakely and M. G. Snyder, *Fortress America: Gated and Walled Communities in the United States*, Working Paper for Lincoln Institute of Land Policy (June 1994).

[15]Where segregated uses are artificially imposed by "routine-minded real estate developers," architectural critics see individuals contriving deliberate differences to distinguish their building from the next. Jacobs at 223-29, citing "impulses to look special (in spite of not *being* special)," the "googie architecture" distinguishing standardized roadside commercial strips. See also Raskin, "On the Nature of Variety," *Colum. U.F.*, Summer, 1960.

[16]Norcross, *supra* note 11, 80.   This 1973 Urban Land Institute report characterized residents as "unhappy, resentful, discouraged, and disillusioned about their associations," with "[a] considerable number of families . . . so angry that they are selling their homes and moving away, . . . to get away from what they think of as straight-jacket controls on their lives." *Id.* The report lamented the "great dissatisfaction" of residents with their associations as a "tragedy" in light of the "many advantages of homes associations"—many of which are touted in the Institute's classic, *Urban Land Inst., Tech. Bull. No. 50, The Homes Association Handbook* (1964, 1966, 1970 eds.). Representative quotes from resi-

associations has mushroomed.[17] In extreme cases, these conflicts trigger

---

dents, included in this report, reinforce the impression of these associations as overly restrictive of homeowner freedom, confused and unprepared for governance responsibilities, and more concerned with details of essentially private owner behavior than with common facilities and legitimate matters of community concern. Norcross, *supra*, at 83-84. Association enforcement of restrictive servitudes engendered far more resentment than enforcement of association dues obligations; the same survey found about three-quarters of the residents to be satisfied with their monthly association dues. *Id.* at 81.

Some 15 years later, two studies generated similar findings of resident dissatisfaction with community associations. *See generally* "Barton and Silverman California Study," *supra* note 1 finding, for example, that 44 percent of the associations reported that in the past year a member of the board had been harassed or had a personal accusation made against him or her in an open meeting, or that the board had been threatened or actually served with a lawsuit. See also the "Williamson and Adams Florida Study," *supra* note 11, describing restrictive covenants limiting structural, landscaping, and interior design changes as "a major *source* of stress," *id.* at 18, threatening "a serious decline in condominium development as the quality of condominium life deteriorates." *Id.* at 4.

[17]"Barton and Silverman California Study," *supra* note 1, at 13, reporting that 5 percent of all California associations surveyed have actually been sued in just the year before being questioned for the study. This is consistent with the picture of increasing CIC litigation generated by several searches of the Westlaw "Allstates" database of appellate state courts (including D.C., but excluding courts in some states prior to 1965).

These searches included some to allow comparison of the growth of all promissory servitude cases and those occurring only within CICs; and a comparison between cases to enforce CIC monetary obligations and those involving only nonmonetary obligations. The results of these searches suggests dramatic growth in CIC litigation in recent years, as summarized below:

Period	with $ suits included	omitting $ suits	assn. as % of all servitude suits
'57-'62	0	[similar	0.0%
'62-'67	2	proportions,	0.5%
'67-'72	6	but includes	—
'72-'77	9	75-80% of all	—
'77-'82	68	servitude/assn.	10.3%
'82-'87	137	suits]	18.7%

$ = suits to enforce assessments

threats of violence or even actual violence.[18]

The Academic Perspective: CIC Living as Homebuyer Choice and "Public Freedom"

In weighing the benefits and costs of CIC living—and the utility of ready judicial enforcement of CIC covenants—the legal academic community has often cast the issue in terms of market and homebuyer choice. CICs are painted by many commentators as increasing home-buyer choice by increasing purchase options to include not only the CIC ownership form generally but also the varied community styles and differing amenities packages enabled by CIC covenants.

Professor Richard Epstein has recently cast issues of CIC covenant enforceability in terms of the tension between private volition and social control. When should the law defer to the intentions of the various

---

By these searches, all appellate servitude cases (not limited to CIC cases or settings) have increased by approximately 60 percent since the 1957-62 period, while CIC suits have increased approximately 13,700 percent during the same period, and by approximately 1,522 percent since 1972-77. The number of appellate cases (which lag at least several years behind association creation) has grown almost twice as fast as the number of associations increase. Compare "Barton and Silverman California Study" at 13, reporting that fully 5 percent of all associations in their study had actually been sued in the year immediately preceding their study. Compare also figures in Galanter, "Reading the Landscape of Disputes: What We Know and Don't Know (And Think We Know)," 31 *UCLA L. Rev.* 4 (1983).

[18]See, e.g., Button, "Condominiums: Welcome to the Board," *Money* 191 (October 1982) (describing perceived necessity for guard to prevent fist fights at association meetings, and quoting a resident likening struggles between association directors and unit owners to "the Hatfields and McCoys revisited"); Poliakoff, "Conflicting Rights in Condominium Living," 50 *Fla. B. J.* 756 (1980) (describing shotgun threat against association president, bite on association president's leg, destruction of condominium guard house). *See also Florida Times Union*, Nov. 15, 1986, at G-1 (describing condominium residents' problems as including "'condo commandos' on Big Brother-like patrol for minor violations of condo rules, and bitter, sometimes literally deadly, political infighting"). *See also* "Barton and Silverman, Common Interest Homeowners: Private Government and the Public Interest Revisited," *Public Affairs Report*, (March 1988) at 16 [hereinafter, Barton and Silverman, "Private Gov't/ Public Int."].

parties, and when to individual freedom of action?[19]

Epstein favors ready judicial enforceability of CIC covenants—limiting "public regulation [of promissory servitudes to requirements of] notice by recordation of the interests privately created."[20] CIC covenant enforcement is an important protection of the creating parties' freedoms of both contract[21] and property.[22] Other commentators share his premise

---

[19]Epstein, "Notice and Freedom of Contract in The Law of Servitudes," 55 *So. Cal. L. Rev.* 1353-54 (1982) [hereinafter, Epstein, "Freedom of Contract in Servitudes"].

[20]*Id.* at 1354.

[21]*Id.* at 1357.

[22]Epstein's argument takes great pains to glorify the CIC covenant enforcer—even in the extreme case where that enforcer is a single homeowner whose strictness is out of step with current views in the common interest community:

> Ownership is meant to be a bulwark against the collective pressures of others; it allows one, rich or poor, to stand alone against the world no matter how insistent or intense its collective preferences. To say that ordinary ownership presents a holdout problem is not to identify a defect in the system; it is to identify one of its essential strengths. If a holdout is adamant, no private party can *force* him to sell . . . at any price. . . . The power of the original party to hold out, to maintain his servitude against his neighbor, marks the vitality of nascent ownership.

Id. at 1366-67. *See also* Rose, "Servitudes, Security and Assent: Some Comments on Professors French and Reichman," 55 *So. Cal. L. Rev.* 1403, 1412 (1982) [hereinafter, "Rose"] and sources cited therein, for characterization of the holdout servitude owner as holding a "genuine interest in his property right," assertion of which against an intimidating outside world might even qualify such a servitude owner as a potential "culture hero."

More recently, Epstein has moderated his defense of holdouts as marking "the vitality of nascent ownership," emphasizing the individual covenanting parties' ability to waive the holdout problem *ex ante* by imposing majority rule governance onto the servitude regime. *See* Epstein, "Past and Future: The Temporal Dimension in the Law of Property," 64 *Wash. U. L. Q.* 667, 717-18 (1986). For the suggestion that CIC servitudes can be more coercive than liberating, *see generally* Alexander, "Freedom, Coercion, and the Law of Servitudes," 73 *Cornell L. Rev.* 883 (1988), which is criticized in Robinson, "Explaining Contingent Rights: The Puzzle of 'Obsolete Covenants'" 91 *Colum. L. Rev.* 546, 577-79 (1991).

that binding one's self to CIC covenants is freely volitional.[23]

The management power and flexibility so delegated to an owners' association—which is created by the "unanimous ratification" of its constituents, and is sometimes small enough to allow each individual's vote to carry significant weight—has been seen as specially enhancing the constituent owners' autonomy where the association is democratically governed.[24] To each constituent owner's original, autonomous consent to the servitudes regime, this argument would add the "public freedom"

---

[23]*See, e.g.,* Ellickson, "Cities and Homeowners Associations," 130 *U. Pa. L. Rev.* 1519, 1520 (1982) [hereinafter, Ellickson, "Homeowners Associations"]; Korngold, "Resolving the Flaws of Residential Servitudes and Owners Associations: For Reformation Not Termination," 1990 *Wis. L. Rev.* 513, 519-20 (relying heavily on judicial commentary to the same effect, rather than on empirical data) [hereinafter, Korngold, "Flaws of Residential Servitudes"]. Compare, "Rose," *supra* note 22, at 1404, describing the law of servitudes, including in common interest communities, as a "quest for signs of continuing assent" to the obligations of a servitude. For nonacademic endorsement of this view, see "RCA Characteristics and Issues," in *Residential Community Associations: Private Governments in the Intergovernmental System?* at 10 (U.S. Advisory Commission on Intergovernmental Relations, 1989) [hereinafter, "ACIR"].

[24]*See generally* Ellickson, "Homeowners Associations," *supra* note 23. *See also* "Residential Private Governments," *supra* note 11, at 261-63 and at 276 where Dean Reichman acknowledges consent as a premise for servitude enforceability, but as a possibly endangered species in CIC purchases:

> The key term here would seem to be "voluntary." Currently, only a small percentage of the housing market is operated under a residential private government system. Home buyers, generally people of some means who can be expected to take care of themselves, therefore have a real choice as to whether or not to join such a community.

See also Note, "The Rule of Law in Residential Associations," 99 *Harv. L. Rev.* 472 (1985) [hereinafter "Illiberal Residential Associations"] at 479-80; Hyatt, "Condominium and Home Owner Associations: Formation and Development," 24 *Emory L. J.* 977, 1006-08 (1975).

to "participate actively in the basic societal decisions that affect one's life."[25]

The Darker Side in Common Interest Communities: Homebuyer Choice and "Public Freedom"

Choice vs. Implied Consent?

Arguments that CIC servitudes enhance individual autonomy by enhancing homebuyer choice are particularly vulnerable in the many instances where CIC homebuyers' original volition proves to be more imagined than real. Homebuyer submission to some aspects of some CIC servitude regimes is increasingly the focus of conscious thought, and express negotiation between autonomous creating parties. However, most CIC servitudes are imposed with little analysis and discussion between parties who, in any case, often have fewer options than consent-based defenses of servitudes suggest. Throughout most CIC life, the "public freedom" to participate in associational governance—which is tightly limited by the CIC's creating documents—often remains unexercised.

Typically, subdivision restrictions are drawn up and recorded by the developer and her attorneys prior to any sales of lots subjected to them—usually without any participation from prospective owners of the lots under development.[26] The developer also often possesses—by ownership of as yet unsold lots in the development, and often by enhanced voting weight or other special governance provisions created for the development period—overwhelming practical voting and governing

---

[25]Frug, "The City as a Legal Concept," 93 *Harv. L. Rev.* 1057, 1068 (1980).

[26]*See generally* W. Hyatt, *Condominiums and Home Owners Associations* (1985) [hereinafter Hyatt], including secs. 1.05; 9.01; 9.04; 9.14; 9.06; 9.07; 10.13; 10.15. Throughout its coverage of the development process, this leading developer's legal handbook treats the owners as recipients of, rather than shapers of, the initial servitude regime. For another description of the developer's practical control in shaping CIC servitudes, see "Residential Private Government," *supra* note 11, at 260-62, 286-91. *See also* Barton and Silverman, "Private Gov't/Public Int." *supra* note 18, 10-12 (1987); "Geis, Beyond the Condominium: The Uniform Common Interest Ownership Act," 17 *Real Prop. Prob. & Tr. J.* 757, 773 (1982).

control of the association from the association's creation until fairly late in the sales period.[27]

Blocking the prospective homeowner from shaping CIC servitudes is also inherent in the prevailing legal doctrines by which servitudes become legally binding. For CIC servitudes to be enforceable among neighbors, the restrictions must be conceived in advance as part of a common development plan, entailing essentially uniform restrictions applicable to lots between which enforceability is planned.[28] Thus, by the time prospective owners are considering the purchase of parcels or units subject to a regime of servitudes, the seller is effectively powerless to change the CIC servitudes even if she were persuaded a change might be substantively wise.

Furthermore, as more and more residential properties are bound by servitude-regimes,[29] and standard forms proliferate,[30] the option to reject the model(s) of servitude-regimes prevailing in a given area is becoming less realistic for those who wish to enjoy either suburban or condominium

---

[27]*See* "Residential Private Governments," *supra* note 10, at 285-88. *See also* Note, "Residential Associations and the Concept of Consensual Governance," 9 *G. M. U. L. Rev.* 91, 99-100 (1986). An extreme example of developer-retained powers is the community of Reston, Virginia, where the developer remains a major figure in association governance some 25 years following the community's creation by virtue of votes assigned to the developer's still unbuilt, unsold lots, and the developer's continuing rights to appoint half the membership of the Reston restriction-enforcement arm. Author's interview with Jack Poganyi, November 16, 1991.

[28]*See generally* 2 *Am. Law of Property,* at Sec. 9.30 (Casner, ed. 1952, 1976).

[29]See *supra* at nn. 1, 3.

[30]Servitudes are often largely boilerplate language, drafted by attorneys who rely on increasingly standardized forms. *See, e.g.,* Bowler and McKenzie, "Invisible Kingdoms," 5 *Cal. Law.* 55, 58 (No. 12, Dec. 1985). The widespread use of standardized servitude language was confirmed in interviews. A handful of private publications have been very influential in recommending specific servitude language. Hyatt, *supra* note 26; G. Buck, *Condominium Development: Forms with Commentary* (1990); P. Rohan, *Homeowner Associations and Planned Unit Developments* (1977); D. Wolfe, *Condominium and Homeowner Associations That Work* (1978). For an earlier publication that has influenced many later drafting recommendations, see *Urban Land Inst., Tech. Bull.* No. 50, *The Homes Association Handbook* (1964, 1966, 1970 eds.) [hereinafter, *Homes Assoc. Handbook*].

living. Objectionable provisions in one set of restrictions will increasingly be contained in restrictions of other area subdivisions. Standardization of documentation throughout entire residential markets is also practically required by government regulatory oversight, either by state real estate agencies or by federal secondary mortgage agencies. Rather than fight bureaucratic tastes, developers regularly simply lift servitude language from government forms.[31]

Available evidence further suggests that few prospective owners intelligently review the restrictions to which they subject themselves upon acceptance of a deed to land burdened by servitudes.[32] The documenta-

---

[31]See Andrews, "A Proposed Common Interest Community Act," 55 *Fla. B. J.* 144, 146 (1981). *See* Interviews by Nathan Simmons of Jeff Morrison, Subdivision Appraiser, U.S. Dept. of Housing and Urban Development, Denver Office (July 14, 15, 1987) (on file with author) [hereinafter, Simmons-Morrison Interviews], confirming that, in order to streamline HUD's review of project documentation, HUD recommends to developers that they follow "to a T" the promissory servitude language set forth in Appendices to applicable HUD Handbooks (#s 4140.3, 4265.1, and 4135.1, for subdivisions, condominiums, and planned unit developments, respectively) in documenting projects for which FHA, HUD, FNMA, FHLMC, or VA financing may be sought. According to Morrison, the majority of developers use language identical to that recommended in these HUD forms. *See also* Letter of Professor James Geoffrey Durham (February 26, 1988) (on file with author), noting that developers Durham represented in the San Francisco Bay Area relied on standardized forms that "reeked of language we knew would satisfy the California Department of Real Estate, FNMA, *and* FHLMC. That did not leave a lot of room for creativity." For summary of secondary financing market agency requirements for approval of CIC projects, see *D. Anderson & G. Buck, Attorneys' and Lenders' Guide to the Common Interest Ownership Acts: Condominiums, Cooperatives and Planned Communities* 30-40 (1989).

[32]*See* Simmons-Morrison Interviews, *supra* note 31, suggesting that as many as 85 percent of homeowners are not even aware of applicable servitude restrictions, or even of the existence and role of owners associations at the time they purchase properties in servitude-regimes. Such purchasers often first learn of restrictions when they undertake a use or modification of their property arguably prohibited by the servitudes. *Id. See also* Letter of Susan F. French (December 10, 1987) (on file with author) (in which the Reporter for the forthcoming Restatement of Servitudes notes that most owners—and even most association board members—in her community's nearly 1,000-unit servitude regime "did not even know that we had CC&Rs that imposed architectural control."); Sargent, To Consent . . . Or Not to Consent . . . Is There a Question?

tion typically makes long, boring reading for laypersons,[33] who rarely retain counsel to review any documentation involved in home purchases.[34] Even those who read the restrictions in advance may miscalculate their own future attitudes toward servitude restrictions over time,[35] perhaps

---

(1987) (student paper on file with author) (reporting interviews with Denver area real estate professionals, describing potential buyers of new subdivision homes as rarely noting applicable servitudes during the period they are deciding to purchase); Interview by Nathan Simmons of Joe Hofmann, Senior Deputy, Technical Section, Subdivisions, California Dept. of Real Estate (July 23, 1987) (on file with author) [hereinafter, Simmons-Hofmann interview].

A more optimistic opinion was expressed by a regulatory official in Florida, where regulation of condominiums by his state agency requires a prospectus offering a simplification of restrictions applicable to condominium projects containing more than 20 units. Interview by Nathan Simmons of Alex Knight, Division of Florida Land Sales, Bureau of Condominiums, Florida Dept. of Housing (July 27, 1987) (on file with author). But *see* Note, "Judicial Review of Condominium Rulemaking," 94 *Harv. L. Rev.* 647, 650-51 (1981) and authorities cited therein, questioning the effectiveness of disclosure statements.

[33]*See, e.g., id.*; Andrews, "A Proposed Common Interest Community Act," 55 *Fla. B. J.* 144, 145-46 (1981). *See also* "Barton and Silverman, Private Gov't/Public Interest," *supra* note 18, at 12; Simmons-Morrison Interviews, *supra* note 31.

[34]*See, e.g.,* "Report of Special Committee on Residential Real Estate Transactions of the American Bar Association," reprinted in 14 *Real Prop. Prob. & Tr. J.* 581, 594 (1979); Note, "Judicial Review of Condominium Rulemaking," 94 *Harv. L. Rev.* 647, 651 (1981); Fishman, "Role of Lawyer and Organized Bar in Real Estate Transactions," 9 *Real Prop. Prob. & Tr. J.* 551 (1974); Payne, "A Typical House Purchase Transaction in the United States," 30 *Conv. & Prop. Law.* 194, 200 (1966).

Neither these sources nor everyday experience suggests any basis for Professor Epstein's assertion that typical CIC servitudes "are not casual affairs. If they are recorded, there is a strong likelihood that *both parties* have been represented by lawyers." Epstein, "Freedom of Contract in Servitudes," *supra* note 19, at 1365 (emphasis added).

[35]Contract doctrines recognizing impossibility and commercial impracticability as excuses for nonperformance, restricting specific performance of particularly personal, long-term contracts, providing a bankruptcy discharge from past debts, and in mandating participation in social security, pension, and elderly health care programs all reflect our legal system's solicitude for people who inaccurately project their self interest over time. *See, e.g.,* Sterk, "The Continuity of Legislatures: Of Contracts and the Contract Clause," 88 *Colum. L. Rev.* 647 (1988);

inaccurately expecting that friendly relations with neighbors will avoid hostile disagreements between residents over enforcement.[36] Such optimistic expectations are often disappointed.[37]

Even a CIC homebuyer inclined to review servitude documentation, and able to accurately project his reactions to servitude impacts over time, may find himself bound to a servitude regime without reasonable record notice at the time he buys that there are servitudes to review. Thus, a covenantee's recordation of a servitude in a deed to some nearby benefited property[38]—a parcel quite distinct from that being purchased subject to the servitude's burden—gives record notice to the later taker of the burdened estate, even where the servitude appeared nowhere in the taker's chain of title,[39] and thus might well not be found by a search of

---

Kronman, "Paternalism and the Law of Contracts," 92 *Yale L. J.* 763, 778-86 (1983); T. Jackson, *The Logic and Limits of Bankruptcy Law* 235-41 (1986).

[36]For exploration of such contradictions in relations of "political friendship," see generally, Yack, "Community and Conflict in Aristotle's Political Philosophy," 47 *Rev. of Politics* 92 (1985). *See also* Silverman and Barton, "Private Property and Private Government: Tensions Between Individualism and Community in Condominiums" (Working Paper #451, University of California, Berkeley, 1986) (exploring this contradiction in the context of community associations). *See also* Sennett, *supra* note 14, at 32, 33.

[37]See *supra* note 16.

[38]The situation typically arises in cases involving reciprocal servitudes, where the grantor includes in his deed to grantee not only a servitude imposed upon the grantee's parcel, but a reciprocal servitude imposed on the grantor's retained land. If the servitude is not also recorded in the chain of title to the grantor's retained parcel, it would not be discovered by a typical search conducted on the occasion of a later transfer of that retained, burdened parcel.

[39]The leading case, supported by the weight of subsequent authority, is *Finley v. Green*, 303 Pa. 131, 154 A. 299 (1931). Cases adopting this view with respect to either easements or promissory servitudes, include *Guilette v. Daly Drywall, Inc.*, 367 Mass. 355, 325 N.E.2d 572; *Huff v. Duncan*, 263 Or. 408, 502 P.2d 584 (1972); *Moore v. Center*, 124 Vt. 277, 204 A.2d 164 (1964); *Reed v. Elmore*, 296 N.C. 221, 98 S.E.2d 360 (1957); *Hallett v. Sumpter*, 106 F. Supp. 996 (Alaska, 1952); *Harp v. Parker*, 278 Ky. 78, 128 S.W.2d 211 (1939). The leading case rejecting the "Finley" result is Glorieux v. Lightpipe, 88 N.J.L. 199, 96 A. 94 (1915), which also has a modern following. *See, e.g., Hancock v. Gumm* 151 Ga. 667, 107 S.E. 872, 16 A.L.R. 1003 (1921); *Buffalo Academy of the Sacred Heart v. Boehm Bros., Inc.* 267 N.Y. 242, 196 N.E. 42 (1935); *Yates v. Chandler*, 162 Tenn. 388, 38 S.W.2d 70 (1931).

official recorder of deed indices.[40]

Even where no servitude binding his lot has ever been committed to writing, the later purchaser is bound to all servitude obligations common to the neighborhood just as if he had consciously assumed them, according to most courts.[41]   From earlier marketing of the CIC, courts infer the parties' intention that all lots be subject to the same servitudes.[42] The courts further hold that the uniform physical appearance of the surrounding area places a later taker on notice of the unwritten servitudes implied into the developer's earlier sales.[43]   Such diluted protection for

---

[40]For a lucid explanation of methods for searching recorder of deeds' indices in establishing title under recording systems, see C. Haar and L. Liebman, *Property and Law* 694-97 (2d ed. 1985). Where computerized title records have been developed, searching beyond deeds to one's own parcel becomes far less oppressive. And though title insurance searches pose their own limitations, such searches will often turn up subdivision restrictions.   The imputation of constructive record notice does not, however, usually turn on availability or use of these improved search techniques.

[41]The best known case is *Sanborn v. McLean*, 233 Mich. 227, 206 N.W. 496 (1925). Accord: *Turner v. Brocato*, 206 Md. 336, 111 A.2d 855 (1955).

[42]*See, e.g.,* "Sanborn" and "Turner," *supra* note 41; *Seaton v. Crawford*, 24 Cal. App. 3d 46, 100 Cal. Rptr. 779 (1972); *Waterhouse v. Capital Investment Co.*, 44 Hawaii 311, 353 P.2d 1007 (1960); *Jackson v. Richards*, 26 Del. Ch. 260, 27 A.2d 857 (1942). *See also Thisted v. Country Club Tower Corp.*, (146 Mont. 87, 405 P.2d 432 (1962); 124 N.J. Eq. 24, 199 A. 758).

Where a promissory arrangement has admittedly been created, the parties' intention that the arrangement constitute a running servitude, binding and benefiting successors, is more generally implied from the nature of the covenant, even where no intent to bind or benefit successors is expressed in the creating documents. *See, e.g.,* R. Cunningham, W. Stoebuck and D. Whitman, *Property,* 475-76 (1984).

[43]In addition to implying servitudes unexpressed by the original parties, "Sanborn" and "Turner," *supra* note 41, each also held that subsequent constructive notice of the unwritten, unrecorded servitudes was afforded by the physical uniformity of the surrounding development.   In their eagerness to enforce servitudes, these courts seem to blur over distinctions between the earlier manifestations of the development plan on which the original servitude implication is based vs. those from which the court infers subsequent constructive notice to successors of the servitude. *See* Cunningham, Stoebuck and Whitman, *supra* note 42, at 503-04 (1984).

For decisions imputing inquiry notice of servitudes from the apparent physical conformity of surrounding lots, *Shalimar Assn. v. D.O.C. Enterprises,*

takers of land subject to hidden claims may be justified as protection against the developer's sloppy documentation or infidelity to his earlier commitments, on behalf of those prior purchasers who relied on existence of an enforceable servitude regime when they bought into the subdivision. But the doctrine also substantially undercuts the wishful suggestion favoring simplification of servitude law by relying only on present recording laws to protect later takers from servitudes they did not create.[44]

Autonomy Trade-Offs Over Time

At the very least, any contracting individual who *asserts* her autonomy by choosing to enter a contract binding over time thereby enters a relation which, by definition, also *restricts* her own future autonomy. As the contract term becomes more and more extended, the trade-off becomes more and more obvious. The contracting individual has, in effect, set her present self against her future self so that, if and when her view of her earlier contract changes, the autonomy of one or the other of her selves—the earlier contractor or the present repudiator—will inevitably be overridden, depending on whether the original contract is enforced.[45]

In some contexts, this trade-off of personal autonomy has been termed a "Ulysses Contract,"[46] underscoring the conflict between present

---

Ltd., 142 Ariz. 36, 688 P.2d 682 (App. 1984); *Hagan v. Sabal Palms, Inc.*, 160 So. 2d 302 (Fla. App. 1966); *Stark v. Robar*, 339 Mich. 145, 63 N.W.2d 606 (1954).

Professor Berger criticized "Sanborn" as ignoring the realities that a developer of multiple tracts would likely build somewhat uniformly regardless of his plans to impose uniform restrictions. Berger, "A Policy Analysis of Promises Respecting the Use of Land," 55 *Minn. L. Rev.* 167, 201-02 (1970). Indeed, filing restrictions with the recorder's office would be such an easy, routine step for the developer that his failure to file could arguably be substantial evidence that no servitude regime was contemplated by the developer.

[44]Epstein, "Freedom of Contract in Servitudes," *supra* note 19, at 1356-58; Korngold, "Flaws of Residential Servitudes," *supra* note 23, at 518. *See also,* French, "Reweaving the Ancient Strands," *supra* note 4, at 1309.

[45]*Compare* Ackerman, *Social Justice and the Liberal State,* 196-99 (1980).

[46]This usage refers to Homer's *Odyssey,* in which Ulysses—anticipating he would soon be tempted to abandon ship by the irresistible Sirens' Song—ordered his crew bind him to the ship's mast, and not to release him despite his later entreaties. Homer's *Odyssey,* Book XII, vv. 158-165, at p. 160 (H. Cottrell, tr.

and future self anticipated by the making of such a contract in the first place.   Acknowledging that a Ulysses Contract might be seen as a "paternalism," exercised by present over future self, Calabresi and Melamed defend the device as not really paternalistic, since it "merely allows the individual to choose what is best in the long run rather than in the short run, even though that choice entails giving up some short run freedom of choice."[47]   For contracts that run over substantial time periods, this formulation of the autonomy trade-off seems to reverse the contracting individual's options.   By the binding contract, the exercise of her freedom by entering the contract is limited to only the present moment of contracting, but is precluded over the long run of the contract term.

Regimentation and Commodification

Contractual restriction of future autonomy, to be offset against present autonomy enhanced by recognizing the freedom to contract, threatens the autonomous nature of our society more seriously when we consider the "escape from freedom" offered by long-lasting servitudes and the tendency of modern servitude restrictions accordingly to regiment even details of individual residential use.   Both classical free market economics,[48] and classical individualism,[49] contemplate the contracting parties as

---

1911).   For use of this reference in discussion of inalienable property entitlements, *see* Calabresi and Melamed, "Property Rules, Liability Rules and Inalienability: One View of the Cathedral," 85 *Harv. L. Rev.* 1089 at 1113 [hereinafter, Calabresi and Melamed].   The term "Ulysses Contract" has also been used in writings exploring problems of consent to medical treatment, Furrow, "Public Psychiatry and the Right to Refuse Treatment: Toward and Effective Damage Remedy," 19 *Harv. Civ. Rts. Civ. Lib. L. Rev.* 21 (1984), or to experimentation, Rhoden, "Commentary: Can a Subject Consent to a 'Ulysses Contract'?" Hastings Center Rep., Aug. 1982, at 26, 28.

[47]Calabresi and Melamed, *supra* note 46, at 1113.

[48]*See* R. Posner, *Economic Analysis of Law* 3 (3d ed. 1986) [hereinafter, Posner 3d].

[49]*See* A. Toynbee, *Lectures on the Industrial Revolution of the Eighteenth Century in England* 148; J. Bentham, *Theory of Legislation* 144-45 (Ogden ed., 1931); P. Atiyah, *The Rise and Fall of Freedom of Contract* 324-29 (1979) [hereinafter, Atiyah].

acting rationally[50] to maximize their own welfare. But our everyday experience suggests that consent to contractual relations may, for example, include the desire to structure one's life according to external dictates—and thereby, as a goal in itself, to renounce some degree of one's own future autonomy.[51]

An individual can submit herself to an autonomy limiting arrangement in a simple, two-party contract or servitude. Once I promise my neighbor, by binding promissory servitude, how my land will or won't be used, my future autonomy will be limited. As such bilateral relations become multilateral, moreover, the likely threat to individual autonomy increases exponentially.[52] Examining some rules of community associa-

---

[50]Posner's view that "man is a rational maximizer of . . . his 'self interest,'" Posner 3d, *supra* note 48, at 1, has figured prominently in much of his writing. *See, e.g.,* Posner 3d, *supra* (in its entirety) and R. Posner, *The Economics of Justice,* at 237 (1983).

[51]*See generally,* West, "Authority, Autonomy and Choice: The Role of Consent in the Moral and Political Vision of Franz Kafka and Richard Posner," 99 *Harv. L. Rev.* 384 (1985). West's main thrust of analysis is that, in day-to-day reality, human beings' motivations to maximize their own welfare in consenting to relationships are often complicated by a yearning to submit to authority—a yearning which, though submitted to freely, is likely to practically undermine autonomous individuality over the longer term. See particularly *id.* at 386-88. West's article stimulated a subsequent colloquy between Posner and West. *Compare* Posner, "Reply to Professor West," 99 *Harv. L. Rev.* 1431 (1986) and West, "Submission, Choice, and Ethics: A Rejoinder to Judge Posner," 99 *Harv. L. Rev.* 1449 (1986).

Professor West's analysis resonates with the view of Erich Fromm, who saw modern humankind as seeking escape from a painfully negative, individual "freedom from" older social institutions—freedom which, as ultimately extended, has tended to "sever all ties between one individual and the other and thereby isolated and separated the individual from his fellow man." E. Fromm, *Escape from Freedom,* 108 (1941). To escape his resulting insecurity and powerlessness, modern man chooses between two "principal avenues of escape in our time": either submission to an authoritarian leader or "the compulsive conforming as is prevalent in our own democracy." *Id.* at 134. Compare Sennett, "The Uses of Disorder: Personal Identity and City Life" 40 (1970).

[52]Part of the increased threat derives from subjecting each individual to majoritarian control, which often includes power to change the original substantive rules when the majority elects to do so. *See* Atiyah, *supra* note 49, at 591. Individual autonomy is further prejudiced because the individual promisor has a less realistic prospect of negotiating for changes she wants in the

tions to which large numbers of people[53] submit themselves, via promissory servitudes—and even assuming consent to the association and its rules was freely knowingly given[54]—one cannot help but question what mix of motives leads lot purchasers to bind themselves to such long-term, anti-autonomous arrangements.

Thus, CICs have not merely restricted lots to residential uses only. They have purported also to restrict resident ages and childbearing practices,[55] religious practices,[56] financial and social compatibility,[57] and

---

rules as the number of promisees with whom she must negotiate increases. *See, e.g.,* the discussion of strategic bargaining and other impediments to servitude modification among large numbers of CIC residents in Sterk, "Freedom from Freedom: The Enduring Value of Servitude Restrictions," 70 *Iowa L. Rev.* 615, 630 (1985).

[53]Thousands of new owners associations are created each year, according to scholarly and industry estimates. *See* "Residential Private Governments," *supra* note 11, at 256, and sources cited therein; *see also*, Ellickson, "Cities and Homeowners Associations," *supra* note 23, at 1520 (1982). More recent and detailed figures on the dramatic growth in numbers of common interest associations, and in housing units subject to association administered servitude-regimes, are presented in note 1, *supra*.

[54]For analysis questioning how free and knowing such consent to servitudes is, *see* discussion in text at notes 26-44 *supra*.

[55]*See, e.g., O'Conner v. Village Green Owners Assn.*, 33 Cal. 3d 790, 662 P.2d 427, 191 Cal. Rptr. 320 (1983); *White Egret Condominium v. Franklin*, 379 So. 2d 346 (Fla. 1979); *Adrian Mobile Home Park v. City of Adrian*, 94 Mich. App. 194, 288 N.W. 2d 402 (1979); *Coquina Club, Inc. v. Mantz*, 342 So. 2d 112 (Fla. App. 1977); *Riley v. Stoves*, Ariz. App. 223, 526 P.2d 747 (1974). *See generally* Note, "The Enforceability of Age Restrictive Covenants in Condominium Developments," 54 *S. Cal. L. Rev.* 1397 (1981); Travalio, "Suffer the Little Children—But Not in My Neighborhood: A Constitutional View of Age Restrictive Housing," 40 *Ohio St. L. J.* 295 (1979); Doyle, "Retirement Communities: The Nature and Enforceability of Residential Segregation by Age," 76 *Mich. L. Rev.* 64 (1977). In continuingly controversial legislation, the United States Fair Housing Act has, since 1988, prohibited discrimination based on familial status, defined to preclude barring families with underage children, except from certain communities for the elderly. See 42 USC 3601, *et seq.*

[56]*See, e.g., Taormina Theosophical Community, Inc. v. Silver*, 140 Cal. App. 3d 964, 190 Cal. Rptr.38 (1983); *State v. Celmer*, 80 N.J. 405, 411, 404 A.2d 1, 3-4 (1979); *State of Oregon v. Rajneeshpuram*, 598 F. Supp. 1208 (D. Ore. 1984). *Compare* Ellickson, "Homeowners Associations," *supra* note 23 at 1528, advocating the enforceability of some religious restrictions.

the family or marital status,[58] of residents. Some associations have also restricted commercial and political speech within the developments they regulate.[59] CICs typically have granted owners' association architectural review boards—or often, the original subdivision developers[60]—veto power over major structural changes,[61] and also over many seemingly minor details of personal behavior and aesthetic judgments.[62] Such

---

[57]*See, e.g., Chianese v. Culley,* 397 F. Supp. 1344 (S.D.Fla. 1975).

[58]*See, e.g., Jayno Heights Landowners' Assn. v. Preston,* 85 Mich. App. 443, 271 N.W.2d 268 (1978); *Green v. Greenbelt Homes,* 232 Md. 496, 194 A.2d 273 (1963); *see also* Annot., 71 A.L.R.3d 693, 725-35.

[59]*See, e.g., Laguna Publishing Co. v. Golden Rain Fdn. of Laguna Hills,* 131 Cal. App. 3d 816, 182 Cal. Rptr. 813 (1982), *appeal dismissed,* 459 U.S. 1192 (1983).

[60]*See, e.g., Syrian Antiochian Orthodox Archdiocese v. Palisades Associates,* 110 N.J. Super. 34, 264 A.2d 257 (1970). Approval by the developer/common grantor of restricted lots was required in about half of the appellate cases examined that addressed architectural review requirements.

[61]*See, e.g., Rhue v. Cheyenne Homes,* 168 Colo. 6, 449 P.2d 361 (1969)

[62]The restrictions in *McNamee v. Bishop Trust Co.,* 62 Hawaii 397, 616 P.2d 205 (1980) required approval "of any alteration or modeling [sic] of the improvements on the demised premises in excess of ONE THOUSAND DOLLARS ($1,000)." This dollar standard was subject to no inflation indexing, though several inflationary years had passed between imposition of the servitude and commencement of the litigation.

Review requirements have been applied to restrict owners' choices of exterior paint colors, *see, e.g., Westhill Colony, Inc. v. Sauerwein,* 78 Ohio L.Abs. 340, 138 N.E.2d 404 (Ct. App. 1956), window awnings, *see Kirkley v. Seipelt,* 212 Md. 127, 128 A.2d 430 (1957), window air conditioners, *see, e.g., Inwood North Homeowners' Assn. v. Meier,* 625 S.W.2d 742 (Tex. Civ. App. 1981), the use of doghouses, *see University Gardens Property Owners Assn. v. Solomon,* 88 N.Y.S.2d 789 (Sup. Ct. 1946), 18 A.L.R. 3d 853, and the type of vehicles residents can park outside their homes, Kenney, *supra* note 5.

> Community associations often control the color of units or houses, who can use the pool, what kind of trees can be planted, what boulders can be moved, or even the color of the curtain liners. The associations in many condos fine residents for taking their trash out during daylight hours. In Florida, a woman was fined for hanging an American flag on her balcony—no hanging objects were allowed on balconies.

R. Louv, *America II,* 109 (1983) [hereinafter Louv]. With widespread patriotism accompanying the U.S. military success in Kuwait, many—but not all—associations backed off enforcement of anti-flag-waving restrictions. See Friedman, "Old

review is guided by standards ranging from extremely intricate technical guidelines,[63] to sweepingly broad criteria,[64] or no limiting criteria at all.[65]

Glory Flies: Waiving Flag Restrictions in Patriotic Times," *Common Ground* 18 (July/August 1991).   Such tolerance of flags can hardly be counted on when no immediate armed conflict is underway to stimulate patriotism. *See generally*, "Residential Private Governments," *supra* note 11, at 269-70. *See also* Note, "Residential Associations and the Concept of Consensual Governance," 9 *G. M. U. L. Rev.* 91, 95-96 (1986) [hereinafter "G.M.U." Note]; *Wash. Post,* January 5, 1986, at B5, col. 1, (describing restrictive servitudes applicable to homeowners in the planned community of Reston, Virginia, which, for example, go so far as to regulate the colors of owners' children's swing sets). *See also* Telephone Interview by Nathan Simmons of Douglas Kleine, former Director of Publications & Research, Community Association Institute (July 9, 1987) [hereinafter, Simmons-Kleine Interview] (on file with author), suggesting that typical servitude-regimes allow *"nothing"* to be done without permission of the architectural review committee.

[63]Consider, *e.g.*, the Park Lane Condominium (Denver, Colorado) requirements restricting any balcony enclosures residents may wish to construct:

> All enclosures shall be clear Plexiglass, 3/16 inches in thickness, framed in dark bronze aluminum "C" frame, 3/4 inches wide. Frames shall be attached to the railings by means of self-tapping screws, #8 placed 2 feet on center. . . . Framed Plexiglass shall extend from the underside of the railings downward for a distance of 30 inches.

[64]*See, e.g., Alliegro v. Home Owners of Edgewood Hills*, 35 Del.Ch.543, 122 A.2d 910 (1956), in which the architectural committee considered only:

> the suitability of the proposed building or other structure and of the materials of which it is to be built, to the site upon which it is proposed to erect the same, the harmony thereof with the surroundings and the effect of the building or other structure, as planned, on the outlook from adjacent or neighboring property.

Id. at 911. *Compare Snashall v. Jewell,* 228 Or. 130, 363 P.2d 566 (1961), requiring approval based simply on "conformity and harmony of external design with existing structures and . . . maximum view for surrounding properties." *Id.* at 568.

[65]*See, e.g., Davis v. Huey*, S.W.2d 620 561, (Tex. 1981), in which the subdivision restrictions provided:

> Refusal of approval of plans and specifications by the developers, or by the said Architectural Committee, may be based on any ground, including purely aesthetic grounds, which in the sole and uncontrolled discretion of the Developers or Architectural Committee shall seem sufficient.

These promissory servitudes thus often involve not only the imposition of specific use restrictions, but also the delegation to an owners' association—and, at the outset of the development's life, usually to the original developer/grantor, directly or via her practical control of the association for some time[66]—of power to alter the regulatory scheme throughout the term of the promissory servitude regime.[67]

Personal Identity and Citizenship

Beyond individual liberty, the growing predominance[68] of progressively more intrusive[69] promissory servitude regimes in many residential markets threatens the related notion of personal identity—at a time when personal identity is already increasingly undermined by modern social institutions. In the long passage from feudalism to modern capitalism, the individual was released from earlier ties that restricted both economic productivity and individual freedom. At the same time, however, the underlying bonds by which each person is connected to the outside world were also profoundly altered.

As with feudal society, evolving notions of property have been instrumental in the ascendance of market economies and notions of

---

Id. at 563. Although such purportedly sweeping grants of authority are usually cut back under an interpretational rule of reason when reviewed by courts, e.g., *Davis v. Huey, supra; Kies v. Hollub,* 450 So.2d 251 (Fla. Dist. Ct. App. 1984), such unlimited language can powerfully slant negotiations against the property owner seeking permission for an alteration from the regulator. This concern may account for occasional decisions holding standardless architectural review provisions void for vagueness. *See, e.g., Lake Forest, Inc. v. Drury,* 352 So.2d 305 (La. App. 1977), writ den., 354 So. 2d 199 La. (1978);

[66]For authorities addressing the developer's usual *de facto* early control of owners associations, see note *see supra* note 26.

[67]*See* "Residential Private Governments," *supra* note 11, at 273-74: *Bay Island Towers, Inc. v. Bay Island-Siesta Association,* 316 So.2d 574 (Fla. Dist. Ct. App., 1975); *Warren v. Del Pizzo,* 46 Or. App. 153, 611 P.2d 309, modified, 48 Or. App. 237, 616 P.2d 1186 (1980). For recognition of problems in notifying later takers of unrecorded burdens imposed pursuant to powers conferred in the recorded declaration, see *FNMA vs. McKesson,* 636 So. 2d 78 (Fla. App. 4, 1994). Compare Winokur, Meaner Lienor Community Associations, *supra* note 7 at 356-58.

[68]See notes 1, 3, *supra.*

[69]*See generally* text and notes at notes 55-67, *supra.*

possessive individualism. The replacement of feudalism with capitalism has required that—progressively, and forcibly if necessary—many life components once-integrated with land rights[70] be broken out into marketable commodities.[71] The new individualism of post-feudal society fostered freer alienability of property in land including, ultimately, alienability of component rights in land.[72] By a process of commodification, the allocative power of commerce has extended to a growing catalogue of newly conceived, increasingly intangible legal entitlements.[73]

The long process of modernization initially ate away at the tangible and spiritual connections between primitive people and the limited

---

[70]Within the feudal manor, a man's property tied him into a single, life-long web of social relations which accounted for home, livelihood, physical security, mate, religious experience and political niche. The man, and the nature of his life, was concretely identified in terms of his particular piece of land. *See* J. Winokur, *American Property Law: Cases, History, Policy and Practice,* 133, 134-36 (1982).

[71]*See* R. D. Sack, *Human Territoriality,* 71-80 (1986) [hereinafter, Sack, *Territoriality*:

[A]n important requirement for the rise of capitalism is an extensive market system. . . . But this can hardly be sufficient, for traditional societies contain both merchants and markets and yet, in these pre-market cases, trade does not fundamentally alter and displace subsistence household economies. . . . [C]apitalism needs to make labor and capital dependent on commerce. This transforms the role of the merchant from a person supplying conveniences to one supplying necessities, and it transforms the role of the peasant from one relying on himself and his community to one relying on the market and the merchant.

See also Grey, "The Disintegration of Property," in *Property: Nomos XXII* 69, 74-75 (J. Pennock and J. Chapman, eds. 1980) [hereinafter, Grey, "The Disintegration of Property"]; Rosenfeld, "Contract and Justice: The Relation Between Classical Contract Law and Social Contract Theory," 70 *Iowa L. Rev.* 769, 790-94 [hereinafter, Rosenfeld, "Contract and Justice"]

[72]*See* Radin, "Market-Inalienability," 100 *Harv. L. Rev.* 1849, 1856, 1860, 1862 (1987) [hereinafter, Radin, "Market-Inalienability"]; Grey, "The Disintegration of Property," *supra* note 71, at 74-75. Rosenfeld, "Contract and Justice," *supra* note 71, at 790-94. *See also* Reich, "The New Property," 73 *Yale L.J.* 733 (1964).

[73]Grey, "The Disintegration of Property," *supra* note 71, at 75.

territory they encountered,[74] and then continued to erode the bonds between people and land that were central to feudal civilizations.[75] In contrast to these pre-feudal and feudal societies, the citizens of the modern community have become far less land-connected—more a collection of specialized individuals than a single, organic entity.[76]

While the earlier, "determinist" theory of urban sociology argued that such individual differentiation in urban life weakens intimate social groups and isolates people,[77] modern sociological research portrays urbanites firmly connected to others. These modernists emphasize that, while each individual's friends are less likely to be friends with each other, urbanites have no fewer intimate relationships overall than their rural counterparts. Modern city dwellers merely select their associates from a wider choice of special interest contexts, these scholars suggest.[78] Still, urbanites "seem to feel more estranged" even if the sociological scholarship suggests they ought not and, at least in "advanced societies," urbanites express less overall contentment than people from more rural settings.[79]

Amid modernity's wondrous technology and science, the individual's experience of various places and times becomes increasingly undifferentiated, as abstraction and commodification proceed apace.[80] Each suburb, each downtown area increasingly resembles others, and the denizens of one not only often visit others, but also relocate again and again[81] within

---

[74]*Compare* T. Strehlow, *Aranda Traditions* 30-31 (1947), describing the Australian Aborigine's view of land, with *The Bible, Genesis* 1:1, 2:7, 3:17-19, 3:24, 4:11-16, 7:1-8:14, 11:1-9, 15:18.

[75]Sack, *Territoriality, supra* note 71, at 66-72, 74, 76-77.

[76]*See id.* at 115-16.

[77]*See, e.g.,* Wirth, "Urbanism as a Way of Life," 44 *Amer. J. Soc.* 24 (1938).

[78]*See generally* C. Fischer, *The Urban Experience* 113-171 (2d ed. 1984).

[79]*Id.* at 193-98.

[80]*See* Sack, *Territoriality, supra* note 71, at 99-100.

[81]According to a survey conducted in 1983, fully 16 percent of available housing units were reported occupied by households who had moved into such units within the previous year. *U.S. Dept. of Commerce, Bureau of the Census and Dept. of HUD, Annual Housing Survey: 1983,* "Part D: Housing Characteristics of Recent Movers," Table A-1 (1985). (For background, methodology, and procedure of study, see "Introduction" at XI-XIV.) 38.6 percent of the U.S. population had reportedly been living in their current residences less than 4 years. *Id.* (22 percent of those who owned their residences had lived in their current residences for this time, while 68.8 percent of renters had such short

and between cities harder and harder to distinguish from each other.[82]

Traditional liberalism has promoted economic wealth and personal freedom by a generic exaltation of each individual's subjective will, exercised to exploit an ever-widening catalogue of entitlements.[83] But in thus honoring equally the will of each individual, traditional liberalism has tended, ironically, to abstract personhood and to conceive of persons as fungible.[84] This strikingly parallels the progressive commodification and abstraction of property[85] as the external objects upon which individual will operates. These processes of abstraction—separating people from things, and rendering both increasingly fungible in modern thinking—have been abetted by technological sophistication in measurement and the resulting greater influence of nonnormative, quantitative, and scientific analysis.[86]

In our time, people have a confusingly contradictory sense of being personally "powerless in the face of the juggernaut of impersonal power that surrounds and molds us."[87] When so many of society's abundant comforts are offered over to the individual consumer pre-packaged in standardized format, designed to anticipate his every desire, the individual's own significance is easily overshadowed. "[I]t is not surprising," writes psychoanalyst Rollo May,

> . . . that the listener is confused at times as to whether *he* is the anointed one, . . . or just the dumb fall guy? . . . In . . . [the] . . . promises of great power and freedom, a *passive* role is expected of the citizen who is to be recipient. . . . Our role, however subtly put, is to accept the blessing, and be thankful.[88]

---

tenures. *Id.*) Of all owners and renters who had moved to a new residence within the previous year, 24.9 percent had reportedly moved from a different county, state, or Standard Metropolitan Statistical Area. *Id.* Table A-3.

[82]Sack, *Territoriality, supra* note 71, at 91.

[83]*See also* note 22, *supra.*

[84]*See* Radin, "Market-Inalienability," *supra* note 72, at 1897. *Cf. See* D. Riesman (with N. Glazer and R. Denney), *The Lonely Crowd* 307 (abr. ed. 1961).

[85]*See* text and notes *supra* at notes 73-76.

[86]*See generally* Sack, *Territoriality, supra* note 71, at 84-9; Atiyah, *supra* note 49, at 602-07.

[87]*See,* R. May, *Love and Will* 187 (1969).

[88]*Id.* at 186 (italics in original). Compare the "follower" targeted by Wayne Hyatt in his advice to CIC developers, cited in note 26, *supra.*

Against this alienating overall backdrop, personal identity requires not only connection of the individual to the world outside, but a sense that one can shape his own life by his own, unique values,[89] rather than merely conform to the values of others.[90] We should pursue a more satisfying balance between modernity's wealth and relative liberty from external control and our forebears' comforting sense of rootedness in a context where each person's unique identity was specifically manifest to his own stable community. As it has done by tradition,[91] property can play a central role in enriching our society's sense of individual personhood.

The home is property that obviously helps constitute a person's identity, fostering the sense of connectedness with context essential for human flourishing.[92] Readily distinguishable from realty held purely for investment, or by a developer for sale to customers, a person's home should provide a unique zone of enhanced self expression and personal privacy. It is, after all, "the scene of one's history and future, one's life and growth."[93]

Economists consider the externalities of one resident's use and the sensitivities of neighboring residents to that use to be qualitatively indistinguishable.[94] Thus, enforcement of some servitudes, for example, servitudes protecting privacy arguably protect the personal property of the

---

[89] *See* R. May, *Man's Search for Himself* 13, 22 (1953).

[90] *See* D. Riesman (with N. Glazer and R. Denney), *The Lonely Crowd* 307 (abr. ed. 1961).

[91] *See* "Reich, The New Property" 73 *Yale L.J.* 733, 772 (1964):
   ... [P]roperty performs the function of maintaining independence, dignity and pluralism in society by creating zones within which the majority has to yield to the owner. Whim, caprice, irrationality, and "antisocial" activities are given the protection of law; the owner may do what all or most of his neighbors decry.

[92] *See* "Radin, Property and Personhood," 34 *Stan. L. Rev.* 957 (1982) at 991-1002; Radin, "Market-Inalienability," *supra* note 72, at 1908.

[93] Radin, "Property and Personhood," *supra* note 92, at 992. *See also* Sack, *Territoriality, supra* note 71, at 195.

[94] See Note, "An Economic Analysis of Land Use Conflicts," *Stan. L. Rev.* 293, 314-15 (1969). See also Winokur, "Mixed Blessings," *supra* note 8, at 19, n. 69.

home more than they infringe upon residents' control.[95] But many existing servitudes—especially those addressing aesthetics—severely regiment conduct and experience in one's immediate home environment. Respect for individual identity surely requires protection of each resident's right, for example, to determine when he takes out his trash, to select the color of his own swing sets, to fly the American (or other) flags from his balcony, to choose his own interior curtains and liners, and to decide how many sixteenths of an inch apart screws are located on his new balcony enclosure.[96]

The burden of persuasion should rest heavily on any party challenging activities integral to one's self in one's own home. In modern society that increasingly abstracts and renders fungible so much in our lives, opportunities to be peculiarly one's self are to be preferred, even at the expense of the neighbors' heightened aesthetic sensibilities to adjacent uses, and their preferences for uniformity and regimentation.

Quite arguably, the conduct of some business activities in each resident's home should remain his or her own choice.[97] Similarly, the ages during which an owner retains his home, and his childbearing and religious practice, and marital or family status[98] are so integral to each person's sense of self and identity that they should also presumptively remain a matter of each resident's own choice, without risking eviction from his home if too many birthdays pass, a child is born, a lover or friend moves in, or a yarmulke is abandoned.

---

[95]Compare, e.g., Radin, "Time, Possession, and Alienation," 64 *Wash. U.L.Q.* 739, 757 (1986). UCLA Law Professor French (also Reporter, *Restatement (Third of Servitudes)*), has posed as pro-personhood restrictions against second-story construction in her own nearly 1,000-unit California CIC regime, where back-yards often have unshielded hot tubs and are highly valued, very personalized spaces. Letter of Susan F. French (December 10, 1987) (on file with author). Servitude protection of these privacy interests in French's community seems very much a protection of personal identity.

[96]Examples of servitude restrictions on these resident choices are provided in notes 62, 63 *supra*. Defense of these restrictions appears at Korngold, "Flaws of Residential Servitudes," *supra* note 23, at 525-26.

[97]Coverage of recent controversies over the conduct of businesses in CIC homes appears in Budd, *supra* note 13.

[98]Examples of servitude restrictions on age, presence of children, and religious practice are presented in notes 55 and 56, *supra*.

Citizenship and Public Freedom vs. Apathy and Neighborly Hostility

In servitude regimes administered by homeowners or condominium associations, it remains doubtful whether the anticipated advantages of participatory democracy and "public freedom" have actually materialized sufficiently in most CICs to offset the limitations on individual autonomy often inherent in CIC life.

CIC residents reflect great dissatisfaction with the community associations that govern their communities. Attendance at association meetings is often sparse, with perhaps a majority of members actually attending only very rarely.[99] Conversations with member residents suggest a view of the association not as each resident's democratic workshop, but rather at arm's length from the individual residents—both a vendor of community services in return for association dues, and the strongly resented regulator of the residents' personal activities at home.[100] This dissatisfaction has spurred a mushrooming spate of litigation.[101] CIC boards, composed and often managed by resident amateurs, have often seemed inept in the crucial tasks of enforcing restrictions against neighbors while maintaining the community association's financial strength.[102] As the structuring of servitude-regimes moves progressively toward vesting more discretionary power in the governing associations,[103] an individual resident's influence over the restrictions to which he is subjected is particularly shaky where the association actively discourages member participation in association deliberations, or engages in harass-

---

[99]"Residential Private Governments," *supra* note 10, at 267; "Barton and Silverman California Study," *supra* note 1, at 13. *See also* Interview by Nathan Simmons of Ralph C. Meyer, Assoc. Professor of Political Science, Fordham University (July 8, 1987) (on file with author).

In a recent study of Florida condominium dispute resolution, 84.3 percent of the 759 responding condominium residents "strongly agreed" or "agreed" that "owner apathy is the biggest problem facing community associations." "S. Williamson and R. Adams, Dispute Resolution in Condominiums: An Exploratory Study of Condominium Owners in the State of Florida" 68 (Human Resources Mgt. Center, College of Business. Administration, University of North Florida, 1987) [hereinafter "Williamson and Adams Florida Study"].

[100]*See supra* notes 16, 17, 18.

[101]*See supra* note 17.

[102]*See supra* note 11.

[103]*See* Simmons-Kleine Interview, *supra* note 62; *see also* Posner 3d, *supra* note 48, at 60.

ment of its members.[104] In the face of such abuses, resident autonomy becomes illusory, particularly if associations remain immune from constitutional constraints imposed on public governments to protect fundamental civil rights—on which effective participatory democracy within the association depends.[105]

DIRECTIONS FOR REFORM

The sheer size and suddenness[106] of the community associations' movement, and the complexity of its components—including condominium, townhouse, free standing, single-family residence, and other planned unit developments, which raise new issues of property, contract, and institutional (e.g., corporate, municipal) law—all suggest that the CIC ownership vehicles will require substantial adjustment and refinement well into the future. Although the law of CICs arose through the law of property and contracts,[107] those doctrinal fields cannot be expected to address fully the myriad of community governance issues inherent in the CIC structure. Even smaller CICs usually are not merely expanded, two-party transactions as contemplated by the traditional real covenant and equitable servitude doctrine. In many instances, CIC problems arise on

---

[104]Fordham political science professor Ralph Meyer is quoted as decrying such association abuses:

Some of them do all sorts of things to control people: they overthrow committees they don't like, keep the press out of their meetings, prevent residents from talking or even attending board meetings, engage in nuisance lawsuits, verbally harass members.

Quoted in Louv, *supra* note 62, at 114.

[105]See "Illiberal Residential Associations," *supra* note 24, at 482-83; "G.M.U. Note," *supra* note 62, 98-101. Several commentators have argued against application of constitutional limits to the enforceability of servitudes in association-administered regimes. See "Residential Private Governments," *supra* note 11, at 275-77, 304-306; Rosenberry, "The Application of Federal and State Constitutions to Condominiums, Cooperatives and Planned Developments," 19 *Real Prop. Prob. & Tr. J.* 1, 28-30 (1984). *But see* Ellickson, "Homeowners Associations," *supra* note 23, at 1528, 1535-39, 1556-63; Comment, "Democracy in the New Towns: The Limits of Private Government," 36 *U. Chi. L. Rev.* 379, 408-10 (1969); Walter, "Condominium Government: How Should the Laws be Changed?" 4 *Real Est. L.J.* 141, 143-45 (1975).

[106]See *supra* notes 1, 3.

[107]See generally Winokur, "Mixed Blessings," *supra* note 8.

a whole different, community-sized scale, and they should not be "addressed" as primarily an appendage to covenant and servitude doctrine.[108] In addition to the difficult, contract-related questions of assuring CIC residents have freely enlisted in the community,[109] CICs thus raise community governance issues in at least the following three areas largely foreign to real covenant and equitable servitude theory:

1. The decision-making structure for resolving issues of community concern, whether anticipated by the original CIC documentation or not.
2. The type of enforcement required (or even permitted) for use restrictions binding the CIC residents.
3. The financial and other means by which each community association can realistically manage and maintain community assets given over to its care in creation of the CIC.

---

[108]In the emerging American Law Institute's new *Restatement of the Law Third, Property (Servitudes)* community associations and CICs are not the primary focus. Reporter Susan French has proposed that the *Restatement's* focus be widened from individual servitudes created in isolated transactions to include "interrelated servitudes implementing entire schemes of land use control in both commercial and residential developments," with a separate chapter "devoted to the operation of unit owner associations." French, "Design Proposal for the New Restatement of Property—Servitudes," 21 *U.C. Davis L. Rev.* 1213 (1988). While many aspects of the planned Restatement are laudable, the subsidiary attention planned for CICs is regrettable. Regarding servitudes and community associations, see generally, J. Winokur, "Ancient Strands Rewoven, or Fashioned Out of Whole Cloth: First Impressions of the Emerging Restatement of Servitudes," 26 *U. Conn. L. Rev.* (1994), and balance of symposium.

[109]*See* text and notes *supra* at notes 19-23, 26-44. A useful, partial method for assuring true assent to joining a servitude regimes is reflected in Article IV of the National Conference of Commissioners on Uniform State Laws' Uniform Common Interest Ownership Act (1982) ("UCIOA"), requiring that unit purchasers be furnished with public offering statements by CIC developers, and resale certificates by unit sellers. The availability of disclosure alone cannot eliminate all free choice problems—especially in the growing number of communities where alternatives to CICs are nonexistent. See Winokur, "Reforming Servitude Regimes: Toward Associational Federalism and Community," 1990 *Wisconsin Law Review* 537, 544-45 (1990) [herinafter, Winokur, "Reforming Servitude Regimes"]; C. Silverman, S. Barton, J. Hillmer and P. Ramos, The Effects of California's Real Estate Transfer Disclosure Requirements: Report to the California Dept. of Real Estate 19 (Oct. 1989).

Though it is well beyond the scope of this chapter to resolve CIC problems in these large issue areas, some comments suggesting directions for reform are appropriate.

Decision-Making Structure[110]

Currently, community associations' decision-making structure is often constrained by both general and specific dictates[111] of its creating documentation, which are amendable only by a unanimous or super-majority vote of all homes in the CIC. In many communities, especially the larger CICs, these amendment requirements render even noncontroversial amendments infeasible.[112]

The problem stifling inflexibility imposed by practically unamendable, detailed restrictions can be loosened for new CICs by drafting restrictions more broadly, leaving discretion to the association, and by building in some structure for reviewing the continued applicability of a restriction over time.   For existing associations whose governing documents are drafted inflexibly, a potential solution might resemble California's Common Interest Development Act, which permits California courts to validate what a judge considers a "reasonable" amendment approved by *most* voting unit owners—though *not* the *super-majority* of all unit owners as required by the Declaration—provided a conscientious effort was made to include all owners in the voting.[113]

---

[110]Community associations have long debated the related question of how to classify an association for purposes of reviewing the legality of its actions. *See, e.g.,* W. Hyatt and J. Stubblefield, "The Identity Crisis of Community Associations: In Search of the Appropriate Analogy," 27 *R. Prop. T. J.* 589 (1993). *See also* Weakland, "Living Under the Due Process Shadow," 13 *Pepperdine L. Rev.* 297 (1986); Rosenberry, "Actions of Community Association Boards: When Do They Create Liability?" 13 *R. Est. L.J.* 315 (1985); Hyatt and Rhoads, "Concepts of Liability in the Development and Administration of Condominium and Home Owners Associations," 12 *Wake Forest L. Rev.* 915 (1976); Kennedy, "The Governmental Entity Analogy: Is a Residential Association Really the Functional Equivalent of a Municipality?" (unpubl. mscpt., 1991).

[111]*See* text and notes *supra* at notes 63-65.

[112]*See, e.g.,* R. Natelson, *The Law of Property Owners Associations* 612-13 (1989) [hereinafter, Natelson].

[113]Cal Civ. Code Section 1356. *See also* Natelson, *supra* note 112, at 613; 1990 *Supplement* to Natelson 125-27.

When decisions address controversies over particular units, rather than general policy principles of an association's governance, individual unit owners must be entitled to fair, nondiscriminatory application of the association's rules.[114] Beyond fair adjudicative application of association rules, however, CICs and their residents may be better served by a less adversarial dispute resolution process such as mediation.[115] After all, the disputants in these cases typically remain neighbors to each other beyond the resolution of their dispute, and preservation (or creation) of a cooperative relationship will predictably be of importance of the parties. While existing data provide conflicting evidence on how widely mediation (or arbitration) would be accepted by CIC disputants,[116] the promise of alternatives to adversarial litigation are so great as to require further exploration of these possibilities.

Enforcement of CIC Restrictions

Many CIC residents resent strict enforcement of use restrictions.[117] On the other hand, community associations often feel bound to other residents to enforce these restrictions strictly. Beyond abstract arguments over which group of residents—the *laissez-faire* proponents or the strict constructionists—are morally right, board members may fear that enforcement flexibility will open the board itself to the risk of having permanently waived a restriction it fails to enforce against every technical violator.[118] The board may also fear liability to individual unit owners

---

[114]*See, e.g.*, G. Korngold, *Private Land Use Arrangements* 370-72 (1990), reviewing judicial oversight of association enforcement of its aesthetic restrictions. For a proposed bill of rights for unit owners, see S. French, "The Constitution of a Private Residential Government Should Include a Bill of Rights," 27 *Wake Forest L. Rev.* 345, 351-52 (1992).

[115]For helpful argument that nonlitigation forms of dispute resolution may be particularly important in CICs, see Korngold, "Flaws of Residential Servitudes," *supra* note 23, at 533-35.

[116]*Compare id.* at 535 n. 121 (more optimistic) with Winokur, "Reforming Servitude Regimes," *supra* note 109, 543, n. 35 (less optimistic).

[117]*See* Winokur, "Mixed Blessings," *supra* note 8, 62-66.

[118]Although selective enforcement has been successfully raised to defend against association enforcement of CIC use restrictions, see, e.g., *White Egret Condominium v. Franklin*, 379 So. 346 (Fla. 1979), success with this defense is—and should be—relatively rare. *See Natelson, supra* note 112, at Section

who claim the right to strict enforcement.[119] A board's perceived duty and potential lability can sometimes blind it to the human stakes affected by covenant enforcement.

Where moderation of covenant enforcement is appropriate, board duties and risks depend on as yet largely undeveloped areas of CIC law. These should be resolved to allow association boards to exercise *principled, nondiscriminatory* enforcement flexibility without fearing waiver or liability. For example, a board's principled decision to enforce a blanket "no dogs" rule only against dogs that bite, bark, or mess on others' land should not risk losing the enforceability of any "no dogs" restriction merely because the board's enforcement is considerably narrower than the sweep of the restriction as written.

Financial and Managerial Viability of Associations

The managerial and financial weakness of community association boards poses serious problems for CICs.[120] Widespread association management problems stem from a range of causes—from inadequate CIC documentation to amateur leadership. Partial solutions lie in "gap-filling" legislation, clarifying questions left uncertain in documents creating CICs, and conferring on associations powers inadvertently omitted from those documents. For example, the Uniform Common Interest Ownership Act ("UCIOA") helpfully sets forth a broad range of association powers,[121] including the often questioned[122] association

---

5.5.4.

[119]Such a claim was made in *Williams v. Glauz*, No. 57759, (Yolo County, Calif., 1987), which settled before trial.

[120]*See* text and notes *supra* at notes 11, 12.

[121]UCIOA Section 3-102.

[122]Especially where the declaration is silent, several courts have refused to recognize association standing to litigate even common area problems on behalf of its members, until legislation mandated that result. Compare *Friendly Village Community Association v. Silva & Hill Construction Co.*, 31 Cal App. 3d 22-, 107 *Cal Rptr.* 123 (1973) (later superseded by statute conferring association standing, see *Orange Grove Terrace Owners Assn. v. Bryant Properties*, 176 Cal. App. 1217, 222 *Cal. Rptr.* 523 (1986)); *Hendler v. Rogers House Condominium, Inc.*, 234 So. 2d 128 (Fla. App. 1970) (also later statutorily superseded, see *Imperial Towers Condominium Inc. v. Brown*, 338 So. 2d 1081 (Fla. App. 1974); *Laurel Park Villas Homeowner's Assn. v. Hodges*, 345 S.E.2d

standing to litigate on behalf of the CIC. Such legislation often defers to contrary declaration provision, but confers helpful powers when the declaration drafter failed to address whether the association holds the power in question.

Legislation can also help coax associations and their attorneys into following good business practice in managing CIC operations. A good example is CCIOA's budgeting provisions, which require annual budgeting,[123] and notice to all unit owners of the executive board's proposed budget changes, but declares such budget automatically accepted unless a majority of all homeowners, or any larger percentage specified in the Declaration, specifically objects.[124]

Finally, with associations responsible for managing and maintaining community infrastructure, they must have the wherewithal to perform those substantial responsibilities. Association standing to litigate on behalf of the association is only one important necessity.[125] Associations also require enhanced power to collect funds owing them. UCIOA addresses this concern by according the association a limited priority over other creditors equal to six months of assessments, including earlier first lienors on a unit in default in paying its homeowner assessments.[126] To facilitate assessment status verification for buyers, lenders, and their title insurors, UCIOA obligates the association to provide promptly a written, binding, and recordable assessment status report.[127] A side benefit of this

---

861 (N.C. App. 1986). Compare *Villa Sierra Condominium Assoc. v. Field Corp.*, 787 P. 2d 661 (Colo. App. 1990) with *Summerhouse Condominium Association Inc. v. Majestic Savings & Loan Assoc.*, 615 P. 2d 71 (1980). For analysis of the necessity of association standing to CIC litigation feasibility, particularly where construction defects are at issue, see W. Hyatt, *Condominium and Homeowner Assoc. Practice: Community Association Law* 113-14 (1988).

[123]UCIOA Section 3-115.

[124]UCIOA Section 3-103(c) .

[125]*See* text and notes *supra* at notes 122.

[126]UCIOA Section 3-116. Where already implemented, these UCIOA assessment super-lien provisions reportedly have not impaired sale of mortgages to Fannie Mae, Freddie Mac, or private secondary market investors. See letter of Connecticut Mortgage Bankers Association Counsel, Norman H. Roos, Esq. Fannie Mae's Seller's Guide, Section 608.02, expressly contemplates such limited assessment lien priority over first mortgages. Freddie Mac regulations are in accord.

[127]UCIOA Section 3-116 (h).

reporting requirement should be some regularizing of association collection procedures.

Associational Federalism

Beyond the specific suggestions sketched out thus far, decision making, enforcement, and financial problems of CICs would also be eased by structural reform of community associations.

For new CICs,[128] decision making can be rendered both more flexible and more inclusive of the CIC citizenry by using federal structures for CICs.[129] Thus servitude documentation might set forth comprehensive restrictions presumptively applicable to all sections of a development, but also afford individual subgroups within the larger association power to alter restrictions applicable to its constituents. Subgroup power to so alter restrictions would be limited by an enumerated set of the community's most basic principles, waivable only by vote of the entire regime.

Thus, for example, each subgroup may be authorized to loosen restrictions on items such as interior window dressing, swing sets, flag poles, balcony enclosures, flower boxes, and basketball hoops, but not authorized to lift the restriction to residential uses. Subgroup divergence from the regime's uniformity might be allowed from the moment of CIC creation, or could be permitted only after the regime has aged. Even relatively large subgroups[130] would make voting on amendments more

---

[128]Existing CICs would need enabling language in their declarations, or legislation, to restructure into the type of federal structure here suggested. See text and notes *infra* at note 133.

[129]Winokur, "Mixed Blessings," *supra* note 8, first proposed returning control of some servitude enforcement to small groupings of neighbors, while other enforcement powers—especially regarding assessments to maintain common assets—would remain with the larger community association. The original proposal ceded to smaller "pods" of 12 units or less control over use restrictions only when the larger regime had aged. At this point, the association would remain available as an enforcement agent for disputes arising within the respective pods. These enforcement pods were to be designated in advance by the regime's founding developer. *Id.* at 80-83. As explained below, the goals of such a federal associational structure can be served by a variety of federal structures.

[130]As developer and community association attorneys gain experience with the inflexible servitude regimes typically imposed in the 1960s and 1970s, they are drafting federation-type structures into servitude documents without any

realistic than where modification of restrictions requires voting (and therefore campaigning) throughout a regime of hundreds or thousands of units. The smaller the subgroups,[131] the more they could also make face-to-face negotiation of changes workable.

Some community association specialists have suggested that community association subgroups not be constituted in advance by the creating developer, but rather by self-selected, contiguous unit-groups within the regime as and when they desire variation in restrictions applicable to their own lots.[132] The size of a consenting subgroup might be based on some minimum number of consenting units, or distance from the units seeking to vary their properties in ways prohibited under the general regime. To control against imposing excessive externalities on units outside these self-selected groups, some sort of limited oversight might be required by either the master association, local administrative agency, or a court.[133]

Yet another federation-based model for servitude regimes is suggested by the master association provisions of the Uniform Common Interest Ownership Act.[134] UCIOA contemplates the possibility of smaller, otherwise independent, nonadjacent community associations delegating selected powers to an umbrella master association. The master association could provide record-keeping, maintenance, and other services, and might also provide a more neutral, private forum for adjudicating designated types of intra-association disputes.

---

statutory mandate. In servitude regimes encompassing hundreds or thousands of units, "neighborhoods" may contain 60 units to about 250 units. Each "neighborhood" within the larger regime is authorized to elect its own neighborhood advisory committee, with authority to advise the central association regarding aesthetics, maintenance of neighborhood common areas, and corresponding assessment of units within the neighborhood. Interviews with Robert M. Diamond, Esq. and Deborah K, Raines, Esq., Falls Church, Virginia, April 10 through 17, 1990.

[131]*See supra* note 129.

[132]Interviews with William R. Breetz (April 21, 1990), and James L. Strichartz (April 25, 1990).

[133]*Compare* California Civ. Code Section 1356, authorizing amendment of a condominium declaration by judicial decree, at the request of more than 50 percent of votes in the association where statutorily imposed procedural requirements have been met and the court deems such amendment "reasonable."

[134]UCIOA Section 2-120.

Quite apart from use restrictions, each of the federal structure variations here presented maximizes economies of scale, which are among community associations' great potential advantages. Small associations floundering due to inept, amateur leadership[135] might well be able to afford professional management in federation with other such associations. Especially as subgroups are kept small, each resident gains influence in shaping the restrictions to which his or her unit is subject, which will likely soften the unit owner's perception of helplessness in the face of association authority. Where apathy currently cripples large associations unable to turn out the voters required for association-wide issues, smaller decisional groupings improve prospects for successfully polling all those entitled to vote on subgroup issues.

Face-to-face discussion of each subgroup's own issues should lessen anonymous resort to intermediaries for resolution of neighborly disputes. More fundamentally, in allocating some issues to the larger regime, while reserving others to a small group of immediate neighbors, the federated community association I propose prompts occasions for negotiation among a group of neighbors small enough to allow personal interaction. Recognizing much of the larger community association's agenda as involving essentially administrative issues to be resolved based on relatively impersonal interests like maintaining property values and providing well kept, quasi-public amenities, this federalism preserves an agenda for more intimate mediation. In so doing, the federal structure may begin to fulfill some modern yearnings for community.[136]

---

[135]*See supra* note 99 and accompanying text.

[136]T. Bender, *Community and Social Change in America* 146-47, 150 (1978). *See also* G. Suttles, *The Social Construction of Community*, 264-68 (1972); Rubin, "Function and Structure of Community: Conceptual and Theoretical Analysis," reprinted in *New Perspectives on the American Community* (R. Warren and L. Lyon, 1983). *See also,* J. Winokur, "Community Associations Institute Research Foundation Symposium on Community and Community Associations," 36 *St. L. U. L. J.* 695 (1992).

IV. Community and Political Life in a Private Government

Editors' Note

Political life exists anywhere that collective decisions must be made. It is widely believed that the political process is less difficult when the people involved are a small group that is relatively homogeneous in background and values. Gregory Alexander reports a puzzling combination of frustration and apathy among members of planned development homeowners' associations in Arizona in "Conditions of 'Voice': Passivity, Disappointment, and Democracy in Homeowner Associations." On the one hand, many residents resented the restrictions the association placed on their use of their own property. On the other hand, they rarely became involved in the association to try to change the way it functioned. Instead, a small and often reluctant group governs the association. Alexander argues that these findings show a general lack of civic consciousness and suggests that "participatory rituals" are needed to draw people into involvement in their association.

In "Shared Premises: Community and Conflict in the Common Interest Development," Carol J. Silverman and Stephen E. Barton review California survey findings on the prevalence of conflict in common interest developments. They do find that social heterogeneity can lead to conflict, but they also find that in a homogeneous community of private property owners the homeowners' common values also create and even intensify conflict. They trace the roots of this phenomenon to the role of private property ownership in the home as a primary means of protecting private life from intrusion by other individuals or organizations. Homeownership in the common interest development incorporates two often-contradictory roles, both protecting them from unwanted involvement with others and involving all owners in a public decision-making process.

A case study of conflict in two similar common interest developments studied by Silverman and Barton illustrates the intensity of feeling and inability to resolve differences that can result from privatized understandings of neighbor relations. One of the two cases demonstrates that residents do have the ability to generate a self-perpetuating civic culture. For all the difficulties, residents can learn to understand the nature of public life within the association and separate their mutual obligations as co-owners and neighbors from their personal feelings and private lives.

In "Community and Direct Democracy in a Limited-Equity Cooperative," Allan Heskin and Dewey Bandy describe several controversial decisions. Their case study provides evidence that the explicit collective nature of the cooperative and the reduced individual financial interest that residents have in a limited-equity cooperative combine to make it easier for them to resolve disputes in a creative manner that preserves trust and cooperation within the community. With the bulk of community wealth held in common and in trust for future residents, commitment to the community is greater. However, the greater range of control exercised by the cooperative over who joins the community opens up a greater range of potential conflicts.

6

Shared Premises: Community and Conflict in the Common Interest Development

Carol J. Silverman
Stephen E. Barton

The relationships between the home, the neighborhood, and local government change constantly, as do the boundaries between them. While private life in the home and public life in the larger society have always influenced each other, today the common interest development (CID) links them in unaccustomed ways. The common interest development is a type of neighborhood with a new mixture of public and private elements—involving both individual and collective ownership of private property. This partly individual, partly collective form of property ownership has profound implications both for the owners' and residents' private lives and for their participation in public life.

In this chapter, we use data from the California Common Interest Development Study (Barton and Silverman 1987) and a study of California homebuyers (Silverman, Barton, Hillmer, and Ramos 1989) to show that residents typically fail to understand the mixed, public, and private nature of the CID because they do not understand the inherent connections between private and public life. Instead, they equate home with private life and government with public life and try to assimilate the neighborhood into the home as a part of private life. They understand private property as moral rights held by private individuals and not as a politically created and government supported mixture of rights and obligations that define social relationships. Conflict and low levels of participation in the public life of the CID result from contradictions between the complex reality, in which private and public life are interrelated, and people's privatized understanding of their individual rights.

PUBLIC AND PRIVATE LIFE DEFINED

There is a large literature on the origins and meaning of public and private life. Originally conceived to represent a body politic separate from the will of the king, the public has come to be identified most clearly with the state (Habermas 1962). Thus public life commonly refers to participation in the democratic process. However, as shown by the phrase "being in public," public life means more than government; it includes all situations where people need not know each other and where any one individual cannot exclude another from participation so long as laws are not broken. When dealing with "the public," people have no idea whom they might encounter. Even in small isolated towns, an outsider always might come and perhaps even stay. People who are together in a public setting may not have a shared past to guide them in their behavior towards each other, lack expectations that they will need to continue to interact with each other in the future, and have no choice over the other individuals who are "in public" with them. As a result, customs and laws are necessary that enable people to share a street or community and participate in public activity together (Lofland 1973).

Private life, in contrast, is bound up with the concept of privacy. The term comes from the Latin root "privates" (Hixson 1986), meaning withdrawal from public life. Originally applied to religious orders, the term took on additional meaning of independence and intimacy in the sixteenth century. The right to withdraw presupposes control over potential intrusions and thus independence from the larger society.

Privacy and private life have long been bound up with domesticity and intimacy. This is exemplified by the home—the "haven in a heartless world" where the family is accorded autonomy and power in its internal affairs, freed from the constraints of the larger society. Private life evolved as the household separated from the larger society and gained the power to choose who could share in the intimacies of family and individual life. Private life extends beyond the household as people establish friendships with compatible others. The defining characteristic of this side of private life is individual choice and control. (The emotional and social ties of the family are another, and very different side of private life.)

Today the private life of the household and the individuals within it are safeguarded within the intersecting institutions of private property and of laws and customs protecting the home from intrusion. The home provides the space where the household feels most free to express itself both as a family and in the use of consumer goods, an additional type of choice and control. This freedom in the home is never absolute; it is constrained by laws restricting the destruction of property and criminal activities and regulating uses that infringe on the larger neighborhood. Nonetheless, the home and the household are the best-protected domain of privacy and freedom from interference by others.

PRIVATE AND PUBLIC IN THE NEIGHBORHOOD

If the state and the family are the purest expressions of the distinction between public and private, the neighborhood, like the corporation, is more ambiguous. The neighborhood is usually seen as part of the private world, since it serves as the location for the household. The business corporation, as a fictitious individual and as private property is also considered private. In both cases, the state deliberately limits its normal ability to intervene. Laws setting the rights of private property owners are publicly created and enforced. But in both spheres the belief in noninterference is so strong that even democratically decided government actions are viewed by many as violations of basic moral rights. A homeowner arguing against a zoning regulation that prohibits adding a second unit to the house, a landlord arguing against rent control, and a business owner protesting limits on hours of operation all see government regulations as an unfair restriction on their individual property rights.

Neighborhoods and corporations are public as well as private, however. Each involves a sphere where unchosen others must interact and where the behavior of one party influences others. While the public nature of the corporation is beyond the scope of this article, the public nature of the neighborhood is key to understanding CIDs. Neighborhoods are public because they are a location of interaction between unchosen neighbors. They are the setting for households who rarely choose their neighbors and often do not get to know them. Thus the neighborhood is the site of close contact and potential conflict between private and public life.

Private life means more than the simple absence of the state; it also means the ability of the individual or household to maintain control over their home and private relationships. Control means the ability to establish freedom from as well as freedom to. These freedoms are exercised within three not well-separated aspects of the neighborhood, as most residents experience it: face-to-face interactions, general sensory knowledge, and the use of property. Residents can restrict the actual entry of others into their homes and use their own space as they desire, within the limits of the law, but cannot control all boundaries. Precisely because neighbors share boundaries with the home, they can pose the greatest threat to total control. Sound can travel through thin walls, trees extend into adjoining yards, and dogs or children wander across property lines. Not only do neighbors actively or passively challenge a household's control over its own space, they may observe and learn more about the household's private life then may be considered desirable.

In order to maintain control of the individual household, then, each household extends its claim to control beyond its own immediate boundaries and even across property lines. Neighbors, particularly homeowners, assume rights to set standards of behavior and use of property within a larger neighborhood space in order to establish freedom from unwanted interactions to preserve their "right" to the neighborhood they moved into. When expectations about the "neighborhood character" are violated, whether by neighbors, businesses, or government, residents can act vociferously, seeking to block activities that they feel violated their rights to *freedom from.* Yet, the strongest challenges come from neighbors, exercising their own perceived rights to *freedom to.* Thus one neighbor's rights to freedom from certain land uses and to a certain type of neighborhood interferes with another's freedom to use property as desired.

Public and private life are never truly separate. Private space is maintained by constant negotiation between members of the public. The rights of private property owners in the neighborhood and in business are all public creations and are maintained by a great many laws and regulations that people, acting as citizens and participating in public life, have argued about and voted on in the democratic process. Neighborhood organizations are the most visible means by which people get together to engage in public action aimed at protecting their neighborhood from intrusion or at setting the rules by which people co-exist within the neighborhood (Barton 1985; Crenson 1983).

So long as the *status quo* is maintained, however, the public underpinnings of private life can be and typically are ignored. As we have argued elsewhere (Silverman 1983, 1987), so long as neighbors possess similar standards of behavior and exterior forces do not intrude, the public aspects of the neighborhood are not salient. Only when there is an external threat, or other people seek to redefine their rights or when a new neighbor with different standards moves in, does public life become salient. Neighborhood organization and activism is not characteristic of most neighborhoods.

Neighborhoods differ in the extent of formalization of the process of public negotiation over local standards and their need to collectively decide upon issues that touch their separate lives. In CIDs there is a structure of ownership, including a mandatory rather than voluntary owners' association to provide governance, which highlights the public aspects of the CID as a neighborhood. The dual public and private aspects of the CID are found in all its aspects: the individual units, the neighborhood and in the formal structure of the association as a mutual benefit, nonprofit corporation. The CID thus makes explicit the public aspects of the neighbor role. As in any neighborhood, coresidents rarely select each other, yet their private lives extend into shared neighborhood space, and each must get along with the others and make, or at least live with, collective decisions about the neighborhood.

PUBLIC CONTROL OVER PRIVATE LIFE IN THE COMMON INTEREST DEVELOPMENT

CIDs have varying mixtures of individual and common property ownership. In cooperatives all land and buildings are owned in common, with individual ownership limited to shares in the cooperative and accompanying rights to occupy particular units. That is, in large measure, why there are so few cooperatives in the U.S. (See Chapter One.) In condominiums, people individually own their own unit, although this may consist of as little as the airspace and paint on the walls of their units, with the building structure and grounds owned in common. In some CIDs, usually in those organized as planned developments, the construction permits individual ownership of separate houses, but the adjoining front walkways, patios or green spaces are collectively owned. In any CID some common property, such as backyards, parking areas, or decks may be reserved for the use of the individual owner or tenant; other property such as roads, green spaces, and recreational facilities may be for the use of the entire development. (See Chapter One for a description of the types of common property and services provided by CIDs in California.)

The property that people own in a CID has conditions, covenants, and restrictions (CC&Rs) as part of the deed defining the property. These closely control what people can do with both individually and commonly owned property. Architectural controls impose "community standards" on individual units—what can be built on privately owned property, or what materials may be used. The CC&Rs, or additional rules the CC&Rs empower the homeowners' association to create, may go so far as to limit the pets residents can own, the curtains they hang, and the permissible plants they can put in the backyard. Other rules delimit the use of common facilities, restricting use to particular times for example.

Owners' private finances are also affected by the collective nature of the association. In ordinary residential neighborhoods, individual owners decide when repairs are to be done on their homes—perhaps using their own labor—and how much money they will spend. In the CID, in contrast, this is decided by a governing board that has a responsibility under the law to maintain the association and to ensure the use of an acceptable quality of labor. In practice, this almost always means hiring outside contractors. If the association approves a special assessment or a large dues increase to pay for legal fees, to fund reserves for future renovations or to make capital improvements, individual owners may be required to come up with thousands of dollars even though they do not support the decision or do not have the necessary income to afford the expenditure. As a result, the individual owner loses control over the decision on when to spend money and how much money to spend.

Homeowners in ordinary neighborhoods can decide on their own to build swimming pools or to upgrade landscaping or exteriors. In CIDs, in contrast, all such decisions are up to the association as a whole. Particularly, but not only when homeowners differ in their disposable income or in their interest in the association, bitter disagreements can occur between owners wishing to upgrade the common areas and those who may not have the funds or wish to spend them for other things.

In ordinary neighborhoods, where residents are not linked by common ownership of property, rules of community living are established by tacit or voluntary agreements, or are established and enforced by local government. The common interest homeowners' association, in contrast, is governed by an elected board of owners with the responsibility for managing the association in the interest of all property owners. Boards collect regular assessments (a median of $1,140 per unit annually in 1987 in California) and sometimes set special assessments, maintain the property, budget for future repairs, and set and enforce what are often an exhaustive set of rules governing people's behavior both within individually owned property and in the common areas. Boards are able, when rules are violated, to revoke use privileges on common property, to impose fines, liens, and even to foreclose on individual mortgages.

With equivalents to the power to tax, to legislate, to enforce the rules and to provide community services, the private Common Interest Homeowners' Association closely resembles a local government, as well as serving as a property manager and a neighborhood association. There are important differences, however. With rare exceptions, voting comes with ownership, not residence. Indeed, in California, the developer is given three votes for every unit owned, compared to one for each new buyer, until 75 percent of the units are sold and control officially passes from the developer to the new buyers. Perhaps the most important difference, however, is simply that this "private government" violates many peoples' belief in the strict separation between private and public life. People who already have great difficulty with the necessity of public life, and with government "intrusion" into their private lives, are faced with an entity that purports to arise from their own private property rights, yet intrudes upon their privacy instead of protecting their homes from intrusion.

In the CID the public interdependence inherent in neighborhood life is very hard to ignore. Collective decisions must be made about the level of maintenance within the development and how to pay for it. The ongoing quality of maintenance, services, and resale values are affected by the willingness and ability of all to pay dues and needed special assessments. The 1987 study of California CIDs found that 30 percent of the associations had attempted to pass a special assessment in the past year and 25 percent were able to do so. The median size of the special assessments was small, $200 per unit, but one-tenth were over $1,000. When a substantial minority does not pay, either the other members of the association must come up with the needed money or all properties suffer. Associations can place liens on property for unpaid dues and even foreclose, but they take a secondary position behind mortgage lenders and may never recover unpaid assessments. One-quarter of the associations in our survey had lost money due to foreclosures within the last two years—five percent had lost an amount equal to five percent or more of the annual budget. If enough owners are delinquent, this can affect the resale price of other units.

This interdependence is shown dramatically in several of our case study associations. One, a low-income association originally subsidized by HUD, had 23 out of 310 units in foreclosure, not paying monthly assessments. The association maintained its high quality housing by using aggressive collection policies, which resulted in some residents losing their homes, and high assessments, a substantial burden for its low-income residents.

Another association, with a largely moderate income membership, took a different course. Its residents were left with numerous, major construction defects by the developer. The association hired a lawyer who successfully won a substantial payment from the developer, but who arranged for the developer to make payments to each individual owner, rather than turning the money over to the association to use in making the needed repairs. The board found itself in conflict with its own lawyer and many members of the association over who should get the money and were unable to collect enough to make the repairs. As a result, individual units became unsalable; some members were considering abandoning their units, and the board decided to seek a means to undo the subdivision and convert the building to single ownership so that it could be sold as rental property to an investor with the resources to make the necessary repairs.

The CID differs from ordinary neighborhoods because it has a formal mechanism for defining and enforcing acceptable community behavior, and the deciding and enforcing body is internal to the association rather than located outside in local government. People may welcome rules because they guarantee certain behaviors and standards of upkeep of their neighbors. However, residents often resent the rules when they apply to themselves, limiting what residents take to be their rights to use private property as they please. There is an inherent contradiction here. One neighbor's rights to a particular neighborhood interferes with another's rights to use and develop their own property.

Neighbors' needs and wants differ, but problems resolving conflicts that arise in CIDs are not simply the result of differences, but also because of the similar basis of the claims that neighbors make. In one case study association, for example, parents of young children wanted a play area. The only likely space was outside the window of a couple who objected to the noise of children playing and were supported by other residents without children. Each side argued over whether the developer had or had not originally promised a playground as part of the development and whether people should have known they were buying into a development with or without such a facility. Although the initial responsibility for the altercation lay with the developer, who had included a playground in some publicity drawings but never built one, the association board of directors had to decide what to do. The resulting ill-will had not abated two years later, not simply because people wanted different things, but because they were similar in being homeowners and in basing their arguments on their moral rights as owners and buyers.

DIFFICULTIES WITH PUBLIC LIFE IN THE CID ASSOCIATION

CIDs are often in some difficulty at the very start, because they have owners who, if they understood the restrictions on homeowners' individual freedom that are inherent in a CID, did not really want to purchase in a CID in the first place and did so only reluctantly because they could not afford a home in an ordinary neighborhood or because few "ordinary" neighborhoods existed in the area they wanted to buy in. Many other owners certainly do not understand the nature of the CID in which they have bought. In a 12-county survey in California of resale buyers, we found that 84 percent of those who bought a home in a CID were not looking for a CID to buy in (Silverman, Barton et al. 1989). Even among those who wanted to buy in a common interest development, there was widespread lack of understanding of the behavioral and financial controls. Although California requires sellers of units in CIDs to provide buyers with the governing and financial documents before the sale is closed, we found that the 27 percent of the buyers who had read their documents closely were also most likely to be people who had violated an association rule—undoubtedly they read them after the fact. Similarly, we found that 16 percent inaccurately thought their monthly assessments could not go up.

Whether because members do not know the rules, or know them but reject them, associations have to deal with widespread rule violations. In the California CID Study, 41 percent of associations reported major problems with rule violations. The most widespread rule violations involved parking (18 percent), late payment of assessments (11 percent), pets (8 percent), common area use (7 percent), and unauthorized changes to dwelling units (6 percent). The most intractable problems, in which associations were often unable to gain compliance, involved the last category, violations of architectural controls—reflecting the depth of feeling attached to control over the home. People would also contest the rules by staying within the letter rather than the intent of the law. We were told of one, perhaps apocryphal, association where a homeowner upset with rigid color restrictions on exterior walls painted his unit with alternating wide bands of approved colors.

We found that rule violations were most common when individual private interests come into conflict. Thus associations in economic decline, where investors replace homeowners and the percentage of rental units is increasing, show more violations. More violations are found in associations with more people at different stages of the life cycle, where people will have different standards of preferred behavior; similarly the presence of children, who often do not follow rules; larger associations, which are almost inherently more diverse; associations whose buildings have shared walls, so that noise and differences over maintenance are more likely; and associations with more rental units, with their absentee owners who can be slower paying their bills, and renters, who are usually excluded from the association because they are not owners and have less commitment to it. (See Barton and Silverman 1987 for the statistical model.)

Rule violations are reduced by stronger public life: by member participation in the association; by self-management, where people do the work of the association themselves; and by neighbors' concern for each other, whether expressed in sociability or simply in the more "public" attitude of looking out for others even when they are not friends.

It is not surprising, given the depth of feeling involving private life and property, that associations where the rules were more often broken are also those where board members were most likely to be harassed, threatened, or sued by the membership. This is not an infrequent problem. In the California CID Study 44 percent of the association boards reported that they were personally harassed, subjected to personal accusations, threatened with a law suit, or actually sued by a member in the past year alone. Several board presidents, for example, told us of being threatened by a resident whose car had been towed. The president was blamed personally rather than the association rules or the city that imposed requirements such as visitor-only parking places on the CID in the first place.

Most residents do not harass the board of their association, of course. The larger membership tends rather to be uninvolved. The situation can be tolerable—in 39 percent of associations in the California CID Study, board presidents reported that members didn't care one way or the other what they did and in 19 percent of associations one board member did all the work. But when that member resigns or when one or more members of the association are unhappy about something, the situation breaks down.

It is often difficult to get enough people to run for the board. (See also Alexander, Chapter 7.) In 23 percent of the associations in the California CID Study there were fewer candidates than there were seats in the last election. As one board president put it: "Apathy reigns supreme—most owners want some unpaid volunteer to make decisions for them rather than attending board or annual meetings. We are running out of fools who will volunteer their time." (Another association member, upon reading this quote, wrote us to say that his association had plenty of fools. He simply needed to know where to send them.) Board members also did not serve for long. The median time on the board was two years—in many associations the length of one term of office.

The governing board of directors of the CID association is the most visible symbol of the CID and its dual public and private nature. The board presides over the affairs of an "involuntary association," quite different from the voluntary neighborhood or homeowners' associations found in many ordinary, though usually urban, neighborhoods. Organized as a nonprofit mutual benefit association, yet covered by a series of sometimes conflicting laws (see Sproul, Chapter Four), the association board must deal with the tensions that arose as homeowners' private preferences clashed with the involuntary structure of the association.

Even governing board members often have troubles with understanding the association. In more than one association, the president had to argue with another board member who did not see why the board should pay to repair something, such as a section of roof, that covered one unit but was actually common property belonging to the whole association. Some board presidents treat the association as an extension of their own homes and exercise personal control over association affairs, not involving the membership or even other board members. It is indicative of the tensions between board and membership that at a California legislative hearing on CIDs, one speaker got tremendous applause when he compared board presidents to boys who wanted to be fire chiefs when they grew up.

The prevailing cultural models that board members have to guide them in their work are not particularly helpful. Boards of directors see their most important task as providing property management services, which makes them similar to a small business except that the board is elected rather than chosen by each individual property owner/consumer. The management model, with its focus on getting the work done, leads board members to discount the importance of member participation and to see conflict and conflict resolution as a diversion from the real work of the association.

The California CID Study found that 40 percent of associations contracted with a management company, 16 percent had their own on-site manager, and 44 percent, mostly smaller and less affluent, were self-managed, doing the work themselves. Boards are encouraged by many managers to consider the association as a business, with primary emphasis on efficiency. In this view, the inevitable disagreements that arise are simply management problems: "the three P's—people, pets, and parking" as they are referred to in the industry. Those who disagree with what boards consider to be rational policy are stereotyped as complainers, or in the worst cases as crazies. Yet, the absence of recognition of the legitimacy of member concerns can cause their voices to become increasingly strident, and they may come to resemble the ways they have been labeled.

Many board members are also interested in promoting sociability among neighbors, which makes them similar to many voluntary community associations. The community association model results in board members seeing disagreement as a breakdown in sociability and as unneighborly activity, something to be avoided if at all possible. The management and community association models are accompanied by beliefs that equate neighborhood life and business with the absence of state intrusion. As a result, the conflict resolution functions of a governing board, which are similar to those of a local government, require board members to draw on a model of the CID as government that they are very uncomfortable with and that seems to contradict the models they prefer.

Since the writings of Jefferson and de Tocqueville, citizens of the United States have been extolled as a natural joiners, working in voluntary associations to accomplish civic ends. It is misleading to consider the common interest development as another example of this. The CID highlights individual property interests rather than common purposes. The average owner does not participate and views the association as an expanded set of services purchased with the home. Disagreements typically are not over the best direction for the association as a whole but rather over what are perceived as individual private property rights. The result of such conflict is to create a distaste for the entire process among those most closely involved in running the association. Fully 30 percent of the board presidents in the California CID Study were so disenchanted with their situation that they said they would not consider purchasing a home in a common interest development again.

CIDS AND LOCAL GOVERNMENTS

The common interest homeowners' association replicates important aspects of local government, bringing public life within a private setting. Hundreds of thousands of people are involved in running these associations without the resources and legitimacy of their publicly elected counterparts. But are the problems of associations any worse than those of a small town government? Certainly problems of apathy, conflict, exclusion, and a focus on the primacy of private property rights do not seem unfamiliar to anyone who studies suburban local governments. Indeed, given the somewhat similar historical origins of suburban governments and common interest developments in exclusionary fears of racial and ethnic diversity and the desire to provide better municipal services, it may be that the problems of CIDs can tell us something about the problems of local government. A small suburban town is often seen by its residents as little more than a form of homeowners' association.

In the absence of comparative data we can only speculate, but we believe the problems of associations are worse because of the ways CIDs differ from small town governments, but many, although not all, differences may be more a matter of degree than of kind.

First, the use of common ownership as a vehicle for meeting public needs violates people's understandings of ownership. When a city levies a tax for road repairs or schools, the idea of contribution for the common good is understood even if some do not agree with the expenditure. In the common interest development, in contrast, the common good is less well understood. As in the case where only some roofs leak yet all pay for repairs, people do not see why they should pay.

Second, elected officials and the police have the legitimacy of their offices. People may contest particular actions yet accept the necessity for there to be a position with the power to enforce laws. In the common interest development the enforcing agent is simply a neighbor and the role of the association board as trustees of the common property and commonly held deed restrictions is not well understood.

Third, the idea of neighbors policing neighbors is not only in contradiction to cultural understandings of homeownership, but also it fails to provide the internal checks and balances that people associate with fairness in the U.S. system of government. In government, there is a separation between those who create the laws, those who enforce them, and those who adjudicate disputes over the interpretation of innocence and guilt and who sentence the guilty. In contrast the association board often serves in all four roles. In a common interest development the same person may write an architectural control, determine that a neighbor is violating it, and mete out the fine. In town government, that responsibility is split between the city council, planning commission, the zoning inspector, and the courts. This absence of separation of powers leaves association boards vulnerable to both perceived and actual favoritism and abuse of powers.

Fourth, in a town, citizenship is based on residence, not ownership. While arguments over property rights may consume much of the energy of a small town government, the government is shaped by people's understanding and the legal requirements of democratic government. This is lacking in the common interest development where ownership of property is the foundation of government and the owner-members have rights more similar to those of stockholders in a corporation than to citizens.

Fifth, the surrounding industry of common interest development professionals generally see the common interest development as solely a business to be rationally managed. While this has similarities to the city manager model of local government that is common in small cities, these professionals do not think of themselves as public servants. Differences among residents are seen as troublesome—either interfering with the smooth operation of the association or as business for lawyers. None of the above legitimizes the political processes in the association.

Finally, the governing board in common interest developments are quite literally the neighbors of the rest of the association. People cannot disagree and then physically separate to the extent that is possible in all except the very smallest towns. It is thus difficult to cool out differences through separation since people are likely to see each other in their daily lives.

By privatizing the process of adjudicating rights and responsibilities, these associations have the potential to further weaken people's understanding of public life. "Just neighbors" are asked to take on a responsibility without legitimacy or often sufficient understanding of what is entailed. The attending professions see the political aspects of the association as "people problems" that are an annoyance and impede getting the real work of property management done. Renters are excluded from the process, further reinforcing the use of a property rights model. The result of all of this is to reinforce the notion that politics is the process by which other people inappropriately interfere with individuals' rights to use property as desired and weaken their understanding of the necessity and importance of public life.

REFERENCES

Barton, Stephen. 1985. *Property Rights and Democracy: The Beliefs of San Francisco Neighborhood Leaders and the American Liberal Tradition*. Berkeley, University of California Ph.D. dissertation.

_____, and Carol Silverman. 1987. *Common Interest Homeowners' Association Management Study*. Sacramento: California Department of Real Estate.

Crenson, Matthew A. 1983. *Neighborhood Politics*. Cambridge: Harvard University Press.

Habermas, Jurgen. 1989. *The Structural Transformation of the Public Sphere*. Cambridge: MIT Press.

Hixon, Richard F. 1987. *Privacy in a Public Society: Human Rights in Conflict*. New York: Oxford University Press.

Lofland, Lyn H. 1973. *A World of Strangers: Order and Action in Urban Public Space*. New York: Basic Books.

Silverman, Carol J. 1983. *Neighbors and Nighbors: A Study in Negotiated Claim*. Berkeley, University of California Ph.D. dissertation.

_____. 1987. "Neighboring, Private Lives and Public Roles," Working Paper No. 468. Berkeley: Institute of Urban and Regional Development, University of California.

_____, Stephen E. Barton, Jens Hillmer, and Patricia Ramos. 1989. *The Effects of California's Residential Real Estate Disclosure Requirements*. Sacramento: California Department of Real Estate, October.

7

Conditions of "Voice": Passivity, Disappointment, and Democracy in Homeowner Associations

Gregory S. Alexander

Both in the United States and throughout the rest of the world, it seems, "participation is . . . in the air."[1] In this country, the neo-republican revival is only one indication of the growing conviction that greater opportunity for direct participation, or what the economist Albert Hirschman first called "voice,"[2] in political decision making is both possible and desirable. Then, as if prompted by neo-republican Americans to remind their fellow citizens of their participatory heritage, citizens throughout eastern and central Europe took to the streets to conduct a

---

I want to thank Colette Y. Fergusson, Cornell Law School 1993, for her extraordinary research assistance. I also thank John Forester, Professor of City and Regional Planning, Cornell University, for his comments and insights on developing democratic cultures.

[1]Gillette, "Plebiscites, Participation, and Collective Action in Local Government Law," 86 *Mich. L. Rev.* 930, 930 (1988).

[2]A. Hirschman, *Exit, Voice, and Loyalty: Responses to Decline in Firms, Organizations, and States* (1970). Hirschman defines "voice" as "any attempt at all to change, rather than to escape from, an objectionable state of affairs, whether through individual or collective petition to the management in charge, through appeal to a higher authority with the intention of forcing a change in management, or through various types of actions and protests, including those that are meant to mobilize public opinion." *Id.* at 30.

series of popular (and peaceful) revolutions that led to the demise of state socialism in 11 European nations.[3]

Accompanying this recrudescence of the participatory ideal is the suggestion that participation is the appropriate ideal not just for politics but for other areas of social life as well. The reason why some people find cooperative ownership attractive is precisely because it is an attempt to extend the ideal of participatory democracy to the economic sphere. That is also a primary reason why many others find cooperative ownership objectionable.

This chapter discusses the role of participation in another area of social life to which political ideals like participation traditionally have seemed inapposite—residential life. It focuses on residential life as a sphere of activity that is private and yet can and sometimes does share some of the characteristics of public life. The aims of the chapter are primarily descriptive and explanatory, not normative. Rather than defend participation as an ideal that is normatively appropriate for either public politics or residential life, I will simply assume for present purposes—even as I recall Oscar Wilde's objection that socialism takes up too many evenings with meetings—that participation is normatively desirable and that its desirability does not depend on whether the sphere of activity is conventionally regarded as public or private. My concern here is with the conditions for participation. Assuming that some political norms are appropriate and feasible for some areas of life beyond formal politics (as they obviously are—equality, for example, is appropriate and feasible for many areas of life outside of politics), is participation one of them? More specifically, is participation appropriate for the residential sphere?

The emergence of homeowner, or (as they are known in the industry) "community," associations as a major form of residential life in the United States has prompted expectations that private governance institutions may realize participation as a political ideal more fully than public governance institutions. Advocates of privatization have argued that homeowner associations (HOAs) as an institution for local governance are

---

[3]Even as I wrote this, the citizens of Moscow took to the streets protesting the Stalinist attempt to oust President Mikhail Gorbachev. Their exercise of the "voice" option not only led the coup attempt to fail, but also appears to have signalled the end of the Communist Party's hegemony in the Soviet Union and perhaps the end of the Soviet Union itself.

superior to cities.[4] They are superior not only in providing private and certain public goods and services more efficiently than the public sector, but also in the senses of creating a greater feeling of community[5] and providing greater opportunities for direct citizen participation in community affairs. Democracy and private ordering are usually understood as incompatible or at least as in tension with each other. Private residential associations may be understood as an attempt to reconcile the two: to realize democracy through private ordering.

This chapter has two objectives. First, it describes the results of a modest survey of resident attitudes toward participation in governance of HOAs in several Arizona residential developments. Second, it offers a theory about why residents of planned residential developments display so little interest in the affairs of their governing HOAs and how a democratic culture might be developed within residential groups like HOAs. This theory supplements the now-standard rational choice theory of impediments to collective governance that is associated with Mancur Olson's famous study, *The Logic of Collective Action*.[6]

In both of these aims, this chapter extends prior work done on homeowner associations, particularly several empirical studies done in California by Silverman and Barton,[7] and nonempirical papers by Ellickson[8] and me.[9] Ellickson's and my papers developed competing models of HOAs that served as the bases for conflicting normative theories about the appropriate role of the legal system in regulating

---

[4]Ellickson, "Cities and Homeowners Associations," 130 *U. Pa. L. Rev.* 1519 (1950). But see Frug, "The City as a Legal Concept," 93 *Harv. L. Rev.* 1059 (1985).

[5]One commentator, for example, has asserted that homeowner associations (HOAs) have the potential to "revers[e] the anti-community trends of the last century" as well as to reinvigorate participatory democracy. Reichman, "Residential Private Governments: An Introductory Survey," 43 *U. Chi. L. Rev.* 253, 263 (1976).

[6]M. Olson, *The Logic of Collective Action* (1965).

[7]See Barton and Silverman, "The Political Life of Mandatory Homeowners' Associations," in U.S. Advisory Commission on Intergovernmental Relations, *Residential Community Association: Private Governments in the Intergovernmental System* 1 (1989); S. Barton and C. Silverman, *Common Interest Homeowners' Associations Management Study* (1987).

[8]Ellickson, "Cities and Homeowners Associations," *supra* note 4.

[9]Alexander, "Dilemmas of Group Autonomy: Residential Associations and Community," 75 *Cornell L. Rev.* 1 (1989).

HOAs. Ellickson described HOAs as contractually based voluntary associations. He argued that because of their contractual character, they should be relatively immune for legal interference. I rejected this contractual model, arguing that HOAs are mixtures of voluntary associations and communal groups. Neither Ellickson nor I tested our models empirically.[10] This chapter attempts to fill in that gap.

My study of HOA residents' attitudes revealed a basic contradiction: The HOA owners whose opinions were surveyed expressed disappointment with the experiences in their developments and the governing associations. The owners were not saying that while some aspects of the rules and governing mechanisms of the development were annoying, they were basically satisfied. The owners were frustrated; some were acutely angry. Yet they haven't responded to their disappointment by expressing their frustration. Rather, they chose passivity. At the same time, the circumstances of HOAs satisfy most of the criteria usually identified as necessary for democratic participation. What accounts, then, for the failure of voice in this setting?

The thesis that I want to suggest is that individuals do not react to disappointment by becoming active participants in the governing process unless a democratic culture already exists within the group. There is a catch-22 in this thesis: if participation in collective governance depends on a preexisting democratic consciousness, how can such a consciousness form in the first place? Democratic culture can be developed through the use of rituals that engage people in increasingly intensive forms of social interaction. HOAs have substantial opportunities for such rituals, but they have not generally exploited these opportunities, probably because of a pervasive lack of understanding of how democratic culture develops.

OBSTACLES TO VOICE:
COLLECTIVE-ACTION PROBLEMS AND HOAs

Apathy seems to be a constant feature of American public life. Taking voting as the most obvious, and in some ways least costly, form of political participation, the percentage of citizens who vote in elections at all levels has steadily declined over the past several decades. Other

---

[10]Alexander did, however, draw on the results of empirical studies by Barton and Silverman. See Alexander at 43-44.

forms of participation are more difficult to measure, but the popular perception is that Americans are a politically passive lot.

The theory of rational choice tells us that we should hardly find these developments surprising. In fact, what is surprising is that the level of political participation is as high as it is. It is now something of a commonplace that collective action of any sort faces multiple hurdles. Jon Elster states the classic obstacle this way:

> The characteristic feature of all [collective-action problem] cases is that any individual contribution generates small benefits for many people and large costs for one person—namely the contributor. Although the sum of the benefits typically exceeds the costs, so that there is a collective interest in the contribution, the costs typically exceed the benefit to the contributor, so that there is no interest in its being made.[11]

Thus, according to this theory, the low level of voting is perfectly explainable by the fact that the benefit to the voter from the marginal effect of her/his vote is greatly outweighed by the cost of voting, primarily time spent. This leads to the famous voters' paradox: why do as many people participate in elections as they do when, according to the assumption of individual rationality, they should not?[12]

A more sophisticated version of the theory of collective action problems emphasizes the free-rider phenomenon. Mancur Olson showed

---

[11] J. Elster, *The Cement of Society: A Study of Social Order*, 18 (1989).

[12] As others have pointed out, the paradox dissolves when the costs of participation are viewed as benefits. This assumption reverses the incentives that lead to the free-rider problem; self-interest leads individuals to participate more, not less. The assumption that participation in public affairs is a benefit rather than a cost, while not universally valid, clearly seems valid for some people at some times. Krier and Ursin, for example, showed that in crisis situations people did not view participation as a cost necessary for the production of a desired result, but as consumption of an intrinsically desirable good. See J. Krier and E. Ursin, *Pollution and Policy* 270-71 (1977).

An alternative theory that explains voting is social-norm theory. While the participation-as-benefit explanation is just a variation on the instrumentalist approach of economic theory, social-norm theory explains behavior on a nonconsequentialist, nonrationalist basis. In the case of voting, there is a relatively strong social norm in western democracies to participate in elections, and it is this social norm that accounts for the level of voting in the United States. See B. Barry, *Sociologists, Economists, and Democracy* 17-18 (2d ed. 1979). On social-norm theory, see generally, J. Elster, *The Cement of Society.*

that individuals are unlikely to participate in collective action even when the benefits to them exceed the costs.[13] The benefits of collective action are public goods. Consequently, individuals have incentives not to participate, with the expectation that others will do the work for them and they will reap the benefits. Since everyone shares the same incentives, however, no one will participate and collective action will not occur.

Of course, the fact is that collective action does occur. People do participate in collective decision making, work in soup kitchens, organize after-school child care centers, etc. Of course, the level of participation is context-dependent. It is widely believed among sociologists and political scientists that participation in group activity is much more likely to occur as the size of the group decreases.[14] The reasons for the importance of size are not hard to detect. The probability that individual participation will have a desired instrumental effect is greater within a small group. Individuals not only have greater incentives to participate in small groups but are also more likely to know about relevant facts and issues. Small size facilitates exchange of information and ideas.

Closely related to, but distinct from, size are the stability of the group and the frequency with which members of the group interact with each other. Individuals participate less commonly in groups to which they and others are unlikely to remain for long.[15] Similarly, participation tends to be greater with stable groups in which members frequently interact with each other. In game theoretic terms, active participation increases within games of repeat players. People have greater incentives to cooperate with those with whom they repeatedly deal. Moreover, repeated interaction facilitates knowledge of other members, and people generally feel more comfortable participating in settings in which they know other participants.

Also closely related to size is commonality of interests and values. People more actively participate in groups characterized by a high degree

---

[13]See, e.g., M. Olson, *The Logic of Collective Action* (1965).

[14]Some evidence confirming this common intuition is provided in S. Verba and N. Nie, *Participation in America: Political Democracy and Social Equality* (1972).

[15]This is an elaboration of Hirschman's analysis of the interaction between voice and exit. Generally speaking, if exit is not an available option, voice is far more likely to be used. As a corollary to this proposition, to the extent that the exit option is not only available but likely to be exercised (because, for example, of the low costs of exiting), the voice option becomes less attractive to actors.

of common interests and shared values. This is much more likely to be true of small groups, but intensely shared values and interests may also be present within large groups (consider, for example, certain political religious groups such as Roman Catholic anti-abortion groups). That is, commonality of interests and values is an independent variable.

A famous empirical study of citizen participation in political life by Verba and Nie[16] emphasized that size can be a misleading factor. Size becomes more important when it is judged along with another factor: the extent to which the locality is a "well-defined social unit," or its degree of isolation.[17] Indeed, Verba and Nie concluded that of the two factors, size and degree to which the locality is a well-defined, bounded community, the latter is more important.[18] Residents of localities that are embedded in urban concentrations tend to be apathetic even though their community is small. Their community lacks a degree of distinctiveness that permits them to identify with the community. As anyone who has driven through the San Bernardino Valley communities east of Los Angeles can attest, it's hard to develop a sense of attachment to the suburb in which you live when it's part of a large concentration of suburbs that all look the same.

Socio-economic status is another important factor in predicting participation, especially in public affairs. Confirming conventional wisdom, Verba and Nie found that with respect to the relationship between social status and political participation, the United States is quite class-biased. The reason is obvious: "[u]pper-status citizens have the time, the money, and the knowledge to be effective in politics."[19]

Less widely recognized than these factors is the role of group power. Gerald Frug has argued that greater participation with groups depends not simply on small size but also on empowerment of the group. "Power and participation," he argues, "are inextricably linked: a sense of powerlessness tends to produce apathy rather than participation, while the existence of power encourages those able to participate in its exercise to do so."[20]

In many, although not all, of these respects, homeowner associations would seem to present congenial environments for participatory group life. HOAs are created precisely for the purpose of giving residents a

---

[16]S. Verba and N. Nie, *Participation in America*.

[17]*Id.* at 233.

[18]*Id.* at 236.

[19]*Id.* at 133.

[20]Frug, "The City as a Legal Concept," at 1070.

structured opportunity to express and resolve conflicts, seek satisfaction for disappointments, and gain empowerment over the conditions of their residential lives. Many planned developments with HOAs are located in suburban areas, and sociologists have told us that the moral order of modern suburbia is characterized by avoidance, which is nothing more than a form of exit.[21] Voice is a largely ignored option in suburban America. A major reason is the character of social interaction in suburbs as loose and fluid.[22] That character in turn can be attributed in considerable part to the conditions, including institutional arrangements, of residential life in suburbs, where typically few, if any, institutions exist to counteract the dispersion and atomization of residents.[23] Planned unit developments, with their common areas, and HOAs represent attempts to reverse these conditions, so that voice becomes a viable alternative to exit.

Various features of HOAs would appear to make them successful environments for participation. Although they vary in size, many HOAs are relatively small. Second, although many planned unit developments are located in large metropolitan areas, many developments are not the indistinguishable speck in a vast sprawl that most suburbs are. Planned unit developments are physically distinguishable from surrounding areas in a variety of ways, including physical boundaries, special entrance ways, and architectural features. Third, while the socio-economic status of HOA members varies somewhat, nearly all planned unit development residents have incomes that placed them securely in the ranks of the middle class. Many are quite wealthy, and their education levels tend to be higher than average. Fourth, the common areas in planned unit developments, which often include extensive recreational facilities, provide residents with opportunities to have face-to-face contact with each. Fifth, while few HOAs have a sufficient degree of sharing of values to permit one to characterize them as communal without exaggeration, residents of planned unit developments certainly have a shared interest in maintaining the well-being, financially, physically, and

---

[21] See M. P. Baumgartner, *The Moral Order of a Suburb* (1988). Baumgartner calls this order "moral minimalism": residents of suburban communities manage their interpersonal conflicts by complaining secretly, avoiding sources of annoyance, responding conciliatorily to complaints, or doing nothing at all. See *id.* at 10-11.

[22]*Id.* at 13.

[23]See *id.* at 62-63.

aesthetically, of the entire development. This fact alone, of course, does not distinguish HOAs from residential areas that possess a fairly high degree of self-identity but which lack a formal governance structure to maintain themselves, but it does tend to provide some degree of homogeneity in all HOAs, more so than many suburbs.[24] This last factor alone theoretically makes HOAs a congenial environment for overcoming collective-action obstacles in group governance.[25]

Finally, with respect to the theory that participation depends on group empowerment, HOAs certainly possess some degree of political autonomy. The degree of autonomy that HOAs enjoy depends to a considerable extent on local law, so it is debatable how extensive their real power is. But nearly all HOAs possess and exercise certain minimal powers necessary for the development's maintenance. These powers include the equivalent of the power to tax, the power to vote, and the power to enforce other rules of the association. These powers and rules are sufficiently extensive as to give them the appearance of a private constitution, an analogy that other commentators have used in analyzing HOAs.[26]

In addition to all of these factors, it is important to emphasize that in HOAs, unlike other voluntary associations, exit is costly. Residents, having made substantial investments in purchasing their units, are to a considerable extent locked in. Of course, if they are subsequently disappointed with their decision, they are formally free to sell their unit.[27]

---

[24]It is hard to quantify this, but my strong guess is that there's greater homogeneity on average within planned developments with HOAs than non-HOA-regulated suburban communities.

[25]See Hansmann, "Condominium and Cooperative Housing: Transactional Efficiency, Tax Subsidies, and Tenure Choice," 20 *J. Leg. Studies* 25, 36 (1991).

[26]Ellickson, *supra* note 4; Epstein, Covenants and Constitutions, 73 *Cornell L. Rev.* 906 (1988).

[27]Frequently, there are formal restraints on selling units in planned developments. HOAs often hold pre-emption or option rights in cases of owner sales. Moreover, owners typically are forbidden from excessively fragmenting their interests by selling to multiple purchasers. Courts have increasingly conditioned the enforceability of such restrictions on a reasonableness require-ment, but they have not been inclined broadly to strike them down. See, e.g., *Laguna Royale Owners' Assn. v. Danger*, 119 Cal. App. 3d 670, 174 Cal. Rptr. 136 (1981); *Holleman v. Mission Trace Homeowners' Assn.*, 556 S.W. 2d 632 (Tex. Civ. App. 1977); *Dulaney Towers Maintenance v. O'Brey*, 418 A.2d 1233 (Md. Ct. App. 1980).

Transaction and other costs, however, constrain disappointed owners from choosing this option. Theoretically, this should make mechanisms for using voice as a response to disappointment more attractive.

The upshot is that on the face of things, HOAs seem to offer favorable, if nonideal, circumstances for participation in group governance. They hold out enough potential for participatory governance to make the predictions about the degree of participation in them credible. They combine some aspects of public government structure, particularly formal empowerment, with some of the social aspects of voluntary associations. These circumstances seem favorable for overcoming the collective-action problems that bedevil participation in the public sphere. At a minimum, these circumstances provide a degree of credibility to claims about HOAs' superiority as privatized forms of participatory governance.

PASSIVITY IN PRIVATE GOVERNANCE: THE MESA-CHANDLER-TEMPE STUDY

To test the validity of claims about the superiority of privatized forms of group governance as laboratories of participatory democracy, I conducted a modest empirical study of several HOAs in central Arizona. Arizona, like other Sunbelt states, is replete with planned unit developments and HOAs. However, no one has empirically studied any aspect of HOAs in Arizona.

Background

In June 1991, a research assistant and I conducted a series of 21 interviews with homeowners and a condominium landlord whose developments were governed by homeowners' associations. The interviewees all lived in suburbs of Phoenix, Arizona. Mesa, Chandler, and Tempe, the communities where the residents lived, are middle-class areas. Most of the residents of these communities are well-educated (Tempe is the home of Arizona State University); many are professionals. Consistent with the character of the communities generally, most of the interviewees were transplants to Arizona.

The developments feature houses built by a developer on three or four variations on the same basic design. The houses are purchased completely finished with uniform exteriors but customized interior fittings. Each development has some common area, managed by a homeowners' association, that each resident purchases collectively when he or she buys the home. The items included in the common area differ with the price range of the house.

The houses described in the analysis section below as falling in the $80,000-$100,000 range have the fewest amenities in the common areas. The homeowners' associations in these areas typically manage the entrance to the development, a green belt area, and sometimes the front lawns and hedges of the residents. Houses in the $100,000-$150,000 range have access to a community pool, a playing field, and in some instances a small lake front area with picnic facilities. The more expensive homes, $150,000-$250,000, have community stables and riding areas, playing fields, pools, and tennis courts. The fees charged for these facilities varied from $21 to $97 per month. The median fee was $39 per month. The monthly assessment was not necessarily higher for the more expensive homes or the best endowed common areas. Rather the assessment was solely based on what the board of the homeowners' association decided. In most developments, once an assessment has been set, a vote of two-thirds of the residents is necessary to increase it.

The boards of these associations consist of between five and nine residents. Elections are held annually at the general meeting to which each resident is invited. Residents can also attend any of the monthly or quarterly meetings held by the board on an open invitation. Most boards publish a monthly newsletter that includes the minutes of the last meeting.

Results of the Survey

The overwhelming majority of those interviewed did not purposefully purchase their homes in the development because of the existence of a homeowners' association. Homeowners in the developments studied regarded the presence of a homeowners' association as only marginally significant to their decision to purchase. Indeed, some were not even aware of the existence of an HOA in their development at the time they purchased. Others, while aware that their development had an HOA, reported that they did not fully understand the purpose or powers of an HOA. Less than 10 percent of the residents interviewed had read the rules before closing on the home.

A typical scenario leading up to purchase went like this. The purchaser initially was drawn to a well-kept neighborhood of neat, substantially uniform houses in a design they found attractive. She or he fell in love with the house and decided to buy. During the closing, the real estate agent told her or him that the common areas of the development are controlled by a homeowners' association. One homeowner, an electrical engineer with a multinational firm living in a home in the $80,000-$100,000 range, explained his decision to purchase this way:

I would have bought my home if it didn't have one [an HOA]. I only learned about the homeowners' association during the closing just before I signed on the dotted line. The most important factors in my decision were price, location, functionality of the home. Presence or absence of a homeowners' association did not sway me one way or the other.

Another homeowner, also a condominium landlord and a judge, said whether there was a homeowners' association was "no factor at all" in his decision to purchase. Over three-quarters of those surveyed attached little importance to the presence of the homeowners' association. Real estate agents appear not to have emphasized the HOA and in some cases not to have mentioned its existence at all. A typical response was:

I wasn't aware that the house was in a homeowners' association until I was doing the paperwork. But the fee was only $21 a month, due twice a year, so I figured it was nothing to be concerned about.

Once the potential homeowner learned that an HOA existed in the development and that purchasing a house in the development necessarily means joining the HOA, she or he was usually interested in only two factors: how high the assessment was and what the HOA would do with the money. A restaurant owner living in a $150,000-$200,000 neighborhood expressed these concerns:

I was not opposed to the homeowners' association so long as they provided facilities that we could not provide ourselves. We were looking for an area that provided courts and that had stables for our horses. You can enjoy a higher standard of living if everyone helps to provide these facilities. I was very impressed with the care and the standard of the facilities for the price. It is such a well-maintained neighborhood. However, I did not ask many questions about the homeowners' association beyond the fee and what was provided. I went into it blindly. I was more concerned about the school district and crime.

If collective governance through an HOA is not a substantial inducement to most purchasers, neither is it a substantial disincentive. The presence or absence of a homeowners' association plays so little on a purchaser's considerations that some buy into an association-governed-development even though they are opposed to collective government of housing developments. A training supervisor at a multinational firm living in a home in the $150,000-$200,000 range stated:

> I was not pleased about the presence of the homeowners' association. I am predisposed to be skeptical about any kind of organization. I worried that people's views would differ from mine and that I wouldn't have time to be a major participant so that my views could be considered too.

Another homeowner said,

> I was aware that it had a homeowners' association, and I didn't like the idea since I don't like restrictions being placed on my property. But the good features of the house outweighed the fact that it had a homeowners' association.

On the other hand, some homeowners were pleased that the development is governed by a homeowners' association. The benefit that most of these individuals associated with an HOA, however, was not the opportunity to practice self-governance, but "keeping up property values." These homeowners felt assured that property values would be maximized over time because there was a mechanism for ensuring that the neighborhood remained well-kept. A resident of a home in the $100,000-$150,000 range said,

> I wanted the community to stay the way it looked when I bought my home. A homeowners' association was the only way I could control my neighbors over time. I can make sure that they adhere to the bylaws.

Despite nearly universal emphasis that residents gave to maintaining property value, less than a quarter of the homeowners surveyed found that maintenance of the cosmetic aspects of the neighborhood was an important reason to buy into a homeowners' association.

The Arizona homeowners were not expecting any other benefits, like a more zealously formed community, to flow from their membership in an association. Most residents expected that the function of the homeowners' association was limited to maintenance of the physical aspects of the environment. Only one-third of those questioned even believed that the purpose of a homeowners' association includes fostering a greater sense of community. Moreover, most of that minority said they expected a closer community to be encouraged only indirectly by the homeowners' association. Common recreational areas facilitate socialization among members of a neighborhood. No one expected that a sense of community would develop solely from self-governance.

Most residents did not understand developments managed by homeowners' associations in terms of self-government. Although the board of management is elected annually from among the residents, a majority of homeowners said they expected to remain uninvolved in governing the association. Homeowners commonly blamed their active lifestyle and the care of young children for their apathy toward group self-governance. A few homeowners said that they could imagine becoming active if conditions deteriorated below their personal threshold values. One accountant in the $80,000-$100,000 range said,

I am not interested in "them" so long as they keep the place nice. If conditions deteriorate I would run. Residents have the right to call special meetings so I would go that route first.

One homeowner said she would attend meetings if they were publicized over a week in advance. Two other homeowners said they had attended meetings in the past but found them too stormy or uncomfortable to return. It appears from this survey that most residents's involvement with the governance of their association was limited to reading the HOA's newsletter.

Only one homeowner felt blocked from access to participating on the board of her homeowners' association. She described trying for a position on the board three times and being thwarted by what she believed were persons on the board who did not want her in on shady dealings. She said that she strongly suspected that members of the board in her homeowners' association were pocketing money from the monthly assessments and doing a poor job of policing the area. She guessed that board members want to prevent her from getting a seat on the board because they believe that she will blow the whistle (price range $150,000-$200,000):

I have attended almost every meeting but I feel stonewalled whenever I try to express my opinions. They know that I know want is going on and they don't want me on the board. We are paying them collectively a lot of money. I could think of better ways of spending it. They don't even publish the minutes anymore—what are they hiding? I get no thanks for questioning the board. I'm treated like a pain-in-the-neck.

Fourteen percent of those surveyed felt similarly discouraged by what one supervisor called the "eighth-grade Mickey Mouse politics" practiced by the board. Almost all the other residents said they had no desire to participate with governing the association.

A few residents said they felt compelled to be more active within the HOA than they actually wanted to be. A condominium landlord said:

> I'm only active by the inactivity of everyone else. I showed up at a meeting to complain for one of my tenants about damage to our roof from the leaking upstairs. Before I knew what was happening they had nominated me to the board, seconded it and were voting. I had no say in the matter. I didn't want to make a big fuss by withdrawing; moreover, there was no one else who wanted to run. Anyone they replaced me with would have been just as involuntary.

The president of one association said that he was urged to become active within the HOA by his frustration with the apathetic attitude of those living in his development ($150,000-$200,000):

> In society today, nobody wants to get involved in anything. Usually at the annual meeting where we elect some of the five board members each year, 15-20 of 415 homeowners show up. We send letters to everyone. Sometimes we threaten to raise the dues to get people to come but it is sad that we have to resort to tactics. We have tried to recruit people.
>
> My toughest job in my two-year tenure as president is getting people to understand that the five board members are not there to be the police for the association. We all have to police it. People don't understand that all of us have to watch out. It's an inherent problem. I wish everyone had to serve a year on the board.

Actually, most people surveyed had not only never attended a meeting but knew neither who is on the board nor the issues facing their neighborhood association.

The apathy toward HOA participation that prevails within the developments we studied does not appear to be the result of general satisfaction with the way the HOA governed the development. In fact, residents expressed substantial dissatisfaction with the rules of the HOA or the way in which the board enforced those rules. The source and intensity of dissatisfaction varied considerably. Seemingly minor matters often triggered the strongest expression of unhappiness. Many residents of one development, for example, expressed anger at a rule prohibiting them from erecting basketball hoops on their property. Despite their anger, these residents did not attend HOA meetings or otherwise voice their disappointment. More tensely observed was the rule that any structure built on a homeowners' property has to be pre-approved by the board. The training supervisor (price range $100,000-$150,000) said:

> I find the rule that you can't build any structure without the approvement of the board to be completely unreasonable. The homeowners' association has got to be kidding; this is my property! I just blow the oppressive rules off. I added on a patio, pool and jacuzzi in my backyard without any permission.

One-fifth of those interviewed supported the notion that those who did not read the rules before purchasing the home, could not now complain that they are opposed to the rules. A high-school teacher said:

> I find the rules to be just perfect. Just enough to guide home-owners but not too much to be intrusive. In any case, no one can complain after they have bought into the homeowners' association that they don't like the rules. It is your responsibility to find out about all that beforehand.

Besides, most residents were comfortable with the fees they had to pay the association. The most popular response suggested that a dramatic fee hike could spark some opposition from now passive homeowners. A computer engineer living in a development with $150,000-$200,000 units said:

> They are not a significant portion of my budget so I don't concern myself with whether they are reasonable for the services provided. So long as they don't raise them, I am not going to ask any questions.

It seems clear, then, that most residents have few concerns that could jolt them into active participation in neighborhood government.[28]

One concern that some homeowners voiced was their opposition to some of the tactics of the board. These homeowners perceive the board as a watchdog agency that checks up on how they are running their own homes. Some feel that the board has intruded on the private sphere of their property ownership with zealous policing tactics. One homemaker stated:

---

[28]Of the five board members contacted, one was a real estate agent whose neighborhood was one of his marketing areas, another was an insurance agent who had all the insurance policies on the common areas in his neighborhood, a third owned a property management company that had the contract for her neighborhood, a fourth was a retired widow who viewed the maximization of her property values as one of her biggest investments, and the fifth was a judge.

I find that the neighbors come to visit outwardly acting friendly
but they are really checking up on you. My neighbors reported
me for having a clothes line in my back yard, out of sight of the
road, when they were supposedly visiting casually.

This whole homeowners' association is a useless headache.
They are the police for the area. For instance, they told me I
can't park on the curb in front of my own house. It makes you
uncomfortable. I can understand trying to keep property values
up, but they harass you. I feel like the homeowners' association
is watching. . . .

However, this homeowner was not sufficiently incensed to attend a
meeting and confront the board.

Other residents use the homeowners' association as a weapon. One-
third of those surveyed had been in contact with members of the board
but some of them were using the board as a sword or a shield. As a
sword the association is used by neighbors against other neighbors to
keep them conforming to the board's dictates. One resident stated: "I
also like to drive around to see if people are keeping up with the rules.
If they are not, I inform the board."

As a shield, the association is used in place of neighborly confronta-
tions. The following remark by a counselor and special education teacher
typifies using the association as a shield:

My neighbor's pool had no draining ditch so the water was
ruining our garden. We asked them twice to do something about
it but they did nothing. Then we took it to the homeowners'
association and action was taken by the board. This was much
more comfortable for us since we can still be friendly with them
and hostile confrontation was minimized.

These various uses and abuses of the association have led some people
to value pleasant, individual confrontation more. One homeowner
reported,

I have become friendly with my neighbors because water from
our backyard was seeping into theirs and they did not call in the
homeowners' association. Instead, they chose to speak to us
personally and now we continue to be friendly.

Our study of Arizona HOAs suggests that there usually is a group of
people who do plan to be active when their schedules permit and others
who would cooperate through active participation if they didn't feel
stonewalled. Others apparently intend to be passive from the very time
they buy into the development, and they exhibit no inclination to change

their minds. The cooperators in our study did not look to the pre-committed defectors for support but monitored themselves to determine if cooperation was worthwhile. In some of the HOAs studied, owners appeared to rush to be among the first to defect. One condo owner described a situation that resembles a chaotic scramble to be among the first to commit to perpetual noncooperation. He attended a board meeting to complain about a leak coming from the condo above his, and he found himself unwillingly elected to the board. "I'm only active by the inactivity of everyone else," he concluded. This individual appears to have felt trapped into cooperating because he had not precommitted to passivity soon enough.

At the same time, while few individuals in our sample were altruists, there were subgroups of individuals who had self-interested reasons to cooperate. Insurance agents, real estate agents, and persons running real estate management firms participated by serving on the board because they were in a position to reap professional benefits from participation (publicity, expanding clientele, etc.). These board members could serve as a readily monitorable group for others who are potential cooperators. Their self-interested incentives are sufficiently consistent with their desire for public action that one would expect this group to behave as unconditional cooperators.

Despite the existence of subgroups of active participants, the overall impression that we gained from our survey was that apathy and frustration co-existed on a fairly widespread basis in each of the developments we studied, although the intensity of disappointment varied considerably.[29] Residents of the HOA-governed developments studied do not appear to be "happy campers." In Hirschman's vernacular, loyalty is not the dominant reaction to their experience. According to the Hirschman model, one would expect residents to react to this experience either by exercising voice or exiting. Voice is for many HOA residents the only realistic option for expressing disappointment. Exit is highly unattractive for most of them. The transaction costs of changing residences are high. Moreover, people who purchase generally have a stronger preference for

---

[29]Of course, it is possible that the disappointment reaction that interviewees expressed in this study is misleading. Various psychological factors may lead individuals to convey inaccurate reactions. The residents who said that they felt coopted to participate, for example, may have been perennial complainers who in fact wanted to participate in order to be valued.

residential stability than do nonpurchasers. People who prefer mobility or who have high expected mobility are more likely to rent than to buy.[30]

The Hirschman model predicts, then, that voice should be an attractive option to frustration in HOA governance. But the result of the Arizona study contradicts this prediction. A paradox exists here: residents are disgruntled, but they neither leave nor participate to change the way their developments are governed. How can this paradox be explained? Why do not unhappy HOA owners respond to their disappointment by articulating it and acting to change the HOA's governance? Why do they seemingly prefer to nurse their complaints in silence?

RITUALS AND THE CREATION OF DEMOCRATIC CULTURE

There's a catch-22 to voice being a viable option in response to disappointment: for individuals to practice participation, there must be a pre-existing participatory consciousness. The question is whether any means exist to create such a consciousness. Put differently, if democracy depends on the existence of a democratic culture, can such a culture be created where no pre-existing participatory consciousness exists for that institution? The answer that I want briefly to explore is that democratic culture can be created as a response to disappointment through the use of various rituals of social interaction.

The Limits of Rational Choice Theory

The theory of rituals as a condition of participation augments rational choice theory. That theory treats all individuals—potential participants—as rational economic actors and participation as the consequence of low transaction costs relative to potential individual gains from participation. This theory is useful as far as it goes, but it fails to capture the observable and experienced complexities of what is involved in participation and cooperation. Any possibility of gaining access to those complexities requires an account that treats individuals as *homo socialis*, rather than merely as *homo economicus*. It requires, that is, sociological and cultural perspective.

Rational choice theory overlooks the role of participatory rituals in creating a democratic culture because of its commitment to methodologi-

---

[30]See Hirschman, *Exit, supra* note 2 , at 33.

cal individualism. It views individuals as the fundamental unit of social activity and reduces all groups to aggregations of individuals. It analyzes all human behavior strictly in individualistic terms, identifying self-interest as the sole criterion for rationality and the dominant source of all human behavior. The study of ritual resists this sort of social reduction-ism. Ritual is "a means of converting the obligatory norms of society into the desires of individuals, of creating socialized sentiments, transforming statuses, effecting cures, acting out mythic charters for social action, and reintegrating agonistic social groups."[31]

It is inherently public and group specific. Ritual mediates individual preferences and the demands of group membership. The meaning of much behavior that is inexplicable in terms of individual rationality becomes transparent when the behavior is read as a ritualistic text. The decision to vote, for example, can be explained in terms of ritual. Voting is ritual by which individuals create and express meaning for their experience as members of a political group. Rituals can be constructed expressly for the purpose of endowing meaning in group life. Passivity and apathy are expressions of experience in which living within a group lacks meaning for individuals. Participation and cooperation depend, then, upon infusing group membership with sentiment and emotion. Creating democratic culture is ultimately a matter of altering the individual's sense of self, not accepting the image of individuality that rational choice theory defines as given but enabling individuals, through group rituals, to regard participation as a commonplace aspect of ordinary life.

Participation as Attention-Paying

In their recent and notable book, *The Good Society*,[32] Robert Bellah and several co-authors emphasize the importance of attention-paying to democracy. Their point is more than the tautology that in order for an institution to realize participatory democracy, its members cannot be apathetic. By paying attention, they mean to include a number of conditions for living actively within institutions. One condition is that institutions must be comprehensible. Their scale must not be so vast or

---

[31]G. Marcus and M. Fischer, *Anthropology as Cultural Critique: An Experimental Moment in the Human Sciences* 61 (1986).

[32]R. Bellah, R. Madsen, W. Sullivan, A. Swidler, and S. Tipton, *The Good Society* (1991).

their purposes so diverse that ordinary individuals cannot understand or relate to their reason for existing. This is one reason why participatory democracy within a multinational corporation like General Motors is unimaginable. One simply cannot comprehend the whole enterprise as a concrete institution. More fundamentally, attending, to paraphrase Bellah and his co-authors, means cultivating human possibilities and purposes.[33] It means developing our capacities by investing ourselves for the long-term rather than looking for short-term pay-offs.

Given the importance of attention-paying to participatory institutions, the crucial question, which Bellah fails to address, is whether individuals' taste for attending is simply given or is contingent. If it is contingent, then the question becomes what conditions affect taste for attending. This question does not amount merely to a matter of overcoming the transaction costs of attention-paying. It is matter of affecting perceptions so that individuals view attention-paying as a benefit rather than a cost. Bellah and his co-authors appear to assume that the taste for cooperation is contingent and can be changed by varying circumstances. This is consistent with sociology's general view that preferences are endogenous and subject to being shaped through various means of norm-internalization. It is strikingly at odds, however, with the economic outlook that preferences are exogenous. The economic assumption seems entirely incompatible with ordinary experience. Individuals' preferences to pay attention or remain distracted change in response to education, social interactions, or changing circumstances. Various social institutions instill in individuals a taste for cooperation. Schools, for example, succeed, although with considerable variation, in teaching children to share, when sharing does not appear to be an innate behavioral characteristic.[34] More germane to political participation, Elster makes this point in discussing how food and music affect perceptions about participating in political gatherings:[35]

> Social and political demonstrations can assume the aspect of a festival and attract participants by virtue of the food, drink or music that is offered. Although these are usually presented as

---

[33]*Id.* at 273.

[34]Ellickson, "Bringing Culture and Human Frailty to Rational Actors: A Critique of Classical Law and Economics," 65 *Chi.-Kent L. Rev.* 23, 46 (1989). See generally A. Etzioni, *The Moral Dimension: Toward a New Economics* (1988).

[35]J. Elster, *The Cement of Society: A Study of Social Order* 45 (1989).

rewards offered to people who have joined the demonstration for other, outcome-oriented reasons, they are sometimes intended to induce participation which would otherwise not be forthcoming. . . . The incentives offered to the participants are not intended to offset the costs of participation; rather, they are intended to make participation costless, indeed pleasurable.

Elster's point can be generalized. Participation in collective action can be increased by socializing members of the group through structured activities that are interactive. More specifically, as interactive social activities take on a ritual-like aspect, group members become more conscious of and familiar with their membership in the group. Their individualistic outlook that leads them to focus on whether the payoff to them of participating is sufficiently high to justify becoming active loses some of its force through rituals of social interaction. Participation seems increasingly to be not only an acceptable choice but even natural.

Participation as Ritual

Participatory rituals typically begin as encounters that are primarily social. Politics may initially be entirely absent or confined to a sideline aspect. Political rallies, for example, typically are staged as activities that have an aspect of the festival to them; candidates's rallies resemble barn-raisings or quilting bees far more than they do legislative meetings. This characteristic is hardly serendipitous. Political organizers for years have realized the value of tying politics to a social occasion. Participants are initially attracted to attend by virtue of the socializing, and the political discussions that come later seem to be natural extensions of the social interaction.

An example of this process of using socially interactive rituals to increase participation in collective action is a technique that some local elementary schools use to expand participation in parent-teacher associations. Parent participation in the PTA or other organizations for parent voice typically is notoriously weak, despite self-interested reasons for participation. Some schools have dealt with this problem by arranging activities that create opportunities for parents to interact with each other without committing themselves to participate in the PTA or other forms of school governance. These activities range from relatively low-commitment activities like family picnics and softball games to more time-intensive activities like building playground equipment.

For these activities to succeed in expanding participation, two characteristics are crucial. First, they must begin as primarily social encounters. It is usually fruitless to organize an initial PTA meeting by asking parents to sign up for committees. Few parents will turn out for what is announced as an "organizational meeting." Most of those who do won't volunteer for any committee. Second, they must be interactive; that is, the activities are occasions for the parents to meet, play, or work with each other as active face-to-face participants, not passive listeners sitting side-by-side. A family picnic or game is far more effective than a music concert. The point of the activity is to develop a sense of familiarity among the participants. Apathy flourishes under conditions in which individuals live in relative isolation of each other. Communication and familiarity are necessary for individuals to act on their shared interests.

Through repeated activities of this sort, active participation with other parents takes on a ritual-like quality over time. Eventually, participation in the PTA becomes a logical extension of the ritual. Participants experience cooperation within a governance institution as a social, not political, activity. What would have initially seemed an unacceptable burden that can easily be avoided by free-riding is now an enjoyable family ritual.

Participatory rituals can be arranged along a spectrum of interactivity. At one end of the spectrum are activities like watching a musical concert or listening to a speech. Such activities are only moderately interactive. The behavior is public and group-focused, but the activity does not require participants to interact with each other continuously or intensively. Individuals can and usually do participate in these rituals side-by-side rather than face-to-face. The sense of participation within a group that this kind of activity creates is thin. At the other end of the spectrum are activities like group picnics, dances, and softball games, which are highly interactive. It is activities of this sort that most directly contribute to developing a democratic culture within a group.

HOAs provide an excellent opportunity to create such rituals. Some associations organize and sponsor activities like baseball games among adults and/or their children, potluck suppers, dances, sports tournaments (tennis, golf), and community improvement projects as a way of bring residents together. Developments in which such activities are regularly offered and have taken on the character of ritual are far more likely to succeed in encouraging residents to participate in the development's governance. An appeal to become involved in HOA affairs is more likely to succeed when it is made in the context of a ritualized activity in which participants already interact with each other in an intensive way.

CONCLUSION

Voice need not be understood solely as a residual response to frustration or disappointment in group life, viable if but only if exit is unavailable. Our study of HOA resident attitudes and practices revealed that even when exit is not an attractive option, individuals sometimes do not express disappointment by exercising voice. Even under these circumstances they will remain mute and passive if the group context lacks a participatory consciousness. The creation and maintenance of democratic culture depends on individuals participating in group life as an aspect of their ritualized lives rather than as a matter of rational choice between two equally available options, like choosing between Pepsi or Coke. Passivity and apathy are not commodities; they are expressions of how individuals understand their lives. Participation can be developed as a ritual that is central to individual experience.

8

Managing Interdependence: The Effects of Neighboring Style on Neighborhood Organization

Carol J. Silverman
Stephen E. Barton

The extensive literature on neighborhood organizations has generally treated them as similar to any other voluntary group that brings people with common interests together. Shared neighborhood is important only insofar as common vulnerability to external agencies creates reasons to organize, or insofar as proximity contributes to friendships that may then reinforce neighborhood political action (Boyte 1980, 1984; Cunningham and Kotler 1983; Hunter 1974). The dominant approach to neighborhood organization thus ignores a special character of relations among neighbors—that they share residential space.

Unlike members of other voluntary organizations, neighbors live alongside each other both during and after their work with the organization. This continuing proximity has implications both for neighbor ties and for behavior within neighborhood organizations. Neighborhood residents can choose between different styles of neighboring, reflecting different ways of dealing with the ties of proximity. These styles in turn affect behavior within neighborhood organizations.

Silverman (1983, 1987) has argued that shared space creates mutual vulnerability and an ongoing relationship of interdependence. Neighbors manage this immediate interdependence through either public or private neighboring styles. The public style of neighboring is characterized by recognition of and efforts at cooperative management of interdependence.

The private neighboring style is characterized by avoidance of such recognition and acceptance of relationships only based on personal compatibility.

In this chapter, our purpose is to document the utility of the theoretical concept of private and public neighboring styles in the analysis of behavior within neighborhood organizations. Based upon case studies of two condominium homeowners' associations, we show that a public style of neighbor involvement, which highlights interdependence, is better able to accommodate differences and strains among neighbors and thus to permit neighborhood organizations to overcome potential schisms among their membership. We conclude with suggestions on how other areas in the neighboring literature might be illuminated by this concept of neighboring style.

RESEARCH

Our research draws upon two case studies of neighborhood associations located in common interest developments—mandatory homeowner associations responsible for maintaining common property and enforcing rules of behavior.

The case studies materials we present are drawn from a larger study of management and governance in common interest developments—condominium and planned development subdivisions with mandatory homeowners' associations (Barton and Silverman 1987). In the study we developed 12 case studies of associations in northern California. In each case study, we reviewed the past several years of association documents, attended a board or annual meeting, and conducted in-depth interviews with members of the board and others who were involved in the association. We also interviewed professionals who work with the associations, mostly managers, accountants, and lawyers.

The 12 case studies were selected to vary on dimensions we found to be important in a statewide survey of associations: size, professionally or self managed, and income of residents. The associations were found by referrals from knowledgeable professionals who would, for example, recommend a small, self managed, moderate-income association. In the case studies we probed a number of issues of concern to us including the methods used by the association to resolve differences. We had already developed the concept of public and private styles of neighboring and asked a number of questions designed to understand how the board understood their relationships to neighbors.

In the course of doing the research, we discovered two associations of similar size and socio-economic status whose board and members had undergone severe conflict over similar problems. The boards had, however, employed very different strategies in handling those conflicts. We do not claim that the specific experiences of these two associations are necessarily typical (although the existence of internal conflict is one of the most typical problems of associations). We do claim, however, that the course of the conflict cannot be understood without understanding the neighboring style used by the governing boards.

It can be objected that the membership is not typical because it is self-selected, made up of those who choose to live in such a community. Some members do self-select, but our research in California found that the overwhelming majority of residents chose to live in a common interest development because it had the best location and type of home they could afford, not because they wanted to be members of a mandatory homeowners' association (Barton and Silverman 1987; Silverman, Barton, Hillmer, and Ramos 1989).

PRIVATE AND PUBLIC NEIGHBORING STYLES

The neighbor role appears to occupy a residual position in an affluent modern society. Due to the widespread availability of resources, most individuals need not have much actively to do with neighbors. Neighboring then becomes a discretionary relationship, dictated by individual interests, circumstances, and compatibilities. Neighbors can, but do not need to, widen private life to the larger neighborhood and include neighbors within it. Activities range from friendly conversations in passing to more involved social relations. When instrumental exchanges do occur, they do not differ in character from those in any other primary relationship where sentimental ties lead people to perform favors for each other.

Elsewhere, Silverman (1983, 1987) defined this aspect of the neighboring role as private since it extends the private life associated with the home into the neighborhood and draws on the private values of individualism and choice. Residents who primarily use the private model draw on the values of individualism and choice in selecting compatible neighbors as confidants or social partners. If they should happen to live in a neighborhood where no person is perceived as similar, or if they should feel no need for neighbor friends because of other involvements, then they have little to do with neighbors.

While active neighboring is a discretionary relationship, the neighbor role is not. A person does not chose to have neighbors, rather they are an inevitable part of any residence. Not only do neighbors share vulnerabilities *vis-à-vis* outside agencies and thereby constitute at least a latent interest group (Janowitz 1952; Greer 1962; Suttles 1968, 1972), they also share residential space. As a result, they must depend on each other to maintain the character of the neighborhood and the privacy of individual households.

Even if neighbors actively have little to do with each other, they are passively interdependent. Their shared vulnerability is heightened by neighbors' expectations about their rights both to privacy and to freedom of action within and around the home. Since one person's right to privacy often conflicts with another's freedom of action, neighbors are faced with the ongoing task of negotiating and maintaining explicit agreements about the use of public space and uses of private space that affect others (see Silverman 1987 for a fuller discussion of this). The neighbor role thus resembles other public relationships that are defined by lack of choice and sentimental ties.

These public aspects of neighboring are fundamental. They exist before any person even acknowledges the existence of the next door neighbor. People can draw on selected aspects of both the private and public styles in constructing their behavior (Silverman 1987). Neighbors need not recognize the public aspects of neighboring, and the two dimensions can conflict with each other.

In contrast, residents who recognize their interdependence are likely to feel a sense of obligation towards their neighbors as well. They look at the public aspects, the mutual vulnerability of a group of residents who do not chose each other but who share residential space and perceive the need for neighbors to look out for one another. Unlike private models, the public model is inclusive; all neighbors are considered to be relevant. While residents who hold the public model can become friends, they need not do so.

NEIGHBOR INTERDEPENDENCE AND NEIGHBORHOOD ORGANIZATION

The public aspects inherent in all neighborhoods are given concrete form in neighborhood organizations. These organizations bring together people because of their shared residence and reflect their collective interests. The public nature of neighborhood organization does not require a commitment to a public neighboring style by its members. Members can participate out of private motives, joining together to enhance individual interests and only incidentally to benefit others. Neighborhood organizations, especially when in opposition to some outside organization, serve to defend the identical individual private interests of their membership. Nonetheless, the very fact of collective decision making makes neighbors' interdependence explicit to some degree.

Though they are rarely studied, the mandatory owners' associations in common interest developments are the most commonly found form of neighborhood association. (See Rich 1980, for a study that treats both voluntary and mandatory neighborhood organizations.) Although it is difficult to obtain reliable estimates, there are probably over 150,000 associations in the United States, far more than the number of local governments or voluntary neighborhood associations. With an average board size of 5 and an unknown number of individuals serving on committees, this means that substantially over 750,000 individuals are actively involved in these associations.

What particularly sets the common interest homeowners' association apart from other neighborhood associations is the basis for the mandatory membership—common property ownership and conditions, covenants, and restrictions (CC&Rs) incorporated into the deed to the property. The term "common interest" refers to this common property interest. The common property ranges from buildings and their common spaces to lawns, pools, and playgrounds to streets within a development. The CC&Rs set uniform rules governing the use of both individual and common property (everything from the colors of doors and window shades to the noise-dampening qualities required of floor coverings to visitor access to a pool), and establish the owners' association and give it the power to finance its activities through regular assessments against each unit. In most mandatory homeowners' associations, tenants are not allowed to be voting members and are not encouraged to be active even on a voluntary basis, while absentee owners are automatically members.

The active membership and the board of directors of common interest associations are volunteers, just as in any voluntary association, but membership is mandatory for all owners. In a strictly voluntary association, members can resolve embittered relations by dividing the association into two groups or by one or both sides abandoning organized activities and returning to private life. But in the mandatory homeowners' association, the organization's existence is independent of the preferences of individual members. The association has responsibilities that require continuing activity on the part of the membership and that affect residents' day-to-day lives. In a common interest development active members who disagree can return to private life but will remain subject to the decisions made by those who run the association. The only true "exit" for members is the sale of their home. In this respect the common interest homeowners' association is similar to a local government, rather than a voluntary association.

The mixed structure of individual and common property ownership means that the common interest association must explicitly deal with interdependencies that voluntary associations can more easily ignore. This does not mean that the nature of interdependence in mandatory and voluntary homeowners' associations is dramatically different. Barton (1985) found that many leaders of voluntary neighborhood organizations understood their role as that of guardianship over collective property, even though no property was actually owned in common. Zoning and related land-use regulations create collective rights similar to those based on property rights created by CC&Rs (Barton 1983).

In sum, while there are important differences between voluntary and mandatory homeowners' and neighborhood associations, they both embody concerns with interdependence among neighbors. The repertoire of neighboring styles available to the leadership may thus have an important influence on their ability to deal with neighborhood conflict over collective interests.

The Setting

Hillside Gardens is a 100-unit low-rise apartment complex constructed on pilings on a hillside in the late 1960s. The units were rented until, with the escalation of housing prices in the late 1970s they were finally sold to individual owners. There were numerous construction defects. Developer after developer took over the project, some going bankrupt in the process of attempting to fix leaking roofs and other defects. Residents were moderately affluent, with the average price of a unit in 1987 over $200,000. Many were older adults who had owned single-family homes in the past, while some others had originally been renters in the complex but were able to convert their leases into deeds.

The Hillside Gardens' board of directors did not budget for future repairs and replacement costs and neglected maintenance as well. The buildings were over 20 years old at the time of our case study. Many of the components had decayed and needed to be replaced, and the association found that it needed to come up with large sums of money to do repairs and build up future reserves.

Greenview Terrace is also a large association, over 300 units, built as townhouses surrounding green spaces. Now 14 years old, the association has had to manage a similar crisis. The developer installed faulty roofs, which wore out after six years, creating numerous leaks. The association's reasonably comfortable membership—units sold for about $170,000 to $190,000 in 1987—were faced with years of lawsuits while interim patch-up jobs failed to halt the major leaks. Although the suit was finally settled out of court, the settlement was insufficient to pay for all legal expenses, intermediate repairs, and the actual cost of fixing the roof.

The two associations were working out similar solutions to their financial problems, using a special assessment to raise money for major repairs that needed to be done immediately and increased dues to sustain maintenance and build up reserves. They were at different stages in the process, however. Our interviews at Hillside Gardens took place immediately prior and after the annual meeting where the need for large sums of reserve funds was discussed. Greenview Terrace resolved its funding problems a year before the interviewing took place.

We were sensitive to the fact that the attainment of closure at Greenview Terrace might have biased peoples' recollections. We interviewed parties from both sides of the disputes as well as some individuals not directly associated with either side. Additionally, we reviewed the monthly newsletters and board minutes from the past several years as well as literature put out by the opposition and found a remarkable degree of consensus, admittedly colored by individual interests, about the course of events.

In both associations, we interviewed a number of past and present board members as well as a few less involved residents. We also interviewed the managers of both associations and attended Hillside Gardens' annual meeting and Greenview Terrace's monthly board meeting. In both associations two factions formed; we conducted interviews with adherents of both sides. In all we conducted eight interviews of one to two hours at each association.

Leadership Neighboring Styles

Individuals we interviewed in both associations used the private model to form friendships with neighbors and to share family life and leisure activities. The pattern was much more pronounced in Hillside

Gardens. The president and several other members of the board were friends, active on the tennis courts, at the swimming pool, and elsewhere. They had dinner together, enjoined friendships with other residents based on similar recreational activities, opened up their homes, and at least in one case became business partners. An ex-board president who no longer lived in the association maintained contact with his friends on the board.

At Greenview Terrace, in contrast, the present board did not speak about their friendships with neighbors. They maintained a more distanced relationship with each other and their neighbors, entering into friendships in some cases but not as a general rule. However, several of the committee members talked to us about their many friendships with others in the association.

In Hillside Gardens the association leadership saw themselves as living in a community of like-minded individuals and saw their role as protecting individual investments and encouraging socializing. The board personally desired a place where they could maintain a set of social ties that took advantage of the many recreational facilities provided by the association. It is indicative that one board member introduced himself to a new resident at an annual meeting not by explaining the association but by seeking to uncover their common recreational and work related activities.

The board of Hillside Gardens desired a neighborly association and used a neighboring vocabulary in explaining the benefits of the association, but for them neighborliness means common social activities among compatible individuals, and a neighborly association is one where people can find others who enjoy similar recreational pursuits

> And we had a barbecue and everyone pitched in. We like to have a lot of neighborliness because that is what this is.

The board seemed most pleased with the job they have done in providing ways of enhancing the social climate of the association. When recounting the board's accomplishments to us as well as to the membership, the present board president stressed the various social activities the board had initiated.

> We have been trying very hard to build a communal interest in terms of a lot of social activities. I thought the culmination of, the nicest thing we did all year long, we had, we decorated all of the five [buildings] at Christmas time. . . . It was really, it was almost spiritual the way everyone got together and decorated their individual units. . . . It was really the high point of the year.

Because neighboring is defined by companionship and therefore compatibility, their definition of neighboring extended only to others who are similar.

> You are living with [over 100] neighbors, some of whom you are going to love and some of whom you hope you will never see again.

Because they desired an environment composed of others like themselves, friendships and similar interests were used as the basis for involving people in committee and board work. One resident of Hillside Terrace spoke of how none of the current board bothered to come to a party to celebrate a long-time renter's conversion to ownership because she was different from the board members and therefore not considered a potential social companion. In one board member's words:

> You get to know one another and you like to bring people like yourself, who think like you, onto the board. . . . I recruited some new friends who moved in . . . and you feel comfortable with people like that.

The board understood that they represented the membership of the association, but collective interests were perceived as grounded in similarities in personalities, financial and recreational interests. The job of the board was to keep the membership happy and to provide opportunities to permit people who shared their interests to express them. The current board president was elected on a platform of lowering assessments. When it became clear during the course of the year that this was not possible and indeed that a large increase in assessments was needed, the board looked to how it could best maintain popularity with the membership. A proposed assessment increase was constructed with an eye to how the membership would view it rather than financial prudence. Although their accountant had recommended a 10 percent dues increase to maintain sufficient operating funds, the board recognized that dues increases were more unpopular than one-time special assessments and opted for the larger special assessment.

> We wrenched the accountant around to make a projection which we think much more palatable. . . .

By contrast, the board of Greenview Terrace used the public model. They saw neighboring as an obligation based on the interdependence of people who shared residential space. They became involved in the association because they felt an obligation to the larger community.

[Satisfactions of serving on the board?] Brings home for you the sense of community. I mean I went in for that reason. I felt I took from the community and I owed to the community.

One president rode his bike throughout the development so he could best meet members and hear their concerns; another spoke of how the best part of being on the board was representing the interests of his neighbors. Unlike the board of Hillside Gardens, they focused on common political action as the basis of community rather than social activities.

[In discussing membership activities after the defeat of a proposed assessment] After [the membership] turned down the $5000, they got involved; they wanted to know why. And that brought us all together. It was very positive.

The board did not recruit friends onto the board and were not friends themselves. Unlike Hillside Gardens where a past president who no longer lived in the association maintained his friendship with the current board, board members outside the association were no longer involved with residents. Instead, they recruited people who were interested and who were willing to contribute to the association by working first on committees and then on the board.

Rather than looking for compatibility, they sought diversity. It was thought to provide a potentially enriching source of decision making and a greater certainty that diverse interests would be recognized. The more people that were involved in decisions, the members said in their interviews with us, the greater the number of potential ways of looking at things, the more debate over the course of action, and the stronger the solutions. For this reason, several of the board members we interviewed spoke of the need to maintain large committees. Small committees did not permit a sufficient diversity of viewpoints. They also mentioned how they had brought in a member of the group that had opposed their solution to the roof problem as proof of the strength of the association. The dissident, himself, although not fully believing that the board would ask a self-described rabble-rouser to run, seemed proud of his position.

He [the current president] always thanks me after the meeting when I disagree with a point or get a point clarified because I don't have all the facts for an intelligent vote. So after each meeting, he always makes it a point to compliment me and give his appreciation for keeping the board honest.

The board knew that a diverse membership meant that people had different interests. They were further painfully aware that their actions might hurt some of their members and felt personally responsible for the potentially negative consequences of their actions. For example, in Greenview Terrace as in Hillside Gardens some individuals were unable to afford the special assessments. In Hillside Gardens this was never discussed as an issue by the current board. In Greenview Terrace, the board sought a solution where the association as a whole would look after its members. They talked about the problem prior to the announcement of the assessment, decided to publish an article in the newsletter detailing how individuals who could not afford the increase or who would be willing to loan money in the association should talk to the board. The board also decided that they, themselves, would lend money if necessary and that the lawyer on the board would donate the legal work.

Conflict and Neighboring Style

The two associations were faced with similar conflicts involving construction defects, defects that did not affect all members equally. In Hillside Gardens, those who intended to sell shortly and those who maintained the property to extract rental income were less interested in putting money aside for long-term repairs; in Greenview Terrace not every roof leaked. Yet, regardless of individual interests or indeed capacity to afford special assessments, money was needed from all equally.

Both boards were faced with making decisions that would directly affect the membership, their immediate finances, the long-term health of their investment, and the day-to-day quality of life in the association. Yet, the two boards handled the conflicts very differently, reflecting their different understanding of the neighboring role. In Hillside Gardens boards used the private style and created deep divisions within the association. In Greenview Terrace, the board acted out their understanding of the public role and accommodated differences among the members.

Hillside Gardens

To briefly review, past boards had neglected ongoing maintenance and failed to accumulate capital to replace and repair the decaying infrastructure. The previous year's board president finally realized the extent of the problem and proposed and successfully obtained a substantial dues increase. He then stepped down at the end of his term of office. The new board included several individuals who had felt personal antagonisms towards the old president and who had attempted unsuccessfully during several prior elections to unseat him and those he supported. This faction had finally been able to canvass sufficient votes to gain a majority on the board. They rolled back the dues increase, stating they would save money through competitive bidding.

When the former president threatened a lawsuit, they responded by bringing in a structural engineer and accountant who found there were serious defects resulting from poor initial construction and neglect and that large sums of money would be needed for reserves. In order to maintain popularity with the membership, the board suggested increasing dues as little as possible and relying on a special assessment of $1,500 a year for the next three years.

The results were presented to the membership at the annual meeting where two board members, including the president, were up for re-election. The current president knew that there would be disquiet from the membership at the size of the required assessment as well as an attempt to unseat the current board majority. Rather than address the bases of conflict, the president held off discussion of the assessment until after the vote had been taken. Instead, he briefly referred to the report and downplayed the buildings problems with several jokes and a "state of the condominium" address that focused on the social activities—i.e., the shared private life—of the association. The current board easily won re-election, amidst the past president supporters' accusation of unethical dealings.

In presenting the reserve study, the president appealed to the individual loss in property values that would occur if the assessment were not instated rather than the collective need to maintain the association. Even though the board now supported the need to raise monies, the past president did not accept their authority. He rose to insist there be someone other than a board member to monitor the large sums of monies that would be collected. The board agreed to this although several members were visibly and vocally upset at the implication they could not be trusted. The ex-president next proposed an end to secrecy and closed board meetings. The membership drifted out, tempers rose, and personal attacks were directed against both sides. With one board member screaming and others walking out of the room, the meeting ended. After the meeting, a board member began legal proceedings against the past president for slander.

In Hillside Gardens the conflict turned into one over individual competency rather than the actual decision to raise money on which there evolved agreement. The board and the opposition did not seek to involve the general membership except to the extent their vote was needed. Rather than relying on education, both sides also sought recourse in the courts.

Greenview Terrace

Greenview Terrace's board also faced a hostile membership but with different results. To review, Greenview Terrace had to obtain large sums to fix its leaking roofs. After several years of legal struggles and battles between opposing slates of candidates, each certain the previous board was incompetently handling the problem, the board finally reached an out-of-court settlement that did not cover all of the accumulated costs. When an initial attempt to raise the additional money through a special assessment failed by a few votes, the board took action to educate the membership.

Unlike Hillside Terrace, which downplayed the problem, the board overstated it. Although they knew the additional costs per unit would be about $3000, they ensured the attention of the membership by stating that $5000 would be due within 90 days. Their hope was to obtain high attendance at a special meeting where the issues would be discussed. At the virtually universally attended meeting, they brought in specialists and obtained the general support of the membership although a substantial minority were angry, certain that the best settlement had not been obtained. Unlike Hillside Terrace where the members' assistance was not solicited, the board called for interested and knowledgeable individuals to help them solicit and evaluate bids for repairs.

One year later, the board increased the regular assessment, an action not requiring membership approval. Those angry with the initial assessment were enraged; they attempted to block further increases by proposing an amendment to the governing documents that would limit the amount assessments could be raised without a vote of the membership. They first appealed to the general membership through normal political behavior.

> I was really torqued. . . . I went around, I was part of a nucleus of homeowners that went around. We rabble-roused and we stirred our fellow homeowners and got other people together and we mapped out the complexes and we farmed out and knocked on doors.

With the failure of their amendment, an angered individual sent notices to the entire membership, seeking others to create political opposition to the board. A group of about 25 individuals met, wrote a newsletter and again went door-to-door with their complaints. They put up their own candidate for the board. When they lost, they asked to form a committee to investigate the high dues and assessments. The board authorized them while warning that it was the board's belief that their actions were not in the best interests of the association. The resulting committee report served as the impetus to a new committee charged by the board with amending the governing documents. When the next election occurred, the board asked the previously unsuccessful opposition candidate to run again, this time with their backing. He was elected and now finds what he saw to be the unreasonable behavior of the board to be grounded in thoughtful consideration.

> I found that the people on the board of directors are a little more human that I thought, including some of the incumbents I was all riled up against. They seem to me like they make reasonable decisions and I am happy to be a part of it.

In Greenview Terrace, then, both sides used normal political channels to further their ends, attempting to create coalitions based on shared positions. The board was always responsive to the position of the opposition, even as they disagreed with it.

Public and Private Models and Community Interdependence

The two conflicts were structurally similar in many ways. In each association, two factions formed over a monetary dispute and used political means to try to win power in the association. In each case, those opposing the current board failed to gain power. But while at Hillside Terrace, the political process only further poisoned relations between the two factions, at Greenview Terrace, the two groups eventually were able to work together as each made concessions to the other's position.

What is the difference between the two associations? It can be argued that in a year the factions at Hillside Terrace will have reached an accommodation. That seems unlikely. The two groups there are actually in fundamental agreement now. They both recognize the need to remedy past errors and to raise large sums of money to do so. Instead, their differences occur over the imputation of motives.

The current board is confident that their behavior is correct. They personalize the conflict, arguing that the opposition is being unnecessarily confrontational and obstructionist.

There has been unbelievable nitpicking over things that the board in its wisdom thought were important to do. There has been factionalism. . . . One past president took occasion, on several occasions, to send letters to everyone. Really, that could have been done in conversation. I fund that intolerant, inefficient, time-consuming, devious, contrary, all of that.

The board saw their association as a friendly and neighborly one, marred by the members of the opposition who refused to recognize this. They used the vocabulary of neighboring in speaking of the opposition. But they spoke of a group that refused to fit in, to be happy with the job the board had done of creating what they saw to be a neighborly community. During the annual meeting, an ex-board president who was married to the incoming president read from an obviously prepared speech where he accused the opposition of not being good neighbors, of failing to recognize the well-intentioned behavior of the current board. They further stigmatized the opposition because they did not fit in.

[As a part of a discussion of the need for someone to oversee the monies that would be collected] Suppose the loonies got back in here. My Lord, if [past president] were back administering the money, I would have heart failure.

The opposition, in contrast, is certain that the present board is making unwise financial decisions.

Oh, there is such a tempest in a teapot. It's unbelievable what they are doing with our money. . . . On an emotional basis the dues were reduced.

A new board came in and threw the budget [the one prepared under the old president] out and went off on their own and didn't know what they were doing. . . . It just gets a little bit frustrating when people on the board don't know anything about property management and they don't really know how to run this place.

They saw the board's social activities and desire to please as interfering with their abilities to govern the association. They located the behaviors they found objectionable in the current board's understanding of neighboring. Board actions deemed imprudent were those designed for popular appeal. The charge of secret meetings stemmed from the perception that a cabal of individuals, based on swimming pool and tennis court friendships, was excluding the rest of the association from their decisions and giving each other privileges.

Now there is a feeling here there is a clique among three
members of the board who have this sewn up because of their
personal ideas. . . . There seems to be a mini-government on the
tennis courts. All the tennis buddies get together and they have
their sphere of influence and the swimming buddies have their
idea.

Two of them [tennis court friends] are on the board so
naturally the first thing they do is resurface the tennis courts,
even though the sewers are leaking.

Unlike the board who, both in their comments to us and in a closed-
ended instrument filled out before the interview, saw themselves as living
in an association of friends, the opposition saw their development as
uncaring and their opinions as disregarded. The ex-board president in a
closed-ended question described it as an association where people go their
own ways and don't particularly care about each other.

The opposition saw the board as working for its friends, against the
past board, and not for the association as a whole and again read the
cause of the problem as being personalities.

They didn't want to continue [past board's] policies. They
wanted to throw everything out. It was like children. Throw it
out. It is discouraging to see adults acting like that.

[The ex-president explaining why he thinks people currently
serve on the board] It's an ego trip. . . . It's the social clique of
the satisfaction among your peers that you are fostering their and
your mutual interest. Witness the attempt to curry favor.

Neither side at Hillside Gardens admitted how small the true differences were between the two sides. While both sides agreed on the
necessary course of action, the history of conflict had poisoned relations
between them. The ex-president wished only to sell his unit and move
elsewhere. He refused to credit the present board with even the wisdom
of coming around to what he had initially proposed. The present board
would not recognize that the past president had even been correct or that
he might be able to help them in their work. They only focused on his
confrontational style and labeled him a looney. It is indicative that we
were never able to ascertain who was responsible for the initial contact
with the accountant and engineer. Both sides took credit for this.

In Greenview Terrace, on the other hand, the board has always been
willing to cooperate with their opponents. While board members see
themselves as working hard for the best compromise solution, they have
always recognized the validity of a diversity of viewpoints and used the

formal apparatus of the committee system to legitimate opposing view-points. Each side still possesses some reservations about the other's at least initial position. The board believes the opposition did not understand the issues; the opposition is still unhappy with the loss of control over personal finances and use of property entailed in the structure of a condominium. But they are able to work with each other.

The board of Greenview Terrace also created hostility among a portion of the membership that failed to understand the reasons for the expenses and, at least in some cases, had stretched their finances as far as they would go just to purchase a home in California's expensive market. But this hostility never took on the personal tone it did at Hillside Gardens. The circular put out by the opposition discussed the actions of the board rather than the personalities of specific members. Furthermore, there never were accusations of favoring friends since the board members were not friends and the recruitment for the extensive committee system occurred among all interested members.

The Greenview Terrace board downplayed the hostilities evident at the large meeting and never mentioned any of the key actors by name. They seemed to believe that such hostility was inevitable and that their job was to educate the membership about the issues. They wished to talk about the process by which the membership came together in support of common goals rather than common social activities. Others, less directly involved, agreed that the attacks were never personal.

> I don't think any of the directors got personal attacks. I think people saw that they were trying to do their best. . . . There was a kind of dissident group that got organized. . . . I think they were people who weren't very much involved and they were shocked by this and they tried to organize and get together and they were finally able to see that the board had been right.

In Greenview Terrace then the two factions also came to agreement. But there both sides made compromises and were able to work with each other. The board recognized the validity of the opposition's right to have a different position even if they did not agree with it. They authorized the opposition to form a committee in part to educate them about the issues so they could more intelligently participate in determining association policy. They then worked together in revising the governing documents and ultimately hammered out a compromise position.

The two boards then acted out their mutual interests in different ways. The differences reflected their styles of neighboring. The private style may lay the foundations for deeper personal relationships as individuals open up their personal lives to each other but it is exclusive and has little ability to encompass difference. Furthermore, except in those cases where the association is sufficiently small and homogeneous to foster friendships among all residents, it also can lead to a fractionalized membership and, when inevitable differences arise, feelings of exclusion and favoritism.

The public style is defined by inclusiveness. It recognizes that neighbors share space and that they need to cooperate to make decisions about the use of that space. Reconciling differences is part of what is meant by neighboring. As evidenced in Greenview Terrace, conflicts do arise but they are ultimately not divisive since they are not viewed as a failure of what should be a sentimental relationship but instead as an inevitable expression of different interests and opinions.

The strength of the public style should not be overstated. Elsewhere Silverman (1983) has shown that it depends on at least a certain level of homogeneity and that when populations grow too diverse residents lose the sense of living in a neighborhood and in turn in having anything in common with their neighbors. Similarly it is to be expected that a sufficiently serious conflict might cause it to break down. But the public style at least has the potential of reconciling differences while the private style does not and indeed exacerbated the relatively small differences at Hillside Gardens.

Neighboring Style and Community Action

This chapter's intent has been to demonstrate the utility of a concept of public and private neighboring styles in the analysis of two organizations' capacity to handle internal conflict. Here, we have spoken about the public and private styles and common interest developments. We suggest that neighboring style may prove important to the analysis of other questions in the literature on community organization.

It has long been a truism of the community organizing field that a "feeling of community" helps sustain organizing. This is normally expressed in the view that a neighborhood with many friendships among neighbors will be better able to organize, as is a neighborhood with high symbolic identification as a neighborhood among its residents (Boyte 1980, 1984; Hunter 1974; Suttles 1968, 1972). We can suggest that an understanding of the public nature of the local community is equally important, and that close social ties can also be a source of division and conflict without such understanding. (Crenson, 1983, is a rare example of a study of neighborhood associations that includes the importance of how people manage tension over their neighboring relations.)

Neighborhood organizations based on simple coalitions of identical interests can have problems. While simple unity of perceived interest can lead to common action against an outside threat, it provides no basis to decide among different interests or to handle internal conflicts; such organizations create no reasons for the membership to act together when there are differences in outlook. For this to occur, there must be a recognition that the relationship itself is important. Family or friends, for example, can balance the importance of their sentimental ties against their differences and work towards a reconciliation.

It can be dangerous for a neighborhood organization to depend on the use of friendship to resolve differences. Disagreements can be severe since they incorporate residents' expectations concerning their rights to the use of their own property or homes, and such expectations are often extended into the larger neighborhood. Friendship, which typically depends on compatibility, can dissolve under the strain and hurt feelings then exacerbate the conflict. But members of an organization who adhere to the private style but who are not friends have no apparent basis to work towards a reconciliation since they do not recognize the validity of the organization as separate from their individual interests. Thus associations based on the private styles of neighboring have no foundation to reconcile differences when the members are not friends, and they have the potential for extremely bitter debate when disagreements cleave friendships. Debates in organizations governed by the private style have the potential to be particularly rancorous since personal relations intertwine with differences in outlook.

The public style in contrast is based on the recognition that neighbors share space and therefore have an interest in getting along with each other. Since residence, not compatibility, is the basis for inclusion people are not expected to automatically agree on issues and differences are not taken as a threat to a personal relationship. Instead, the public style recognizes the need to work together towards reconciliation as an inherent part of neighboring. Since the organization embodies the collective aspect of the neighborhood, its functions must include arbitration of differences. For these reasons we suggest generally that the neighboring style will affect the organization's capacity to deal with internal differences. Organizations governed by the public style incorporate such adjudication as a normal part of their work.

The literature has long grappled with the free-rider problem posed by Olson (1965) and applied to neighborhood organizations by O'Brien (1975) and others. Given that any particular individual reaps the collective benefits of the organization, he or she has insufficient motive to join unless other benefits, such as increased control over the determination of goals, outweigh the costs of participation. Recent literature has expanded the scope of benefits to include the moral benefits gained from helping others and the expressive benefits of acting out one's beliefs (Ethridge 1987).

People who use the private neighboring style very probably do weigh the individual costs and benefits of organizational activity, consciously or otherwise. The current board of Hillside Terrace, for example, quite frankly admitted to joining the board to have increased control over finances and to using friendship as a means of recruiting new individuals onto the board.

Adherents of the public style, in contrast, start with the necessity of the group working together because of shared space and the attending collective obligation to maintain appropriate social relations within that space. The legitimacy of the group is thus recognized and the obligation each person owes to it given credence. Thus one board member at Greenview Terrace spoke of how the community had given to him and he owed to it. In another association not discussed in this chapter members were successfully instilled with the ethic that all needed to take their turn on the board. Therefore, associations where members take the public style should have a higher rate of participation than organizations where many neighbors are friends. In such organizations, people participate not simply because they want more control over decisions or because they enjoy helping others but also because they recognize that they must depend on each other and that the organization embodies this collective interdependence.

The hypothesis of higher rates of participation has been at least tentatively supported by the quantitative survey data gathered in our larger study. Associations whose presidents report that the members look out for each other but are not necessarily friends do have higher rates of participation, even after such conditions as size are considered (Barton and Silverman 1987). At present we know little about the effect of neighboring style on the ability of neighbors to create organizations at all, but there is some indication that organizing is more difficult where the private style is most prevalent (Silverman 1983).

We conclude that the recognition of interdependence and acceptance of unchosen mutual obligations that underlie the public style of neighboring can be important factors in the practices of neighborhood organizations. The study of how community social relations affect the functioning of neighborhood organizations must take into account the qualitative differences between public and private neighboring styles rather than simply treat neighboring as unidimensional. We face the further challenge, however, of discovering how the individual understandings of people active in a community organization are turned into an organizational tradition, with continuity beyond a small group of individuals. In a society in which privatized understandings are the norm, how does the public style emerge? How is it sustained?

REFERENCES

Barton, Stephen E. 1983. "Property Rights and Human Rights: Efficiency and Democracy as Criteria for Regulatory Reform." *Journal of Economic Issues*, Vol. 17, No. 4 (December): 915-30.

_____. 1985. *Property Rights and Democracy: The Beliefs of San Francisco Neighborhood Leaders and the American Liberal Tradition.* Berkeley, University of California Ph.D. dissertation.

_____, and Carol J. Silverman. 1987. *Common Interest Homeowners' Association Management Study.* Sacramento: California Department of Real Estate

Boyte, Harry C. 1980. *The Backyard Revolution: Understanding the New Citizens Movement.* Philadelphia: Temple University Press.

_____. 1984. *Community is Possible: Repairing America's Roots.* New York: Harper.

Crenson, Matthew A. 1983. *Neighborhood Politics.* Cambridge: Harvard University Press.

Cunningham, James, and Milton Kotler. 1983. *Building Neighborhood Organizations.* Notre Dame: University of Notre Dame Press.

Etheridge, Marcus E. 1987. "Collective Action, Public Policy and Class Conflict." *Western Political Science Quarterly*, Vol. 40: 575-92.

Fischer, Claude. 1984. *The Urban Experience.* San Diego: Harcourt Brace Jovanovich.

Greer, Scott. 1962. *The Emerging City.* New York: Free Press.

Hunter, Albert. 1974. *Symbolic Communities.* Chicago: University of Chicago Press.

Janowitz, Morris. 1952. *The Community Press in an Urban Setting: The Social Elements of Urbanism.* Chicago: University of Chicago Press.

_____. 1978. *The Last Half-Century: Societal Change and Politics in America.* Chicago: University of Chicago Press.

Lofland, Lyn H. 1973. *A World of Strangers: Order and Action in Urban Public Space.* New York: Basic Books.

O'Brien, David. 1975. *Neighborhood Organization and Interest Group Processes.* Princeton: Princeton University Press.

Olson, Mancur, Jr. 1965. *The Logic of Collective Action: Public Goods and the Theory of Groups.* Cambridge, Mass.: Harvard University Press.

Rich, Richard C. 1980. "A Political Economy Approach to the Study of Neighborhood Organizations." *American Journal of Political Science*, Vol. 24: 559-92.

Silverman, Carol J. 1983. *Neighbors and Nighbors: A Study in Negotiated Claim.* Berkeley, University of California Ph.D. dissertation.

_____. 1987. "Neighboring, Private Lives and Public Roles." Working Paper No. 468. Berkeley: Institute of Urban and Regional Development, University of California.

_____, Stephen E. Barton, Jens Hillmer, and Patricia Ramos. 1989. *The Effects of California's Residential Real Estate Disclosure Requirements.* Sacramento: California Department of Real Estate, October.

Suttles, Gerald. 1968. *The Social Order of the Slum.* Chicago: University of Chicago Press.

_____. 1972. *The Social Construction of Communities.* Chicago: University of Chicago Press.

9

Community and Direct Democracy in a Limited-Equity Cooperative

Allan David Heskin
Dewey Bandy

INTRODUCTION

As the number of condominiums, planned unit developments, housing cooperatives, and mutual housing associations has increased there has been a growing interest in their nature and operation. Many have seen them as interesting experiments in local, small-scale communities with their own form of government (Silverman and Barton 1987). In an ever larger country dominated by representative forms of democracy and holding on to a nostalgia for its small town past, small scale governments are seen as a partial return to direct democracy within a community setting (Bender 1978).

Those of us committed to community and direct democracy may have been too quick to assume that these common interest settlements would be communities in the full sense of the word and that their form of self-governance would be akin to direct democracy (Louv 1983). We have tended to equate community and direct democracy with small scale (see Dahl and Tufte 1973). But while small scale is a great aid to the formation of community and the operation of direct democracy, it is by no means sufficient. Given the experience in the United States with representative democracy, which separates people from most decision making and from each other, and with private property, which encourages a high degree of individualism, we should be surprised to find either that community is attained or direct democracy practiced, even in small-scale housing associations.

COMMUNITY AND DIRECT DEMOCRACY

Community in its highest form requires a degree of inclusiveness, contemplation, and safety that is rarely found in this society (Peck 1986). This should not be confused with a "pseudocommunity" consisting of mere physical proximity or small scale. Its essence is found not in friendship but in a spirit of neighborliness in which community members are able to relax their preconceptions, ideologies, prejudices, and values sufficiently to hear, understand, and accept others whose outlook and values are different from their own—an experience only some of us have undergone (Barber 1984; Peck 1986).

Direct democracy is premised on the existence of community and calls for a high level of cooperation and activity among the community members. In direct democracy the citizenry of the community are bound together more by common participatory activity than by the contractual civic bonds of representative democracy (Barber 1984). Decision making becomes a collective search that favors reasonable, pragmatic, and equitable solutions over outcomes that are procedurally correct or that correspond to legal principles.

In a representative system decision making is delegated to elected representatives who are held accountable to the citizenry by the possibility of being voted out of office (Williams 1983). Citizen participation occurs either through the electoral activity, "watch dogging" the government or the pressing of claims upon elected representatives to reach a particular decision. Often the citizenry is relatively inactive until their interests are threatened or a crisis is upon them (Barber 1984). Where the citizens are organized it is usually as a special interest group rather than as a community. Political participation in representative democracy tends to take on an adversarial, bargaining, or logrolling nature (Mansbridge 1983).

In direct democracy this interest group struggle would ideally be replaced by the civility of reciprocal empathy and respect among participating members. Conflict is not repressed, but rather is seen as an occasion in which private interests can be reformulated "in terms susceptible to public accommodation (Barber 1984, 119)." In short, the "us and them" engendered by the representative form of special interests are interpenetrated into a collective "us" through a consensus linking "public and private interest" formed in open and public dialogue (Yack 1985).

COMMUNITY ASSOCIATIONS

Barton and Silverman (1987, 1989; Silverman and Barton 1994), in a pioneering study of community associations in condominiums and planned developments, have found an environment in many of their study sites that is far different from a community. Often they found unresolved conflict rather than consensus formation and contractual legalisms rather than collective problem solving. In retrospect, given the structure of condominiums with their individual ownership of each unit, the substantial percentage of absentee ownership, property values to be protected or enhanced, and the litigious tendencies in our society, their findings are hardly a shock.

Their work raises the question, however, of what would happen in a different environment without these variables. We are fortunate to have such a case that we will present in this chapter of a recent variant of the stock cooperative—a limited-equity cooperative. The stock cooperative is an old form of collective ownership in which a corporation is formed to own the property and individuals buy shares and the right to occupy a unit. While the cooperative owns the property, much of the value in these stock cooperatives resides in the negotiable share and thus blurs the distinction between the coop and condo. There are many such stock cooperatives that vary little from condominiums.

The limited-equity cooperative is quite different. Most importantly, property value is simply not an issue. Typically, the share has a nominal value, and it is not allowed to increase in value by more than the inflation rate applied to the nominal base. The growing equity in the property may not be distributed to the members and upon sale of the property or dissolution of the cooperative the equity must go to a charitable organization. With a minimum share value, the primary incumbrance on the property is in the form of a blanket mortgage covering all the units rather than individual mortgages as in the case of the condominium. While in a condominium default on an individual condo owner's mortgage affects primarily that owner, in a limited-equity cooperative, default by an individual can affect the entire cooperative. This turns every individual's financial performance into very much of a public rather than private matter.

Often limited-equity cooperatives are subsidized by the government as a means to provide housing for low- and moderate-income people, who are thus insulated from housing price increases in the market economy. In the case of low-income people receiving federal rent subsidies this insulation is total, with the monthly payments keyed to their income rather than the costs of operating the cooperative. While there is a cap on the level of subsidy, on the whole issues of who would benefit from and who would pay for a particular proposed expenditure that would increase monthly costs are reduced or removed.

As a matter of California state law, no absentee ownership is permitted (Black 1985). Once all the shares in a limited-equity cooperative are sold there are no nonvoting, nonmember renters and voting absentee owner-members to confuse the democratic process. In condominiums, in contrast, renters are typically excluded from membership in the governing association and may be denied use of common facilities. While the paper work requirements are not much different in limited-equity cooperatives and the people equally conflictual, their low or moderate income and the limited value of the property restrict their ability to engage in costly litigation.

THE ROUTE 2 COOPERATIVES

The case study we will present is of a federation of five limited-equity cooperatives in Los Angeles known as the Route 2 cooperatives. The Route 2 cooperatives trace their origins back to 1975 when the State of California Department of Transportation, (CALTRANS) abandoned its plan to extend the Route 2 freeway through the Echo Park-Silver Lake district of Los Angeles. CALTRANS had purchased much of the property for a 2.4 mile freeway corridor extension and had been renting out the housing in the corridor pending the construction of the freeway. Rents were low in the corridor, and the housing was primarily occupied by low-income, working-class people. Both the neighborhood and the residents of Route 2 are ethnically diverse. About two-thirds of the residents of the corridor are Latino, about a quarter are Anglo, and about four percent are Black and another four percent Asian.

The neighborhood had shared generously in Los Angeles' real estate boom, and CALTRANS was anxious to sell the real estate in the corridor on the open market to realize a speculative profit on its investment. The residents protested that such a sale would displace them and further the gentrification taking place around them. In five years of direct action, political lobbying, courts fights, and the rest, the residents prevailed over the state transportation agency and won the right to buy and convert their housing to coops.

Having gained the right to buy their housing, the Route 2 residents formed a housing development corporation dominated by the residents, attracted various sources of funding, hired a staff, and went about forming their coops. They divided the corridor, which had within it more than 100 contiguous and noncontiguous parcels of land containing more than 270 housing units, into five coops ranging in size from 33 to 98 units, and federated the five coops under the umbrella of the development corporation. With the help of the staff, they put together rehabilitation plans, signed section 8 contracts for federal subsidies, and found lenders to finance each of the cooperatives.

How they did this, itself, is a good story in working-class planning (see Heskin and Bandy 1986), but here we will focus rather on how the Route 2 people have governed their cooperatives. In their development, in the federation and in the operation of the individual coops, the residents have repeatedly been faced with extraordinary issues that go to the core of community and direct democracy. At times, they have approached the community and direct democracy ideal.

We have selected three stressful incidents that arose out of the operation of the coops that allow us to explore the major dimensions of community and direct democracy we have just discussed. These are: the question of admission into the coop of a family politically objectionable to a member, an embezzlement by a president of one of the coops, and a dispute among neighbors called the "invasion."

THE ADMISSION CASE

The first case involved an admission interview before one cooperative's membership committee. The coops have long waiting lists and must choose between applicants when they have a vacancy. They each have membership committees that usually interview between three and five applicants when a unit becomes vacant. Membership on the committee is open to any member in the cooperative who wants to serve. Typically the neighbors living next to the units are invited to participate in interviews. Great deference is often given to the preferences of the neighbors if they choose to attend.

Questions of financial eligibility are settled before these interviews. The committees are usually most interested in how the various applicants might contribute to the operation of the cooperative. If this criteria does not significantly differentiate the potential applicants, the committees often choose the person in the greatest need.

The management committee of this coop is a good example of the cooperatives' ethnic mixture. It was made up of one apolitical Anglo, who is married to a Chicana and was the president of the coop, an apolitical Chicano, who is married to a Filipino and was secretary of the coop, a Latina who is the daughter of a Mexican and Cuban marriage, and two Central Americans, one of whom is a political refugee from El Salvador and an active union member, and the other, the head of the membership committee, who moved north for economic rather than political reasons.

The committee interviewed three applicants at its meeting for a three-bedroom section 8 unit in one of the rougher neighborhoods that this particular coop had housing in. Two applicants were very shy Mexican immigrant families with little to distinguish them from the thousands of immigrants who have moved to Los Angeles in recent years. The third applicant was a Nicaraguan family composed of a former captain in Somoza's army (he had been an accountant rather than a field officer), his wife, a former army nurse, and their children.

The couple from Nicaragua stood out in the interviews. They were aggressive in inquiring about the coop and the obligations moving in entailed. They had been sharing a single-room apartment with two other families since coming north and were anxious to find a place of their own. They stated that, if they were accepted into the coop, they would take their obligations seriously and would contribute their skills to the group. The two shy Mexican families did not actively engage the committee.

When the interviews were over the committee began to discuss the families interviewed. It was clear that the Nicaraguan family stood out. The president and secretary of the coop were attracted by the applicants' aggressiveness and the family's potential for contributing to the coop. The political Central American member responded with horror at the thought of a Somozista moving into the coop. In Spanish, she tried to express her anguish with the other Central American, who is almost fully bilingual, translating.

The officers of the coop responded with a two pronged approach. One was that they could not hold what people did before they came to this country against them or they would have lots of trouble with a great many of the present residents of the Route 2 project (there are Latinos from 14 different countries living in Route 2 who are on all sides of the political disputes in Latin America); and the second was a liberal, civil libertarian position that one cannot hold a family's politics against it in such matters. The Salvadorian member responded that this was not a matter of politics. This man and woman were part of a murderous army; they were not simply Republicans as opposed to Democrats.

The discussion raged on for quite a while, but the Salvadorian member never said anything directly against the particular Nicaraguan people before the committee. Her attack was rather on who they represented and the background from which they came. She said for example, that people *like this* would never participate in or support the coop no matter what they said in the interview. The apolitical North Americans were not comfortable with this systemic rather than personal criticism.

The officers of the coop knew what the Salvadorian was talking about when she said that the applicants would not support the coop. One of the other coops had problems with a Guatemalan resident who claimed to be the brother of a recently assassinated general in that country, and another with a Cuban who organized against the whole Route 2 project stating that limited-equity cooperatives were communistic. On a personal level, however, they felt the applicants before them were a very different kind of people. They saw that he was aggressive and tough, but they felt the particular area he was moving into needed aggressive, tough people to help clean it up.

The two remaining members of the committee were less involved in the discussion. The remaining Chicana member liked the people and was largely oblivious to the political questions. The other Central American sided with the Salvadorian but only mildly. When the vote came, the two Central Americans voted, one each, for one of the Mexican applicants and the other three members voted to admit the Nicaraguan family. The political person was very upset, but the other Central American who was also a member of the board of directors of the coop said she would support the committee's position when the matter came before the board.

The Salvadorian member of the committee was not immediately satisfied and a few days later she indicated that she wanted further discussion of the matter. The president of the coop felt the first process was fair but agreed to hear the member out at the next board meeting. However, she did not show up at the appointed time, and the board went on to approve the admission of the Nicaraguan family.

The Salvadorian stayed away from the meetings for a week or two but has returned to serve on the membership committee that one of the Nicaraguans had subsequently joined. Later, the Salvadorian and the wife in the Nicaraguan family were both elected to the board of the coop by the membership where they serve together amicably.

A basic principle of our ideal of community and direct democracy is inclusiveness. It would be nice to associate the cooperative directly with the formation of this inclusiveness, but in this case the inclusiveness predates the formation of the cooperatives. The very mixed nature of the membership and the neighborhood in which the cooperatives are located was a given in this situation. In addition, from the very beginning, the leadership of the organizing effort openly took pride in the mix and repeatedly included statements of nondiscrimination in their presentations at meetings. These little statements of openness almost became a pledge of allegiance often repeated by the membership as the process continued.

The main threat to this openness in the cooperatives has been from seeking to obtain admission to this scarce resource for one group or another in what Barber (1984) would call an attempt at unitary democracy. In unitary democracy decision making is consensual, based on the common ideals of a homogeneous group. In creating a unitary democracy admission would be based on "blood and brotherhood," usually based on ethnicity or religion, in an effort to create a homogeneous community. Such efforts, however, have met with hostility from the leadership of this diverse organization and have decreased over time.

Although the cooperative form itself did not generate the theme of inclusiveness, the nonprivatized structure of the limited-equity cooperative may well have contributed to the continual regeneration of the ideal. The ownership of the limited-equity cooperative is seen, in part, as a public trust because of its dedication to low- and moderate-income occupancy. While an individual family has the right to occupy a unit the property all belongs to the collective. This helps overcome the appeal of exclusivity as a means to protect private property values or make community life more comfortable.

In this case at hand another factor is also instructive. The process was very open. Membership on the membership committee was open, and the discussion leading to a collective result was passionate and engaging. Even after the meeting, the process remained open to the unhappy member to try and convince the majority of her position. Only when she declined the opportunity to restate her case was the decision made. After that the process again remained open. While she absented herself for a period of time, she was welcomed back and later was elected to the board. In what makes the case particularly pleasant, the process was further opened when the protagonists later joined together on the membership committee and governing board.

This example seems exemplary of the process of community making elaborated by Dr. Scott Peck (1986), an expert in building community in small group settings. Peck sees community as beginning with proximity. This proximity does not instruct the membership on how to proceed and, as Barton and Silverman found, people often simply attempt to avoid collective engagement because conflict and chaos may result. While there are various ways to end this conflict and chaos, Peck believes that a suspension of preconceptions and beliefs, and openness to one another is necessary if community is to be the outcome. Much as the Route 2 people accepted the applicants at face value and refused to automatically laden the applicants with the baggage of their history, members must be open to one another.

This situation might have been handled differently in a stock cooperative and would certainly be different in condominiums. There is a long history of various forms of discrimination by membership committees in stock cooperatives (Mandelker et al. 1981). In most condominiums, the transaction between buyer and seller is outside the jurisdiction of the collective entirely. There is no membership committee and the seller makes the selection based on the payment offered—absent some form of illegal discrimination.

It should be noted, of course, that housing is a limited resource, whether in cooperatives or condominiums. As such, they are not totally inclusive. The coop in this case seeks people who can contribute and will likely participate in the operation of the cooperative. Within the low- and moderate-income group eligible for admission to the cooperative, this will mean that more advantaged people may win out over the least advantaged. There is a discomfort on the coop committees about having to choose at all, but it is a structural constraint that cannot be avoided.

THE EMBEZZLEMENT CASE

The second case further illustrates the open, participatory process that should unfold within the context of the community ideal. This case, which took place in a different Route 2 coop, involved the embezzlement of some of the coop's reserve funds by the board president. In the early days of the project, he had carried almost the entire load of running the affairs of this coop. He had befriended and helped many of the people in the coop, and they, in turn, had considerable affection for him. He, like many of the coop residents, always lived on the edge of financial disaster. He was in and out of all sorts of jobs including cab driver and delivering flowers and had been trying for some time to get a college degree.

The president had a history of substance dependency that made his behavior erratic (he was often late and sometimes inebriated at meetings he was to conduct), but he was exceptionally sharp when sober. People were not happy with this pattern of behavior, but mostly looked the other way because of all the "good" time he put in. He would sometimes say that Route 2 was like therapy for him. It gave him something constructive to do that kept him out of trouble.

Unfortunately, in the last few months of his presidency, his dependency got the best of him, and he took funds to support himself and his habit. When the problem was discovered, the other board members of the coop board met, immediately removed him as president, and secured the remaining funds. The coop was insured for this eventuality so the problem did not result in a substantial financial loss to the coop. What to do beyond removing the president then became the issue. Should they prosecute him and should he be evicted?

When the now former president was confronted with the loss, he immediately confessed and stated his intention to make good the loss. The remaining board members did not believe that the former president, who had somewhat fallen apart, would be able to keep such a promise, but, out of deference for their former leader, they wanted to give him a chance. They told him he would have to act quickly because they would have to notify their insurance company to protect the coop, and they told him of the fact that they were considering prosecuting and/or evicting him. Interestingly, he said he would rather be prosecuted than be evicted and lose his home of many years.

After long deliberations the coop board decided that they would move to evict the former president and not prosecute unless they had to for insurance purposes. The discussion in the board meetings included questions of what would be best for the coop and what would be best for their friend and now past president. Their feeling was that a clear statement had to be made that this type of behavior would not be tolerated and that given the nature of his addictive behavior in the past only the sharpest of actions might bring him around.

Coop members who either had first hand experience as former substance abusers or who had substance abusers in their families said that remaining as a guilty, defrocked, criminal, the past president in the coop might fit the self-degrading image that accompanied addiction, but it would not be good for the individual involved. This seemed to be an important argument to at least one member of the board who was having a hard time voting for eviction. It at least blurred the lines between whether evicting the past president was hurting or helping a close friend.

The former president did not accept the decision of the board and demanded a hearing before the whole coop. Because of the seriousness of the situation, his request was granted. A meeting was called to both elect his replacement on the board and hear the past president's plea. The meeting was an extraordinary one, reminiscent of William Hinton's (1966) description of a mainland Chinese commune gathering.

After the election, the past president addressed the assembled membership confessing his crime, stating that he had been sick, and asking for enough forgiveness for his mistake that he might be allowed to remain in the coop and make recompense in any way he could. The coop members recognized his past service (some felt he had almost earned the amount of money he took with all the time he had put in) and thought he had "guts" to get up in front of everyone and confess like he did. The discussion was going back and forth between the "forgive the mistake" position and the "we can't condone this activity" position with the forgive position appearing to be winning.

Finally, one member, who was not on the board of the coop but was a leader in the federation, took the floor and made an impassioned plea for eviction. She began by describing the coop venture they had all set upon, and how it was not easy to work together. She too was poor and had access to the development corporation money in the past. She had often looked over at the corporation's checkbook when she didn't know where the next dollar was going to come from to feed her children, but knew if she stumbled and "borrowed" some money that the whole effort could fail. She said it was not the money the past president took that bothered her. It was the breach of trust. Her position was that the coop's only chance of making it was if they could truly trust each other. Her argument swung those assembled toward eviction and the decision was made and carried out by the board.

No one felt good about participating in this decision. It was not comfortable to wield the heavy hand of justice, but the consensus was that it had to be done. Stuart Henry (1983), writing about decision making in cooperatives in England, discusses how the "network of intimacy" formed in cooperatives often makes disciplinary action difficult (pp. 181-197). He quotes one coop member as saying disagreement seldom occurs "because we know, trust and respect one another's perhaps differing feeling about a situation, we take each other into consideration, and make as much effort as possible to accommodate one another in most situations . . . " (p. 183). This is true about those in positions of responsibility in Route 2. In this case, however, the past president had gone too far. He broke the chain of trust that bound the people together, and they decided to expel him from the group.

This case is indicative of the political process required in direct democracy. The decision-making process occurred through a public discourse that involved legal concerns, personal compassion, community values, and collective history. What is important here is the participatory process admitted all these differing concerns into the decision-making process to be shifted out by public dialogue. In a more formalistic proceeding these concerns might never have entered into the process.

The decision-making process discussed here was indicative of what Barber (1984) calls "public talk." Public talk is much more than the simple public advocacy of private interests. It "entails listening no less than speaking, . . . it is affective as well as cognitive, and . . . its intentionalism draws it out of the domain of pure reflection into the world of action" (p. 174). It is a form of conversation that permits a community to discover its mutuality, clarify its values, develop affinity, and take action. Public talk provides the vehicle through which individual interests, concerns and conflicts can be located and acted upon within a public context.

Public talk both derives its vitality from community and also contributes to building it. As the embezzlement case bears out, public talk is not conversation among strangers. It occurs between members of a community who personally know one another, who have worked and struggled together. This sense of knowing and common experience allows the admission of the affective, common experience, history, and personal character into the dialogue. At the same time it is precisely at these moments of intense communal tension and crisis that public talk can be the means through which community can be reaffirmed.

Finally this gives us a look at the principle of safety required for the formation of community. The people here used the term trust, but it is very much the same idea as having a safe environment in which the kind of openness discussed in the previous case is possible. It is ironic, however, that here exclusion is required to maintain inclusiveness. Peck (1986) discusses how difficult it is to maintain community once attained and gives a somewhat similar example of exclusion involving an alcoholic member of a support group. It is a failing of the collective that leaves a hole in the totality. It creates the type of sadness felt in this case.

There is little doubt that this situation would have been handled much more formally in the stock cooperative or condominium. In the condominium, evicting the past president wouldn't have been an option. Instead, the collective would have had to seek legal judgment against the individual, and perhaps foreclosed on the unit, not to get him out but to recover the money. The collective would have had to go on with the embezzler in its midst unless he was sent to jail or unable to repay the money without selling the unit.

THE INVASION

The third case, the invasion, was an extraordinary event. Because Route 2 is made up of scattered-site, existing properties, the disparity between amenities at various properties can be significant. In this particular situation a 12-unit apartment building with virtually no back, front or side yard abutted two duplexes with very large front and back yards. The people in the 12-unit building had been complaining for some time that they had a major parking problem because of a high rate of vandalism against cars parked on the street and that they should be given access to a part of their neighbors' backyard for parking.

Needless to say the people in the duplexes, who had many children and saw their back yards as safe play space for their children, were not supportive of the idea of yielding part of their space for automobiles. The plan to provide parking was acknowledged in the rest of the coop as having some merit given the amount of space, but the press of other business in the coop put this particular problem on hold for later consideration.

One day four men in the 12-unit building consumed enough beer to conceive and execute a forced takeover of part of their neighbors' backyard. They passed around a hastily drawn up petition among the residents of their building that would have been the pride of any anarchist band. It said that, since the property was collective property and not private property, it should be more equitably distributed. Then, in a screaming Saturday afternoon they took over a strip of the backyard, uprooting and replanting plants and moving fences closer to the houses in order to create space for parking. The police came and left with their heads shaking, saying that it was an internal matter for the coop.

The leader of the invaders was a very active member of the board of directors of the coop. He was Anglo as was another member of the invaders. One of the other men was Latino and the other Asian, in true Route 2 integrated fashion. Unfortunately, the invaded were all Latino and the issue was colored by the ethnic conflict between the Anglo board member and the Latino residents.

Not surprisingly the incident generated an emergency board meeting of the coop. It was a difficult meeting because the other members of the board believed that the idea of redoing the backyards had merit and had substantial attachment to their very active, fellow board member. On the other hand, no one could argue that the invaders went about their business properly or that the invaded families had not been wronged. The invaded families came to the meeting demanding relief.

The first action of the board was to declare the disputed territory a no-persons land, posting signs that declared that occupation of this land would lead to immediate eviction, their ultimate sanction. The second act of the board was to remove the invasion leader from the board and replace him with the Latina spokesperson for the invaded. It was felt that this would be a strong message to their former colleague that he had not acted properly, and they knew he would be terribly disappointed by his exclusion from board. It would also ensure that the decision-making process that followed would be fully open to the injured parties and demonstrated to the community at large that the board would not treat its own members above "the law."

The third act of the board was the setting up of a series of negotiating meetings in which the parties involved and representatives from all other parcels in the coop (some 30 parcels are in the coop) that wished to participate would meet and negotiate out this and any other property distribution disputes.

The negotiations ended with the agreement that parking spaces would be made available from the backyard that was invaded. In return, the invaders constructed new fences around both the back and front yards of the duplexes. This secured the front yards so that the children would have sufficient safe play space.

The board had sought an equitable distribution of the resources of the coop balancing the needs of the parties and sought to maintain both the integrity of their process and the board itself. They were satisfied that they had been fair, the community appeared satisfied, and peace was restored although it would be an overstatement to say that harsh feelings between the invaded and invaders about the incident had been completely dispelled.

This case seems to illustrate what was meant by Barber when he wrote that conflict, rather than being repressed, must be used to "reformulate private interest in terms susceptible of public accommodation." The board took advantage of the issue to deepen the community in the coop and broaden the democracy that had existed. The essence of direct democracy is not the documents that legally bind the members of a community but common participatory activity. The board went to the essence when they immediately reformulated their own membership in order to internalize the issue within their own ranks. At the same time, they opened up the decision-making process to representatives of all parcels in the cooperative. The matter was not to be resolved by legalisms nor in closed sessions, but by a dialogue over an equitable resolution for the whole community.

In removing the offending board member, the board also acted to maintain the social equality necessary for direct democracy to function. Proponents of direct democracy going back to Rousseau have recognized that the participatory process can be overwhelmed if some members of the community have greater status, power, and influence than others (Pateman 1970). The board accentuated its leveling approach when it went further and called for a committee of residents of every parcel in the coop to negotiate out this and other similar disputes.

This is a set of events that could never have occurred in the same way within a condominium association. Such a dispute in a condominium would have been a "big stakes" affair entailing property rights that would substantially effect the value of condominium units in question. Because the value of the property would be threatened lawyers would very likely become involved. Ultimately, the dispute itself would have been resolved based on formalistic legal criteria aimed at determining who legally owned the property.

In the cooperative, however, as the incident indicates, the invaders viewed the property as collectively owned but inequitably distributed. Direct action was resorted to by the invaders since as moderate-income working-class people, they could scarcely afford a lawyer. The invaded while justifiably upset at the action also had limited access to attorneys. The dispute itself was not seen as about property rights. Rather what was at stake was the equitable nature of the community.

CONCLUSIONS

It would be wrong to infer from these examples that Route 2 is a utopian example of community and direct democracy. Many of the people in Route 2, as elsewhere, are difficult to involve and remain alienated from the process. In an incident following the invasion, a member of that coop who was passing out newsletters, had to go home and get his wage stubs to prove to an aggressively nonparticipating, cynical resident that he was a volunteer activist for the coop and not paid for his efforts.

There are also cases of people responding to the close scrutiny of living in a coop by building high, solid fences. Conflict avoidance behavior is not uncommon, and immediate neighbors will often fail to confront one another over violations of coop rules and instead leave enforcement to other residents around the corner or a block or more away in these scattered-site cooperatives.

From time to time, leaders have emerged in one coop or another that are less open and less able to maintain the participatory process. One coop had a series of near violent encounters before a governing board less in the spirit of community and democracy discussed in this chapter was dislodged by people wishing to return to the more open past.

We have painted a very dramatic picture of life in these coops. It should be noted, however, that not only is it not utopia, but that much of what goes on in the cooperatives, as in condominiums, is much more mundane. The coop board and committee meetings are not always so filled with exciting issues, and life goes on in the coops as it does in condominiums.

We have learned from this exploration that much of what is in the literature about community and direct democracy has validity and can work in practice. Openness, participation, and public talk can lead to resolution of conflict and community building. This can, however, be a very time consuming process, and people desiring community and direct democracy must be willing to work through the chaos.

The increasing number of collective living associations, whether condominiums, cooperatives, or other forms, have presented problems that are not easy for people accustomed to the privacy and independence of "the American Dream" of individual homeownership to solve. The rough and tumble stories we have told in this chapter have their match, when it comes to ferocity, in the other forms of associations. We have argued that the structure of the limited-equity cooperative encourages the development of both community and direct democracy, while the structure of condominiums impedes them. Whether we chose the community, direct democracy approach or another may well boil down to both our awareness of the possible options and our evaluation of the relative costs and benefits of the various approaches. What is certain is that these institutions will continue to be fascinating, fertile fields for observation and research.

REFERENCES

Abel, Richard. 1982. "The Contradictions of Informal Justice." In *The Politics of Informal Justice,* ed. Richard Abel. New York: Academic Press.

Alper, Benedict, and Lawrence Nichols. 1981. *Beyond the Courtroom: Programs in Community Justice and Conflict Resolution.* Lexington, Mass.: Lexington Books.

Barber, Benjamin. 1984. *Strong Democracy: Participatory Politics for a New Age.* Berkeley: University of California Press.

Barton, Stephen, and Carol Silverman. 1987. *Common Interest Homeowners' Associations Management Study.* California Department of Real Estate.

_____. 1989. "The Political Life of Mandatory Homeowners' Associations." Advisory Commission on Intergovernmental Relations, Washington, D.C.

Bender, Thomas. 1978. *Community and Social Change in America.* Baltimore: John Hopkins University Press.

Black, B. 1985. "Cooperative Options of Low- and Moderate- Income People" Working Draft.

Dahl, R., and E. Tufte. 1973. *Size and Democracy.* Stanford: Stanford University Press.

Henry, Stuart. 1983. *Private Justice.* London; Boston: Routledge & Kegan Paul.

Heskin, Allen, and Dewey Bandy. 1986. "The Importance of Class." *Berkeley Planning Journal* 3(1): 47-66.

Hinton, William, 1966. *Fanshen: A Documentary of Revolution in a Chinese Village.* New York: Vintage Books.

Louv, Richard. 1983. *America II.* New York: Penguin Books.

Mandelker, Daniel, et al. 1981. *Housing and Community Development: Cases and Materials.* Indianapolis: Bobbs-Merrill.

Mansbridge, Jane J. 1983. *Beyond Adversary Democracy.* Chicago: University of Chicago Press.

Pateman, Carol. 1970. *Participation and Democratic Theory.* Cambridge: Cambridge University Press.

Peck, M. S. 1986. *The Different Drum: Community-Making and Peace.* New York: Simon and Schuster.

Silverman, Carol, and Stephen Barton. 1994. "Shared Premises: Community and Conflict in the Common Interest Development." In *Common Interest Common Interest Communities: Private Govern-*

ments and the Public Interest, ed. Stephen E. Barton and Carol J. Silverman. Berkeley: Institute of Governmental Studies Press.

Williams, Raymond. 1983. *The Year 2000.* New York: Pantheon.

Yack, Bernard. 1985. "Community and Conflict in Aristotle's Politics." *The Review of Politics* 47(1): 92-112.

V. International Perspectives on Condominium Governance and Management

Editors' Note

It would be natural to suspect that the difficulties faced by common interest homeowners' associations in the United States are a result of peculiarly American understandings of the meaning of private property ownership and the long tradition of American individualism. In other societies condominium apartment ownership is more widespread than ownership of single-family houses, and there are lengthy traditions of cooperation and recognition of obligations to the group.

Nothing could be more striking, then, than the comprehensive survey of Japanese condominium management by Tsuneo Kajiura. Describing a society so often thought to be virtually the opposite of the United States, Kajiura reports the same list of problems between the developer and the new homeowners, between the homeowners' association and management companies, and between the homeowners and the homeowners' association. Problems also result from the exclusion of renters from the association, and the tendency for absentee owners not to participate in it.

Homeownership in the U.S. is widely perceived as one of the most important forms of social integration. Current or expected homeownership virtually defines membership in the "middle class" to which Americans claim membership. But membership in the homeowners' association is also a potential means of linking people with the larger society, although there is little evidence showing that such membership in an "involuntary association" strengthens civic culture.

Bernard Lazerwitz and Yona Ginsberg are concerned with the condominium association as a means to integrate new immigrants into Israeli society. Three-quarters of the population of Israel live in condominium apartments. Even more different, from the U.S. perspective, the condominiums do not have private covenants and restrictions governing resident behavior and the external appearance of property. Instead, report Bernard Lazerwitz and Yona Ginsberg, when residents have problems with a neighbor in these matters they rely on the law and go to the local government for enforcement. Israeli condominium associations simply deal with the physical building management and perhaps engage in social activities. They argue that condominiums strengthen ties among building residents, but that severe conflicts over maintenance expenditures are common and that the associations fail to develop links to the surrounding neighborhood and to government.

In the United States, condominiums are generally considered a tool of land speculators and conservatives. Efforts to protect working-class neighborhoods from displacement and gentrification often focus on preventing conversion of rental units to condominiums. They are also commonly thought of as a means of privatization, as with the sale of government "Council housing" in the United Kingdom or the HOPE program that was created in the 1980s by the United States' Secretary of Housing and Urban Development, Jack Kemp, to sell public housing to tenants.

Jan van Weesep describes the rapid growth of condominium ownership in the Netherlands, where it is used as a tool for urban renewal that is sensitive to current residents. There conversion generates funds that provide subsidies to renovate a large sector of rent controlled housing. The condominiums themselves, he reports, are often plagued by difficulties in coming to agreement on maintenance and repairs, just as they are in the U.S., Israel and Japan.

10

Social Control within the Israeli Condominium System

Bernard Lazerwitz
Yona Ginsberg

BARRIERS TO RESIDENTIAL COOPERATION

The impact of living with neighbors from a variety of class, ethnic or religious groups, or different family life cycle stages is a lively topic in both the social sciences and among ordinary people. Do such residential experiences loosen, harden, or leave untouched the opinions, stereotypes, and interaction patterns of neighbors? Does it result in increased social integration? How are actual or potential conflicts among neighbors handled?

Residential integration and cooperation have been the subjects of research endeavors and publications for a number of years in a variety of countries. The major research questions for a long time have been:

1. To what extent can the different social groups that compose modern urban societies occupy the same buildings, blocks, or neighborhoods?
2. What are the gains and problems that result from having different social groups in the same buildings, blocks, or neighborhoods?
3. How stable are such arrangements?

A careful examination of the research literature struggling with these three questions indicates that residents report most satisfaction with "homogeneous neighborhoods," i.e., with neighborhoods whose residents follow a similar style of life. The components of such a lifestyle are formed by items such as behavior towards public and private property, educational standards for one's children, participation in voluntary associations, ease in expressing one's self in speech and writing, communication patterns between husband and wife, ways of rearing children, time spent with relatives and friends, drinking and smoking habits, and leisure time behavior of family members.

The research literature is not that clear about the ability of different ethnic groups to live together. This depends on the involved ethnic groups being pretty equal with regards to social status and, even more, having the same, or fairly similar religions. If the contacting ethnic groups are not traditional "hate targets" for one another, and lack religious barriers, status equal ethnic groups can be expected to get along reasonably well in the same building, block, or neighborhood.

Class differences are strong barriers to residential cooperation. Keller (1968, 66) points out that working-class people living in a middle-class neighborhood feel inferior in status and withdraw socially to the company of their own families and other working-class people. Middle-class people living in working-class neighborhoods will join local voluntary associations to find status equal people or move out of the neighborhood as soon as they can. She (1968, 84) also emphasizes that major class or lifestyle differences among neighbors can lead to considerable friction, social withdrawal, or moving away. Bracey (1964), after contrasting United States and English suburban developments, concludes that discord among neighbors appears to be a class-based problem. Heraud (1968) points out that the English "New Towns" have reached community class heterogeneity only by building different neighborhoods for the different classes.

Perhaps the two most thorough treatments of the thinking behind social cooperation via residential integration can be found in the articles by Sarkissian (1976) and Marrett (1973). Sarkissian, concerned about American and English thinking on this topic, points out that proponents of residential integration feel:

(a) Residential level contacts among the members of different classes will expose the lower-ranking classes to the "higher standards" of the upper-ranking classes. These higher standards can cover a variety of items such as personal hygiene, property maintenance, aesthetic practices, personal ambitions, and motivating children to higher educational achievements.

(b) With class mixture at the residential level, neighborhood schools will be under much greater pressure to be "good schools." School authorities might get away with furnishing inadequate education to working class children, but middle-class parents will not permit them to do this.   Hence, working-class children going to school with middle class children will be attending much better schools.

(c) Mixed residential situations enable people to get to know one another across whatever social barriers might separate them. In this manner, the members of the various residential social groups can develop realistic knowledge of one another, stereotypes are reduced or eliminated, and intergroup hostility mitigated.

(d) The middle-class residents of a combined working-class/middle-class neighborhood can furnish the necessary local leadership where the working-class residents cannot.

(e) Class mixture at the residential level will expand the market for local services. Hence, working-class residents living with middle-class residents will have available a greater variety of services and shops at more competitive prices than they would have if they lived by themselves.

Furthermore, according to Sarkissian (1976), the discussion of residential integration through all these years has failed to clarify the basic question of at what residential level—community, neighborhood, block, or building—are planners to seek what percentage of social mixture? She concludes that we really lack enough research on the residential mix concepts to clarify the ideologically based thinking devoted to this topic.

Marrett (1973, 180-83) explores the same set of issues for the United States. She states that successful efforts at residential integration across class lines hinge on the involvement of working-class families who differ only on job types and income from middle-class families. Residential integration should not be viewed as a means for changing the lifestyle of working-class families. Residential mixture across class lines is a complex thing that can result in many problems besides its hoped-for advantages.

Back in 1961 and 1968, the well-known sociologist and city planner Herbert Gans contributed several insightful articles on this issue of residential integration and cooperation. In his first 1961 article, he maintains that homogeneity of characteristics is more important than living near to one another for friendship formation. In his second 1961 article, Gans explains that design plans can encourage or discourage social contact among neighbors, but that it was common backgrounds, interests, or values that changed such social contacts into something closer. Again, in this second article (p. 177), he declares that a mixing of all ages and class groups can well produce a polite, but distant set of social relations. To get more positive contacts, a moderate degree of social homogeneity is necessary. Otherwise, social conflict is as likely an outcome as is social cooperation.

As do many of the researchers mentioned here, Gans points out that people with better educations and higher incomes can feel that their children are harmed by living among less advantaged neighbors. He agrees with Marrett that it is the upwardly mobile working-class families who can benefit most from contacts with middle-class families. Ideas and values are most readily diffused from one class to those just above or below it. Consequently, the positive effects of residential integration are more likely to be achieved under conditions of moderate population heterogeneity. Extreme heterogeneity is likely to inhibit communication and to create mutual resentment.

What one wants, Gans suggests, is enough consensus among neighbors to prevent conflict: positive, but not necessarily intense, relationships between neighbors with respect to common needs and obligations; and the possibility for some mutual visiting and friendship formation in the immediate vicinity for those who want it.

THE ISRAELI CONDOMINIUM SYSTEM

An estimated 73 percent of Israel's population lives in condominium buildings (Werczberger and Ginsberg 1987). The first national condominium law was passed in 1952. This initial law was revised in 1969. Israeli law requires that the owners of apartments in a condominium building ought to meet at least once a year in order to elect a building management committee. This committee typically consists of a chairperson, a treasurer, and a secretary. In turn, this small management committee has the task of running the building. This consists of hiring and overseeing a gardener, a person or company to clean the common areas of the building such as its halls and stairways, hiring someone to do minor building repairs, and paying utility bills for the common areas such as stairway electric lights. Before any atypically large expense is incurred, the management committee must get the approval of a majority of the owner families. The assembly of all the building's families decides upon the annual family fees that are paid monthly and collected by the management committee.

According to the law, all apartment owners have to pay for the maintenance of their building. This includes regular maintenance such as cleaning of the staircase, gardening, etc., and other repairs or renovations. Even if apartment owners do not use a specific building facility, such as an elevator, all owners have to pay for the maintenance of such basic facilities.

The inspector of land registration acts as a judicial authority in cases of disputes, and his decision is final. There are two kinds of conflicts that can be decided by this inspector. The first deals with any conflict over the obligations of owners in building maintenance such as painting the outside of the commonly owned building. The second involves trespass disputes such as the persistent parking in an auto space assigned to some other apartment. These suits can be started by individual apartment owners or by building committees.

There are some conflicts that need to be handled in a civil court. These are primarily quarrels among neighbors not related to the maintenance or functioning of a building such as complaints about loud and persistent noises.

Another mechanism for disputes is the "Association for Better Housing," sponsored by the National Housing Ministry. The association can act as an arbitrator and usually its decision is accepted by apartment owners. In 1989, about 6 percent of the apartments in the city of Tel Aviv were involved in appeals to this association.

Note that this system operates on a volunteer basis. Building committee members are unpaid. Furthermore, they typically have limited experience in the intricacies of building repairs and maintenance. Problems are solved as they occur; skilled workers are hired as needed. Unlike some other countries with extensive condominium systems, such as Italy, the United States, or Canada, even large-scale Israeli condominium projects seldom have resident managers or a contract with a firm whose specialty is the maintenance of condominium buildings.

Typically, though, problems are handled by private negotiations between a financial delinquent and his or her building neighbors. Not infrequently, neighbors will undertake to pay additional building fees to cover the obligations of a suddenly impoverished neighbor or of an aged pensioner. Studies have shown that the Israeli condominium system is a popular institution that functions reasonably well. Churchman and Ginsberg (1980a) report their survey respondents asserted that the functions of building committees were to supervise the maintenance and cleanliness of condominium common property and to collect monthly building fees. These researchers report that 92 percent of their respondents were satisfied with their building committees.

Israeli public housing authorities work hard to enable residents living in their projects to buy their apartments and to form building committees. Given the relatively high cost of Israeli apartments and the limitations of Israel's mortgage system, many residents of public housing projects are skilled workers earning adequate salaries. Given Israel's welfare orientation and governmental efforts for new immigrants, a wide range of people have the right to enter public housing projects. Rapid population growth, the initial poverty level of many new immigrants, and the goal of moving population away from Israel's large cities has required a constant supply of public housing projects.

The Impact of Major Social Barriers on the Israeli Condominium System

The Israeli condominium housing system can only work if the residents of jointly owned buildings at the least are able to talk to one another, agree on what maintenance and operational aspects need to be done, and agree to pay the required bills. Can such a housing system function across religiosity, class, ethnic, and family life cycle barriers? These questions can be investigated through studies of two Israeli neighborhoods. The first is composed of a mixture of middle-class Orthodox and secular Jews. The second is a new, mainly working-class, housing project.

The Religious Barrier

Chaldea is a prestigious neighborhood in one of Israel's main cities. The neighborhood is composed of four-story and larger condominium buildings (with from 9 to 45 apartments in each building). There is no purposeful religious clustering within buildings, and there is generally only one religious family in any building (for study details, see Tabory 1989).

The neighborhood population is largely middle and upper class. Just over 70 percent of the religious and 40 percent of the nonreligious have a university education. About 90 percent of the respondents in both groups are in the labor force, and many of them are professionals.

Neighboring

Respondents were asked how often they neighbored with persons of different religiosity levels. Table 10.1 shows that most of the respondents rarely had contact with persons of different religiosity levels.

Participant observations in the neighborhood indicated that religiously segregated patterns strongly affect all social activities. While several religious women take part in a gymnastics class held two evenings a week in the local general school, these women mainly socialize among themselves outside of class. The religious men have organized their own weekly basketball game in the gym rather than take part in the general game open to all respondents. On the Sabbath religious residents congregate in one specific area of the local park.

While the religious inhabitants do not completely isolate themselves from the nonreligious, they also do not go out of their way to foster close relationships with them. As a rule, they do not want to become overly close to the nonreligious, and they do not want their children to play with their children. (Religious children in the neighborhood may be seen playing among themselves with only minimal and occasional contact with the nonreligious, even between children of similar age and sex who live in the same building.)

Given all this, it is noteworthy that this elite religious group chooses to live mixed with much less religious, but status equal, people. (It is the ultra-orthodox groups, such as Hassidim, who choose to live in religiously segregated neighborhoods.)

The religious residents consistently state that they are satisfied with the area, and their primary reason for possibly wanting to move is to live in an even larger apartment or in a private house. If they were to move, they would either want to remain in the neighborhood or move to one that is basically similar to it. They rule out the possibility of living in a neighborhood that is limited to religious families. Since this elite religious group is integrated into Israel's economic life, residential segregation could endanger their economic status.

Yet these considerable gaps are bridged to a significant degree by residents belonging to the same socio-economic classes, by their having middle-class lifestyles, and by their being members of the same major Israeli ethnic group. On such a foundation, adequate communication can take place among all types of families, despite a considerable degree of social segregation by religiosity, so that the condominium system, and its building committees, work quite well. The buildings are well maintained.

Table 10.1.   *Frequency of Helping, Visiting, and Going Out With Religiously Different Persons in the Neighborhood*

Frequency	Religious with Nonreligious (%)	Nonreligious with Religious (%)
Daily	6	4
Weekly	13	3
Several Times a Month	11	5
Several Times a Year	13	4
Rarely	57	84
Base	100	100

Chaldea residents are proud of the social and physical qualities of their neighborhood. Members of both religious groups participate in building committees and share in the leadership.

Class, Ethnic, and Life Cycle Barriers: Lion Neighborhood

The planned neighborhood to be examined contains major differences in class, ethnicity, family life cycle, and religiosity.   Indeed, such differences were deliberately built into the project. What adjustments or distortions happen to the Israeli condominium system when it has to confront such differences? Is such a neighborhood stable?

The Physical Neighborhood. At the time it was studied, Lion Neighborhood contained 314 apartments in 31 buildings, which had been built in five elliptical rings. Three of these five rings contain an eight-story structure of 30 apartments each. The other structures consist of a ground floor plus three additional floors. The two ground floor apartments in 18 walk-ups (36 in all) are larger ones reserved for large families.

After its construction, the walk-up section of the development was available to those families who had entry "rights." Such families were those living in condemned slum structures, low-income families with many children, young couples living with their parents, families relocated due to slum clearance and urban renewal projects, and new immigrants to Israel.

The firm that did the construction was also allowed to build three high-rise structures with a total of 90 apartments. Of these 90 units, 12 ground floor apartments were reserved for aged couples, selected according to welfare criteria. The remaining 78 were sold on the private market at a profit, repaying the construction company for the small profit it received from the walk-ups. Physically, the high-rise apartments contain the same number of rooms as most of the walk-ups, namely two bedrooms, one bathroom, a kitchen, a small living room, and a medium sized porch area for laundry and storage. Many of those who moved into the high-rises were young couples who were entitled to special mortgage rights issued by the National Ministry of Housing.

The residents of each building were required to establish a building committee responsible for its proper maintenance. This included the right to collect a monthly maintenance fee from the families of each building.

In addition to these building committees, the public housing authority aided the establishment of an overall committee for Lion. At first, this committee was elected at large from among all the residents of the project. After one year, a new system was inaugurated whereby the overall committee was elected by the chairpeople of the individual building committees.

The People of Lion. As of the date of the study, the average family size was four persons. The total Lion population was 1,216 people. Lion had 287 families and 27 vacant apartments.

The combination of being a public housing project with strict limitations on the size of apartments and a project with lots of people per family gives Lion just about four times the population density of its city as a whole. Clearly, this density adds to the noise levels within the project as well as probably giving its residents a sense of "crowding."

Lion's Social Subgroups. Much of Lion's heterogeneity is due to the differences between its more homogeneous social subgroups. Lion can be broken down into the following categories:
1. 73 high-rise building young families,
2. 32 immigrant families in the low-rise Lion buildings,
3. 33 young couple families in the low-rise Lion buildings,
4. 36 large families in the low-rise Lion buildings,
5. 105 other relocated families in the low-rise Lion buildings,

6. 9 aged persons or couples in the ground floor apartments of the high-rise structures.

Lion family heads can be divided into two basic subgroups. One is composed of the young high-rise families and the young couple families in the walk-up buildings. Both of these groups generally have heads under age 30, with almost none above 40. However, the life cycle picture is quite different among the other subgroup family heads. Among them, the majority of family heads are over 40 years of age. Recent immigrant heads and the other relocated family heads resemble one another on age distribution while the heads of large families are the oldest of all.

Predictably, the young couple and high-rise family heads are generally Israeli-born. The heads of the other relocated families are only 19 percent Israeli-born; of large families only 11 percent are Israeli-born; and, of course, all recent immigrant family heads are foreign-born.

Almost all relocated family heads are of Middle Eastern-North African backgrounds. Three-quarters of the young couple family heads have the same backgrounds. High-rise family heads are evenly divided between the two basic Jewish ethnic groups, European and Middle Eastern-North African. Finally, almost all recent immigrant family heads are of European background.

At the time it was studied, there were 621 children in Lion. Moreover, 7 percent of the children belong to high-rise families, 7 percent to the families of the recent immigrants, 6 percent to the young couples, 28 percent to the large-size families, and 52 percent to the "other" relocated families. Furthermore, 91 percent of the high-rise children and 93 percent of those from the young couples are, as would be expected, under six years of age.

Children 6 to 17 and 18 years old or older are overwhelmingly from large and "other" relocated families. Hence, while their family heads form 50 percent of Lion family heads, the children of these two subgroups are 90 percent of the children 6 to 17 years of age and 93 percent of the children 18 years old and older.

Table 10.2 gives the educational levels of Lion family heads. At one extreme of the educational scale are the recent immigrants; 47 percent of the husbands have done some graduate work or have graduate degrees. At the other extreme are the husbands of both relocated family groups of whom 75 percent have no more than elementary schooling. The young couples in the low- and high-rises fall in between. The low-rise young couple husbands are nearer to the husbands of the relocated families; and

Table 10.2. Education for Various Subgroups of Lion Family Heads, January 1981

Education	All heads	High Rise Heads	Recent Immigrant Heads	Young Couples Heads	Large Families Heads	Other Relocated Families Head
Elem. School or less	48%	16%	4%	31%	74%	73%
Some High School	13	13	0	41	9	11
High School Graduate	21	37	14	28	17	13
Some College	7	15	21	0	0	3
B.A. Degree	3	6	14	0	0	0
Graduate Work or Degree	8	13	47	0	0	0
Base	100%	100%	100%	100%	100%	100%

the high-rise young couple husbands are nearer to the immigrant husbands. None of the low-rise young couple husbands went beyond high school. Fifteen percent of the high-rise young couple husbands have some university education, 6 percent have undergraduate degrees, and 13 percent have graduate education or degrees.

Lion neighborhood has about double the religious percentage of the Chaldea neighborhood. Furthermore, its religious families are working-class Jews who stem from the "oriental Jewish tradition." The synagogues of Lion are often formed by those who stem from the same Moslem community or country. Historically, their orthodoxy has been less rigid, and they are now more tolerant of some religious "deviations" such as listening to radio broadcasts of Saturday (Sabbath) afternoon soccer games.

The net result is that the type of secular person common to the Chaldea neighborhood is a relative rare person here. Few revolt against "oriental Orthodox Judaism." Religious and less religious families live and let live. They can readily neighbor with each other for many of the less religious families follow the religious dietary laws. Participant-observation showed that children's play groups are formed much more on the basis of who lives near to whom without the play group split into religious and nonreligious typical of the Chaldea neighborhood.

Apartment ownership is most characteristic of the high-rise families, and automobile ownership of recent immigrant families. Table 10.3 also shows that young couples mainly rent rather than buy in Lion. (However, it was only after they had lived in Lion for about a year that young couples were permitted to buy their Lion apartments rather than rent them.) Most of the relocated families, especially the large ones, have also bought. Car owning is not a common feature of Lion families.

All in all, it is hard to find much of a common basis among any sizable proportion of the families living in the low-rise buildings of Lion. The low-rise structures are home for young couple families, immigrant families, large size relocated families, and the so-called other relocated families. This combination of families scattered throughout the 28 low-rise buildings gives sizable differences in life cycle between the young couples and the others; in education, occupation, and ethnicity between the recent immigrants and others; to some extent, on education and occupation between the young couples and both groups of relocated families; in native-born proportions between the young couples and the other families; in number of children between the large relocated families and the rest; and in religiosity between the relocated families and the rest.

Table 10.3. *Ownership for Various Subgroups of Lion Family Heads, January 1981*

Ownership	All heads	High Rise Heads	Recent Immigrant Heads	Young Couple Heads	Large Families Heads	Other Relocated Families Head
Owns a Lion apartment	60%	83%	68%	21%	66%	54%
Owns auto	26%	38%	79%	24%	20%	10%

A sizable percentage of Lion residents belong to the middle class. If one includes in that social category the 73 high-rise families (apart from the high-rise aged families), the recent immigrant families, and the 10 young couples families whose heads were high school graduates, then 115 project families fall into the middle class. Lion had 287 occupied apartments. Hence, 40 percent of Lion can reasonably be assigned to the middle class. Also, 25 percent of its heads are of European background.

But what happens to the concentrations of the middle class and European background families? As seen in the preceding tables, the high-rise families are middle class and about half of its heads are of European backgrounds. This means that in most of Lion, apart from the three high-rise structures, 20 percent are middle class at best. Also 20 percent are European. For all practical purposes, then, Lion can be divided into two parts. The first part consists of the middle class, well-mixed as to ethnic backgrounds, similar in family life cycle and religiosity, families of the high-rise structures. The second part consists of a heavily working class, heavily "Oriental" in background, "rest of Lion" sector.

In this "rest of Lion" one finds the immigrant families placed one to a building. This means that the middle class, European subgroup lives, in effect, in a working-class, "Oriental" background environment that is quite foreign to them.

Also scattered, though usually two to a structure, one finds the young couple group who do fit the social characteristics of this second part of Lion. However, these young couple families are at a different life cycle stage than are the other families in their buildings.

Then, while half of Lion's family heads come from the relocated families, their children form 80 percent of all Lion's children; 47 percent of the children under 6; 90 percent of the children 6 to 17; and 93 percent of the children 18 years and older. Among the children of Lion, then, there is a much larger working-class to middle-class ratio than found for family heads.

This Lion split into high-rise and low-rise sectors also shows itself in neighboring patterns. Among high-rise families, 43 percent report within-building neighboring and only 6 percent report any neighboring in other Lion buildings. This is the highest within-building neighboring percentage and the lowest other building neighboring percentage of all Lion subgroups.

Condominium Leadership. To what extent do these wide differences by life cycle, education level, and ethnic background affect within-building leadership? Were the heads of the several building committees handling day-to-day maintenance from any particular group? They were not.

Taking one's turn as a chairperson of a building committee is a matter of volunteering to do a necessary job. It is not a position of power. Rather, it is a routine administrative task of overseeing those hired to clean and repair the building, collecting building dues, and paying bills for the hall lights. The building committee chairperson's duties, then, are task oriented.

Of the eight persons who had headed a high-rise building committee, three were members of a European background couple, two were from Asian-African background couples, and three were from mixed background couples. Indeed, five couples had children and three did not.

The high-rise couples did not find their educational or ethnic differences barriers to the formation of effective building committees. Their shared building committee involvement helped bring about the kind of interaction that leads to a more realistic understanding of immediate neighbors. Friendships might be a byproduct of such interaction, but not necessarily so.

The barriers formed by family life cycle, class, religiosity, and especially ethnicity, were all too real. The condominium character of Lion did create more social interaction among residents of the same building. In turn, such interaction led to more understanding of different social types and the ability to work together with them for building maintenance.

Among the low-rise buildings, there was a wide range in building committee effectiveness. Nonetheless, most low-rise buildings developed adequate to excellent building committees. Working-class leadership emerged and proved itself capable of running a condominium system.

The Successful Condominium Building

From the findings of research on Lion, two key variables can be identified for a successful condominium building. They are within-building friendships and effective building committees. Also these are two key variables that can be influenced by the teams that design a project and its buildings and oversee who lives where in it (more detailed information can be found in Schwartz 1986).

Project and building designers and organizers need to avoid introducing social and physical barriers to friendship formation. This happens when building and project residents differ too much from one another or physical barriers are built that block people from encountering one another on a day-to-day basis. Hence, what the designers and organizers do affects within-building friendship formation potential. This, in turn, affects the building committee's capacity to function.

How do within-building friendships influence building committees? From both participant-observation and survey materials, it was found that such friendships included frequent visits to other apartments within one's building. Such visits resulted in exchange of local information, attitudes, and gossip. Keller (1968, 44-46) refers to such interaction among friendly neighbors as "the latent functions of neighboring." Such latent functions not only pass on information, but also aid in the formation of building and locality norms and the creation of social control mechanisms.

Based on the foundations of such within-building friendships, building committees are able to command much more support by their residents in reaching decisions, trying new things, and having an effective enforcement mechanism of common, mutually agreed upon, building norms. In short, such building committees are able to bind their residents into an effective unit of joint property owners.

Yet, there are some voices that question that a significant amount of within-building friendships has only positive benefits. Rather, Cooper (1975) and Rainwater (1970) note that such friendships can result in residents' complaining about a loss of privacy. Complaints about inadequate privacy did not come to the fore in Lion. Then, too, Ginsberg and Churchman (1985) found in their study of Haifa condominium living that residents report being able to form warm building friendships without losing their feelings of privacy.

In line with the findings of Kasarda and Janowitz (1974) and Fischer et al. (1977), here too, more within-building friendships are associated with more participation in community life. For example, a group of Lion wives lived in a building with a high degree of friendship and often visited each other. This same group of wives were active in Lion voluntary organizations and were the core of a group of women who sought to resolve some Lion problems. Similarly, most of those who became active in the central Lion committee, and in other committees, were first active in their own building committees.

Involvement in Lion community life was not reduced by more quarrels among neighbors. Similar to what Gans (1969) found in Levittown, here too, the existence of quarrels in buildings encouraged residents to enlarge their participation in local voluntary associations. Solving such within-building quarrels also was associated with more participation in Lion voluntary associations.

Considerable amounts of within-building friendships, lots of participation in local neighborhood life, and more support for improved neighborhood organization do not keep residents from moving away from Lion. Furthermore, residents with more effective building committees and with greater success in solving building quarrels were more likely to have plans to move from Lion than the residents of less organized and less successful buildings.

One ought to view plans to leave a neighborhood as a normal social event that is very difficult to prevent. Moving out ought not to be the major measure for the adequacy of a neighborhood organization. Rather, it is a better idea to measure the success of a neighborhood organization as did Franck (1983). She combines the two variables of (1) the image of the neighborhood, and (2) plans to move into a new, single variable called community attachment. Then she uses this new variable to measure the success of the observed neighborhood organization process.

These findings are supported by what Rossi (1980) concludes—that families wishing to improve their housing do so by moving. Since Lion apartments are almost all about 80 to 100 square meters, families wishing more room have to move. Despite the degree of attachment to Lion, when family space needs demand, and finances permit, families have no option but to move.

Indeed, this is certainly so for the young families of the high-rises and the financially better-off new immigrant residents of the low-rises. Wekerle (1977) and Michelson (1976) point out that urban families seldom chose one housing unit for life. Rather, people can be satisfied with one kind of housing at a specific stage in their family life cycle, yet seek out another type of housing at another stage.

AN OVERVIEW OF THE ISRAELI
CONDOMINIUM SYSTEM

Family Quarrels

What about problems resulting from quarrels between families living in the same building? What does a building committee, or its chairperson, do about such quarrels? Little to nothing. Building committees typically wait for such problems to be settled between the quarreling families. Sometimes a building committee just learns to live with the fact that some families of their building are not speaking to each other.

It may be difficult for "insiders" such as building committee members to intervene in these quarrels. It is easier for someone outside of the building to be a neutral umpire in these instances.

Social Leadership

Building committees hold a narrow view of their functions. Theirs is but the technical job of overseeing the cleanliness and general maintenance of the building, and its garden, together with collecting the monthly "building dues" required to finance building cleaning and maintenance. There is considerable reluctance to go beyond these limits. Building committee members need not be neighborhood leaders. Rather, they are merely residents taking their turns at a very specific set of jobs.

Of course there are neighborhood leaders. These are the people who are both willing and able to help settle family quarrels and to concern themselves about a variety of other neighborhood affairs. However, these local leaders typically work on "outside the building" issues such as local traffic flow problems.

The great fear of condominium residents is that the peace and quiet of their homes within the buildings will be even more disturbed by sanctions against one boisterous building family. Hence, people tend to be long suffering before taking any sort of action against such a family. In short, it is necessary for a building committee to have a considerable amount of within-building support and a clear-cut set of building behavior norms before even thinking of any action against a deviant building family.

Obviously, this condominium system, and its associated building committee, is a very flexible device. Depending on a building's leadership, its families can do, or fail to do, a good deal with regard to building cleanliness or maintenance. The learning opportunities for cooperative living can be considerable for a building's older children. For example, some building committees hold periodic cleaning days during which those corners of their structure which are frequently missed by cleaning crews are gone over. On such days, a responsible adult from the building directs the building's children in this kind of a clean-up job. Some times such supervision can also be organized by the children themselves and directed by a high-schooler. What these children clean, they are quite reluctant to dirty again.

Better Off Buildings

The ability to handle a considerable number of building committee problems by spending a bit of money, such as paying more for a cleaning crew to pick up after untidy building residents in addition to their other tasks, gives middle- and upper-class buildings an advantage over working-class ones in the Israeli condominium system.

A building is lucky to have some residents having special skills needed for building maintenance. For example, a building can have an electrician or plumber living in it who would be willing and able to handle some maintenance problems. Such skilled people will do a better job for no money when it involves their building. Clearly, such resident skills are more common in working-class buildings.

In working-class buildings, there are fewer financial resources for high-grade building and garden maintenance; because the work of cleaning buildings is very low in prestige, working-class families are reluctant to form their own cleaning crews despite their need to limit maintenance costs. If voluntary cleaning efforts fail, as they often do, then working-class families will neglect, or ignore, such problems. What we find here resembles what American researchers have often reported about United States working-class neighborhoods, namely that working-class residents have consistently been pointed out to be less concerned about the "beauty" of their property or general building and ground maintenance.

Troublesome Relations

Areas of controversy that attract the attention, even deep involvement, of the building committee, and its chair, are those revolving around the commonly owned property and facilities. A typical area of building conflict is that over a building-wide heating facility. Building committees and building residents can quarrel bitterly about its cost and when to start and end the running of the joint heating system; both as to the times of the winter season and hours of the day. In the warmer parts of Israel the common solution to this better issue has been to disconnect the jointly owned heating equipment and to let each family decide upon its own heating equipment and hours. In the colder parts of the country, the controversies still rage. Now, building contractors have stopped providing a common heating plant for new buildings. The less equipment people own in common, the less they have to quarrel about.

Connecting with City Hall

Building committees suffer from concentrating too much on their own structures. There is quite limited communication from one building committee to another even when their buildings stand next to one another. What communications they have are about trading names and addresses of building service personnel.

The major social gap is that between the various building committees and city hall. The Israeli condominium system typically has a weak, often no, neighborhood committee to work with neighborhood residents and their building committees.

In middle-class neighborhoods, the absence of any real neighborhood level structure does not block joint action with regard to neighborhood problems. A temporary neighborhood committee and leadership group often emerges for the duration of an acute crisis. Such crisis leaders will roam the neighborhood, call and chair meetings, contact building committees, and so on. After developing a neighborhood consensus, and armed with the proper petition signatures, these leaders converge on city hall to seek an adequate solution to the problem at hand. After such a solution is reached, these leaders disappear into the rounds of their own lives, and their committees disappear.

Social Integration

Does this Israeli condominium system have any meaningful impact on social integration? By condominium system, of course, are meant features such as the annual meeting, the frequent, more informal discussions about building maintenance and cleaning that go on among building families, membership in a building committee, the various laws and recognized procedures governing jointly owned residential property, and the building norms and gossip chains used to define rules for families and family activities.

The Israeli condominium system does require that families both living together and owning together have to communicate among themselves. The need to talk frequently about housing matters does force people to become acquainted with one another.

Of course, apartment prices produce economic stratification. But people from a variety of ethnic, religious, and life cycle groups do achieve the same economic level and can buy apartments in the same building. They typically work well together on building committees.

It is likely that the Israeli condominium system does produce more tolerance among children when their apartment buildings contain other children of fairly equal socio-economic status, but of differing ethnic or religious backgrounds. If children can live together, often play together, go to school together, and eat together with other children of similar socio-economic status, but otherwise of different social characteristics, they become more tolerant of different social types.

THE ISRAELI CONDOMINIUM SYSTEM, SOCIAL INTEGRATION, AND NEIGHBORHOOD PLANNING

Within the class boundaries of private and public housing, there are considerable differences on ethnicity, religiosity, and family life cycle. We have looked at religious and secular family interaction in Chaldea, an elite private housing neighborhood. We have studied Lion neighborhood with its mixtures of class, religion, life cycle, and ethnic combinations. Indeed, public housing projects composed solely of working-class families still have a wide variety of ethnic and religiosity groupings. (The so-called Asian-African Jewish group is really composed of quite a variety of ethnic groups ranging from Moroccan Jews to Egyptian and Iraqi Jews, to the Jews from Yemen, Iran, India, and Ethiopia.)

Does "living together-owning together" change the mental pictures these different groups have of one another? All the evidence we have both in this book and the cited literature indicates that the answer to this question is "Yes, within the same building." Residents of the same condominium building do form a more realistic, more humane and understanding picture of the other families living there. When their building committee organization is a better one, this realistic, sympathetic understanding of one another is even greater.

However, such realistic understanding is only partly carried over to unknown and different families living in different buildings.   The condominium system fails to bridge the social gap between buildings. For that, apparently, one needs some sort of project-wide or neighborhood-wide organization.

The cumulative effect of living in a variety of condominium buildings from childhood on is also unknown. While there is little carry-over effect from one's present building to other buildings, there may be carry-over from a person's first building to the residents of his, or her, second or third building. A typical Israeli adult might well live in one building until his early twenties. Then, he or she might rent in several buildings. After marriage, there can be a young couple's apartment. Then, maybe, one or two more apartments before settling into a final building in their late thirties or early forties.

As the class divisions of Israel grow increasingly more heterogeneous with regard to ethnic background or religiosity, it is likely that ordinary life cycle housing turnover will provide people with condominium living experiences involving a fair variety of social types.

Additionally, the ability of some of the working-class building committees of Lion to work with, and aid, multi-problem families shows how flexible a well-organized building committee can be. Yet, this same finding indicates the limits of tolerance of Lion building committees. Multi-problem families whose personal difficulties caused them to be noisy, uncooperative, hostile, or otherwise disruptive of the peace and quiet of the other families of their building, were forced out. The other building families petitioned the public housing authority to move them to other locations.

Yet, as seen in Lion, building friendships are important as a base for the more effective building committees and, more indirectly, neighborhood organization. It does help the quality of building committees to have residents similar enough in social characteristics and lifestyle to have the potential for creating mutual friendships. The religious barriers of the middle-class Chaldea neighborhood are high enough to block meaningful friendships. This religious difference had little disruptive effect on building functions because: (a) such committees are instrumental ones, (b) the religious families were very capable ones and wished to fit into their local condominium system, (c) the religious families were not numerous enough in the various residential buildings to form any sort of within-building subgroup, and (d) the families of Chaldea can afford to spend money on their buildings.

The barriers to effective building committees, like so many other voluntary association activities, are class-linked. Upper- and middle-class families have both the social skills, voluntary organization experiences, and money needed to establish adequate building committees. Most working-class families lack enough of the same factors to form, in a ready manner, equally adequate building committees.

One can conclude that Israeli condominium housing rests on instrumental neighboring. Buildings will be maintained and some degree of mutual tolerance developed through considerable social barriers. Indeed, as has been pointed out previously, given enough professional help on crucial skills, even working-class families can do an adequate job of forming effective building committees through the social barriers of religiosity, ethnicity, and family life cycles.

The Potential of the Condominium System for Neighborhood Planning

The set of social forces that evolved the Israeli single-building condominium system was not responding to neighborhood needs. The "project-wide neighborhood-wide" scope of the first instances of Israeli condominium housing resulted from a neighborhood project committee being in charge of its facilities and maintenance. Its residents were brought together by a sponsoring social institution and had common ideological motivations.

All this ceased when condominium structures began to be built by private contractors on a building-by-building basis. Then, the "semi-kibbutz" urban projects were not longer designed.

Governmental efforts to create project-wide or neighborhood-wide committees in the public housing projects, built after the creation of the state of Israel, have not been very successful. The residents of these projects were not members of any common social movement. Their various project-wide committees owned nothing and managed very little. Rather, the project was under the direct supervision and control of various national and municipal housing authorities.

Better neighborhood committees could do a variety of tasks. For example, Israel has developed a fairly sizable, and active, auxiliary police force that extends down to the neighborhood level. A neighborhood central committee could be the local address for this auxiliary police network and could both staff and run it under the overall supervision of the police.

Then, there is the neglected problem of quarrels between neighbors. The neighborhood central committee could provide conciliatory services for people having troubles with neighbors. Such a service could be staffed both with part-time volunteers and a few professional workers who could have social work backgrounds. In traditional or highly religious neighborhoods, rabbis could be utilized. (Such a conciliation service now operates in Winnipeg, Manitoba, Canada. See Winnipeg Free Press 1987, 1988.)

North American and Israeli Condominium Systems. Condominium housing projects are a growing segment of the American and Canadian housing stock. Condominium housing in these two nations is not built and governed on a building-by-building basis, as in Israel. Rather, condominium housing typically is built with a sizable number of buildings that are formed into projects governed by an overall committee. One might characterize these Israeli-North American differences by saying that in North America, by Israeli standards, condominium projects are "neighborhoods with a neighborhood government."

The North American condominium project governing committees are composed of varying percentages of elected representatives of condominium housing unit owners and representatives of project developers. Silverman and Barton (1986) report that some local authorities expect project developers and residents to provide and pay for a variety of customary urban services.

In Israel, builders drop out of the picture after a building's apartments are sold and its various guarantees expire. Also, each condominium building is entitled to a full range of locality services. Condominium rules as to external appearances are municipality rules.

North American condominium project boards frequently turn to a variety of real estate companies for partial or full-time services in maintaining their projects. This is not done in Israel. Rather, each building committee contracts on a task-by-task basis for whatever work is needed. With fewer housing unit owners to deal with than in the much larger American and Canadian projects, Israeli building affairs can be conducted on a face-to-face basis.

According to Wekerle et al. (1980), Silverman and Barton (1986), and Barton and Silverman (1987), American and Canadian projects have become harder to govern than single Israeli condominium buildings.

Wekerle et al. (1980, 176-78) states that Canadian condominium builders, mortgage banks, and project boards all complain that condominium housing unit owners behave too much like tenants rather than home owners. Canadian condominium owners, she states, feel alienated from the condominium system and considerably constrained by project rules and their governing bureaucracy.

Silverman and Barton (1986) report similar problems in American condominium projects. Residents of such projects, they point out, resent the constant tension between their individual desires with regard to housing and neighbors and the demands of project governing boards and developers.

Such tensions and conflicts are much lesser problems in the single-building Israeli condominium system. Indeed, Ginsberg and Churchman (1985) found in their research that a solid majority of Israeli condominium residents are satisfied with the way their building committees function. Silverman and Barton (1986) report that condominium project residents can, and do, lose their housing units because they fall way behind in their required project fees. It is unheard of in Israel for someone to lose a housing unit for such a reason.

The project-wide governing system of North America would seem to offer a solid basis on which to build effective neighborhood committees. This evolution into neighborhood committees has not taken place. Since projects are customarily a small proportion of their area's housing units, their governing boards do not carry enough weight to create a movement toward neighborhood committees. Yet, where projects form all, or a large proportion, of a neighborhood, their governing boards do, in effect, become neighborhood committees that own property and that function as would the ideal type Israeli neighborhood committee.

Popenoe (1971 and 1985) contrasts Swedish and English urban designs with those of the United States. In general, he defines the Swedish system as being one of high-density low-rise housing and the U.S. one as a low-density low-rise system with England falling in between. Clearly, Popenoe regards Swedish suburban and urban design as providing a better range of urban services for a wider range of social groups than the system developed in the United States—apart from the more spacious and luxurious American suburban home. (Yet, the discussion of the Swedish housing system provided by Lundqvist 1983, makes it clear that most Swedish apartments are rented.)

Clearly a great deal of additional research is needed, both national and international, to understand the potential of the different varieties of condominium systems for better urban living. This includes any possible superiority of condominium systems over massive rental systems such as Sweden's. Hopefully, this monograph is a step in that direction.

REFERENCES

Barton, Stephen, and Carol Silverman. 1987. *Common-Interest Home-owners' Associations Management Study.* Department of Real Estate, State of California, Sacramento, California.

Bracey, H. E. 1964. *Neighbors: Subdivision Life in England and in the United States.* Baton Rouge: Louisiana State University Press.

Churchman, Arza, and Yona Ginsberg. 1980a. "High-Rise Housing in Israel: Advantages and Disadvantages for Residents. *Journal of Urban and Environmental Affairs* 12: 77-84.

_____. 1980b. "Many Entrance Buildings: Residents' Attitudes and Behavior Patterns." Jerusalem: Ministry of Works and Housing (Hebrew).

Cooper, Clare. 1975. *Easter Hill Village.* New York: The Free Press.

Daun, Ake. 1979a. "Why Do Swedish Suburbs Look the Way They Do?" *Current Sweden* 6 (November), Stockholm: The Swedish Institute for Building Research.

_____. 1979b. "Social and Economic Problems of Swedish Housing Environments." *Man-Environment Systems* 9: 195-99.

Fisher, Claude. 1984. *The Urban Experience,* 2d ed. New York: Harcourt-Brace-Jovanovich.

_____, Robert Jackson, C. Anne Stueve, Kathleen Gerson, Lynne Jones, and Mark Baldassare. 1977. *Networks and Places: Social Relations in the Urban Setting.* New York: The Free Press.

Franck, Karen. 1983. "Community by Design." *Sociological Inquiry* 53 (Spring): 289-313.

Gans, Herbert. 1961a. "Planning and Social Life: Friendship and Neighbor Relations in Suburban Communities," *Journal of the American Institute of Planners* 27 (May): 135-40.

_____. 1961b. "Homogeneity or Heterogeneity in Residential Areas?" *Journal of the American Institute of Planners* 27 (August): 176-85.

_____. 1968. *People and Plans: Essays on Urban Problems and Solutions.* New York: Basic Books.

_____. 1969. *The Levittowners.* New York: Vintage Books.

Ginsberg, Yona. 1984. *Subsidized Tenants and Their Non-Subsidized Neighbors.* Jerusalem: Ministry of Works and Housing (Hebrew).

_____, and Arza Churchman. 1985. "The Pattern and Meaning of Neighbor Relations in High-Rise Housing in Israel." *Human Ecology* 13: 467-84.

Heraud, B. 1968. "Social Class and the New Towns." *Urban Studies* 5 (February): 33-58.

International Committee for the Evaluation of Project Renewal. 1985. "Summary of Findings and Recommendations." Report submitted to the Minister of Housing and Chairman of the Jewish Agency. (June), Jerusalem, Israel.

Kasarda, John, and Morris Janowitz. 1974. "Community Attachment in Mass Society." *American Sociological Review* 39: 328-39.

Keller, Susan. 1968. *The Urban Neighborhood.* New York: Random House.

Lundqvist, Lennart. 1983. *Housing Tenures in Sweden.* Stockholm: The National Swedish Institute for Building Research.

Marrett, Cora. 1973. "Social Stratification in Urban Areas." In *Segregation in Residential Areas,* ed. Amos Hawley and Vincent Rock. Washington, D.C.: National Academy of Sciences, 172-88.

Michelson, William. 1976. *Environmental Choice, Human Behavior, and Residential Satisfaction.* New York: Oxford University Press.

Popenoe, David. 1971. *The Suburban Environment.* Chicago: University of Chicago Press.

_____. 1985. *Private Pleasure, Public Plight.* New Brunswick, N.J.: Transaction Books.

Rainwater, Lee. 1970. *Behind Ghetto Walls.* Chicago: Aldine Press.

Rossi, Peter. 1980. *Why Families Move.* Beverly Hills, Calif.: Sage Publications, 2d ed.

Sarkissian, Wendy. 1976. "The Idea of Social Mix in Town Planning: An Historical Review." *Urban Studies* 13 (October): 231-46.

Schwartz, Chaya. 1986. "The Organization Process of a New, Heterogeneous Urban Neighborhood in a Public Housing Project in Israel." Unpublished Ph.D. Dissertation, Department of Sociology, Bar Ilan University, Ramat Gan, Israel (Hebrew).

Silverman, Carol, and Stephen Barton. 1986. "Private Property and Private Government: Tensions Between Individualism and Community in Condominiums." Institute of Urban and Regional Development, University of California, Berkeley, California. (Paper presented at the 1986 convention of the American Sociological Association session on Social Change in Local Communities.)

Tabory, Ephraim. 1989. "Residential Integration and Religious Segregation in an Israeli Neighborhood." *International Journal of Intercultural Relations* 13: 19-35.

Wekerle, Gerda. 1977. "Residential Choice and Housing Satisfaction in a Singles High Rise Complex." In *Human Response to Tall Buildings*, ed. Donald J. Conway. Stroudsburg, Penn.: Dowden, Hutchinson and Ross, 230-39.

_____, et al. 1980. "Contradictions in Ownership, Participation and Control: The Case of Condominium Housing." In *The Consumer Experience of Housing: Cross-National Perspectives*, ed. Clare Ungerson and Valerie Karn. Westmead, England: Gower Publishing Ltd., 170-91.

Werczberger, Elia, and Yona Ginsberg. 1987. "Maintenance of Shared Property in Low Income Condominiums." *Housing Studies* 2 (July): 192-202.

Winnipeg Free Press. 1987. "Dispute Center Resolves Neighborhood Disputes." August 30, p. 4/sw.

_____. 1988. "Centre Fixes Neighborhood Beefs," January 6, p. 30.

Zito, J. 1974. "Anonymity and Neighboring in an Urban, High Rise Complex." *Urban Life and Culture* 3: 243-63.

11

Condominium Management in Japan

Tsuneo Kajiura

A collective house, either a row house or apartment house, where units are individually owned will be referred to as a condominium in this chapter, and herein I shall describe the various problems of condominium management in Japan. In the United States, however, the term "condominium" is not always limited to an apartment house in a legal sense, as they may include detached houses that share common spaces. In Japan today, the greatest number of common interest developments are condominiums. Condominiums are often referred to in Japan as mansions, but this word has a different meaning in the United States and other countries.

TYPES AND NUMBERS OF COLLECTIVE HOUSES IN JAPAN

For this discussion of condominiums, the types and number of collective houses in Japan will be described first. Prior to the Second World War, there were a great number of wooden houses in the large cities of Japan, such as Tokyo and Osaka. But this situation has greatly changed in the past quarter of a century. In a survey conducted by the Department of Public Service of Osaka City in 1940, 95 percent of all houses in the city were wooden row houses, and approximately 90 percent were rented houses. At that time, row houses or apartments built with reinforced concrete or stone were extremely rare.

Since the 1950s, however, the trend to build housing units with reinforced concrete has been growing. It began during the 1950s when the central government started providing funds to public corporations and to the Japan Housing Corporation for the development of housing projects. Private corporations were not eligible for these funds, however, and most could not yet afford to build houses constructed with reinforced concrete due to its higher cost. But by the end of the 1960s, even private developers were building mostly with reinforced concrete.

At present, the total number of collective houses throughout Japan totals about 13,900,000, and these structures make up 37 percent of all available housing in the country (Housing Survey 1988, Japan Statistics Bureau). Of that total number, 11,400,000 are apartment houses and over 2,500,000 are row houses. As for building materials, only 3,270,000 of that total number of apartment houses were constructed with wood and the remaining 7,850,000 were built with reinforced concrete. Of all those built with reinforced concrete almost two million have privately owned units, and 1.5 million are over three stories tall.

While the number of condominiums is relatively small compared to the total number of houses in Japan, almost all of them are located in the larger cities, making their presence in those places quite noticeable. Also, their number is increasing rapidly every year, thus they play a very important part in the formation of housing policies. Of the total number of condominiums in Japan, 53 percent are in the Tokyo metropolitan area, 26 percent are in the Osaka metropolitan area, six percent are in the greater Nagoya area, and the rest are located in the other main cities throughout the country.

The first condominium in Japan was built in December 1955. At that time, there were no special laws to regulate this housing type and its management methods. The law governing condominiums was passed in April 1962, and enacted from April of the following year. The law is described as governing compartmental ownership of buildings. After this law was enacted, many more condominiums were built. Every year the number of condominiums in Japan increased by tens of thousands of units and is the most rapidly growing form of housing. See Figure 11.1.

According to a survey conducted by the Japanese Ministry of Construction in 1988, the average number of units per condominium is 81.4 units. Most condominiums contain 40 to 60 units; however, large condominiums exceeding 200 units comprise almost seven percent of all condominiums. The average number of floors in a condominium is seven, although middle-rise buildings have an average of only five. As for the area of individual dwelling units, there are some units exceeding 100 square meters, but most units have an average of 65 square meters with two or three bedrooms and one living room. According to a study

Figure 11.1. *Construction of Condominiums*

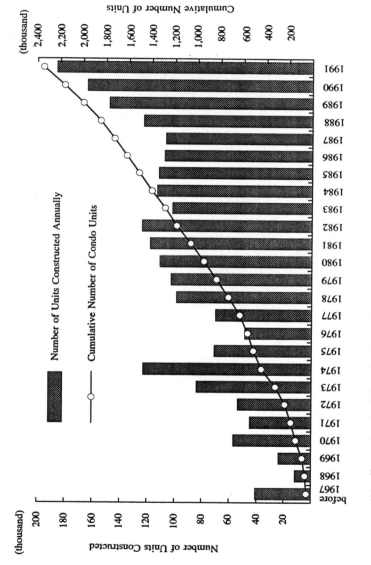

Note: The number of units in condominiums of three stories or more is estimated from the "Building Construction Survey" (Economic Bureau, Ministry of Construction). Since this number has been estimated from the "Building Construction Survey," it is different from the total number of condominiums according to the 1988 Housing Survey.

by a private research institute, the average unit built in western Japan in 1986 had 66.7 square meters.

Originally, only those people in the elite social class with very high incomes could afford to live in condominiums, but since the early 1970s the population of middle-income occupants in condominiums has exploded. Today condominiums are the housing choice for a diverse range of people, including almost all the social and income classes. The construction style of condominiums reflects the different classes of the occupants, ranging from the smaller, narrow buildings to the deluxe, luxury buildings. Table 11.1 shows the percentages of people living in condominiums in cities with populations of over 50,000 people, and these percentages are divided up into five quintile income groups. The figures show that most condominium owners do fall into the higher income groups.

One kind of apartment house available in Japan is the cooperative housing complex. These apartment houses are designed and built by an association of individual unit owners who desire to create a particular living environment. The first cooperative house in Japan was built in Tokyo in 1968, and this housing option has become more and more popular with people who want to live in condominiums. They differ from other apartment houses in that the owners first form an association, then decide on a design for the apartment house, and then each individually creates a plan for their individual unit. After the apartment house is completed, it is owned by the unit owners and it becomes a condominium.

There are other kinds of common interest housing available in Japan, such as town houses and detached houses that share common spaces. Although we have no accurate measure, we do believe that both of these kinds of housing have steadily increased over the last 15 years. In group housing developments, the owners first create a building agreement that regulates management of the common spaces, maintenance of the building design, and maintenance of the living environment.

VARIOUS PROBLEMS WITH CONDOMINIUM MANAGEMENT

As the development of condominiums has increased, various problems with their management have emerged. The first problem is the decline of living conditions in neighborhoods, such as obstruction of sunlight to adjacent houses by middle- and high-rise condominiums. Civil

Table 11.1. *Condominium Households by Income Quintile in Cities with Population of 50,000 or More.*

	I	II	III	IV	V
Percentage of Households in condominiums	6.7%	12.2%	22.1%	34.1%	25.0%

Source: Kinki Branch Housing Section, Architectural Institute of Japan, "Study on Private Condominium Management," 1980.

actions to halt or to alter the construction of these condominiums have been seen throughout Japan at an increasing rate. Due to this influence, a law to control sun shadow was passed in 1977.

Another problem with condominiums concerns major discrepancies between what owners are promised before they buy and what they actually receive once the purchase is made. For example, the initial pamphlet describing the condominium may promise parking facilities, but the owners will find out later that they must purchase parking rights separately from the developer. Or perhaps, the first floor is described as a pilot in the pamphlet, but the owners find out after their purchase that the developer has retained ownership of this space for other purposes. Another common discrepancy is with the proposed direction of the building. The pamphlet may say that the building will face 43 degrees east of due south, but it is actually built at 70 degrees east. This means that the amount of direct sunlight in the units is much less than promised.

In an effort to curb the problems with false promises by developers and with defective construction, the Administrative Management Agency of the central government recommended in 1979 that the Ministry of Construction and other appropriate government agencies take the necessary measures. Administrative guidelines, such as prohibition of extravagant advertisements and the mandatory explanation of all pertinent information to the potential unit buyer, have been imposed upon developers by these government agencies. These measures have resulted in significant improvement, but problems still exist.

Another major problem with condominiums concerns flaws in the construction of the building, which often contributes to the problems mentioned in the previous paragraph. Unfortunately, construction defects are quite common in condominiums and are often expensive to correct. It is ironic that most of these flaws result from corner-cutting on the part of the developer. The following are examples of this problem: (1) A housewife wiped off the ceiling of her kitchen with a wet cloth, and a large quantity of water fell to the floor. Poor waterproofing on the roof and a large crack in the external wall were responsible for this accident. (2) A bedroom was contaminated when a large amount of soot was expelled from the ventilating duct. The investigators found that a large gas stove in a first floor restaurant was connected to the same system, and a malfunctioning fan caused the air to flow inversely. (3) Drainage pipes were installed incorrectly. Faulty connections and poor angling of the pipes caused them to clog frequently, thus dirty water leaked under the flooring.

The next problem related to condominiums pertains to administrative issues. For example, the condominiums' sites are often registered as a possession of the developer when it actually belongs to the unit owners. Also, the developer sometimes fails to pass along the drawings and specifications of the building to the unit owners, making repairs or remodelling quite difficult and confusing.

The last problem I will mention here concerns the management difficulties that have appeared with the rapid expansion of this housing form. This discussion must be broken down into four separate elements, the first of which is related to the operation of Management Associations, particularly with establishing agreement between unit owners. According to the housing law passed in 1962, the bylaws that govern the association cannot be changed without approval of all the unit owners. However, sometimes the developer creates a situation that does not match that which is described in the bylaws, and this creates confusion for the association about how to initiate appropriate changes.

The second element of this problem is related to the repair and maintenance of condominium buildings and facilities. All too often, the Management Association does not have the funds or an efficient plan for conducting periodic large-scale repairs to common spaces that lead to unnecessary dilapidation. The third element of the problem concerns the business conducted by third-party management contract companies hired by Management Associations. Frequently, the association does not know which outside company to trust with their business and ends up dissatisfied with the quality of work that is done or the amount of money they were charged for the work. Also, on-site managers are often ill-trained and unqualified, which leads to complaints about the person's competency. But the on-site manager often has grounds for complaint about the demands made upon him and about the kind of conditions he is offered. Thus it is quite difficult to find on-site managers who make good partners with the association.

In addition, from the latter half of 1980 to 1990, a new type of problem has occurred. Real estate traders buy a number of units in the same condominium in an attempt to force out other unit owners. Finally, the rising number of rental units and instances of nonresidential use are making efficient management difficult.

Countermeasures for These Problems

To correct the management problems listed above, the following administrative policies and community actions have been taken. First, a revision of the government law regarding condominium management was passed in 1983. The main improvements were as follows: (1) changes in the bylaws and alterations to common spaces can be passed by a special majority decision of 3/4 the total number of votes and 3/4 of the total unit owners. (2) Management Associations now have the choice of changing from a cooperative organization to a corporate organization. (3) Further rights and duties of the tenants were specified. (4) Regulations were created to determine actions taken against those tenants who violate the association bylaws. (5) The decision to rebuild the condominium must be passed by at least 4/5 the total votes and 4/5 of the total unit owners at the association meeting.

In addition to changes in the law, a number of other actions have been taken to improve the conditions of condominium management. First, the Ministry of Construction created a set of model bylaws and a model management agreement to provide administrative guidance for developers and management contract companies. This government agency also created a registration system for condominium contract companies, but unfortunately it is not yet mandatory.

Next, Management Associations have increased their influence and effectiveness by creating additional organizations. Also, many Management Associations have formed an outside group of expert consultants to conduct building inspections and to develop repair plans. This organization is a nonprofit group of professionals, mostly engineers and lawyers, and they have earned the nickname of the "Mansion Doctors."

Finally, regional federations of Management Associations have been created throughout Japan. These organizations provide a forum for sharing experiences regarding condominium management and have also been quite effective in dealing with citizen and community issues. These federations hold regular meetings and often publish newsletters.

These actions have resulted in an encouraging degree of improvement in the above-mentioned problems. Long-term repair plans developed by associations, as well as provisions made for repair expense, have resulted in more suitable and timely repairs. General operation of the associations has improved, and the bylaws are more suitable for actual conditions of management. Finally, unit owners are slowly gaining an important understanding of the issues involved in condominium management, and this helps to reduce a number of unnecessary misunderstandings between occupants and managers.

Although progress has been made, the following problems are still causing great difficulty. First of all, Management Associations too often make expensive mistakes due to inexperience and insufficient planning. For example, funds that belong to the association are sometimes deposited into the accounts of the contract companies. Also, condominiums are often under-occupied making the expense of management far greater than the funds actually taken in by the association. In this situation, the assessment per unit increases, and the association may stop utilizing outside contract companies in an effort to cut expenses. However, it is difficult for the association to find anyone who is willing to perform management tasks voluntarily.

REGULATIONS FOR CONDOMINIUM MANAGEMENT

Now I will explain more about the existing laws that govern condominium management in Japan. The Compartment Ownership Law is essential for the continuation of effective management of condominiums. This law states that a management organization is formed by all unit owners in every condominium and is called the Management Association (it is the approximate equivalent of the homeowners' association found in the United States). The Management Association has the option to hold meetings, determine bylaws, and choose an administrator, but these things are not actually required by law. However, if the association does not actively exercise these rights, it becomes an association in name only and does no good for the management of the condominium.

Bylaws

Normally a draft of the bylaws is created by the developer, and it is rare that it undergoes drastic changes before being ratified. A meeting is usually held to formalize the bylaws, and they must be passed with 3/4 the total number of votes and by 3/4 the total number of unit owners (these totals are not always the same since the number of votes is generally determined by unit size). However, if all the unit owners signed the bylaws when they purchased their unit, there is no need for such a meeting. Furthermore, the original draft of the bylaws is considered effective from the sale of the first unit in the condominium. Each prospective buyer is asked to read and sign a copy of the draft, signifying their initial agreement with them. If a prospective buyer is not willing to sign the drafted bylaws, they are not allowed to purchase a unit. This rarely happens as most buyers are more interested in the living environment, the price, the facilities, and the unit itself. Most people do not bother to read the bylaws closely if they have already decided that they like everything else about the condominium.

Because of these factors, most bylaws created by the developers become the first bylaws of the condominium and are referred to as the primary bylaws. These primary bylaws should be advantageous for developers and management contract companies, yet not at the expense of the unit owners. Furthermore, the bylaws should be equitable and follow principles of common sense. Although the primary bylaws can be changed, such changes are not easily made. Given these circumstances, the developer has a great responsibility to create sound bylaws to begin with.

As to the contents of the bylaws, the Compartment Ownership Law states that issues related to management or use of buildings, grounds, and annexed facilities by mutual unit owners can be determined in the bylaws, except for those items already determined by government law. Although government law does provide regulations for some specific items, most areas are left up to the discretion of the individual associations and the particular needs of their condominiums. The main subjects covered by the bylaws are common spaces, building and ground use, the ratios for payment of management expenses, voting ratio requirements, and administrative matters such as meetings and elections.

Meetings

The general meetings held by each Management Association are quite important because they help foster agreement between unit owners. Meetings are normally called by the administrator and must be held at least once a year. Unit owners can request a general meeting with 1/5 or more of the total votes and of the total unit owners. When an association does not have an administrator, the meetings must be called by the unit owners themselves.

Notification for each meeting must be issued to each occupant at least one week before the meeting is to be held, and it must state the proposed agenda and purpose of the meeting. The time period for notification can be changed in the bylaws with the appropriate number of votes. Renters may attend the meetings, if they have the approval of the owners, but they can only express their opinions. They will be allowed to vote only if they are the authorized deputy of the person who owns the unit.

Administrator

The unit owners in the Management Association have the option to select an administrator to represent them, and this person can be chosen from among their members or from an outside source. However, the chair of the association is most often selected for this role. The administrator performs external management business with the authority of the entire association. In the case that the association decides to become a corporation, they need not select an administrator. Rather, the law requires that an incorporated association choose or elect officers who are responsible for management business. It also stipulates that there must be at least 30 participating unit owners in order for them to form a corporation. According to the Housing Survey conducted in 1988, only 13 percent of those associations studied have chosen to form a corporation. This figure supports the general feeling among associations that there is little to be gained by this action.

For those organizations that have chosen to remain cooperative organizations, the administrator has the duty to maintain the bylaws, record the minutes of all meetings, and keep track of any written agreements made by the unit owners. The administrator is also responsible for holding at least one general meeting every year and to report all business affairs for the association in the meeting. According to the

Compartment Ownership Law, the administrator can be penalized up to 100,000 yen if he neglects to perform his duties.

Definition of Common Spaces

The Compartment Ownership Law divides the areas of a condominium into two parts, that which is categorized as having exclusive ownership, and that which is used by every occupant and is referred to as common space. According to the law, the portions of the condominium complex that are naturally part of the common spaces are those shared areas such as stairways, passageways, halls, structural columns, roofs, and external walls. However, the text of the law simply states that common space is any and all areas of the building and grounds that are used in common and does not specifically name which portions. There are two types of common spaces, those that fall into the category of natural common spaces as mentioned above, and those that are determined specifically in the bylaws.

Bylaw Violators

In a community living environment such as a condominium, it is necessary for each occupant to be respectful and considerate of the other occupants, and furthermore that they do not purposely cause trouble for others. Creating a comfortable community life is very important and cannot be accomplished without the efforts of each occupant. The law states that unit owners shall not do anything that is harmful to the building itself, or take any action that goes against the common interest of the condominium community. Unfortunately, there must be planned measures for those instances in which unit owners or occupants do violate the bylaws.

When the Compartment Ownership Law was revised in 1983, certain articles were added regarding bylaw violators, stating what specific actions should be taken against them. There are three basic legal actions that an association can take against bylaw violators in a court of law: the first is a claim for suspension, the second is a claim for temporary expulsion from the condominium, and the third is a claim for forced sale of the unit. A claim for suspension is made when the administrator invokes the court to prevent or stop a violator from breaking the regulations of the bylaws. In this case, the administrator for the association or the entire group of unit owners is listed as the plaintiff, and a majority decision in a general meeting is required to instigate this action.

If this action does not correct the situation, the plaintiff may take a claim for temporary expulsion of the violating unit owner from the condominium. The intention is that further negotiations may be more effective once the person is removed from the unit. In order to take this action, the association must hold a general meeting and pass the decision by both 3/4 of the total votes and 3/4 of the unit owners. The person who is charged with violating the bylaws must be given the opportunity in the meeting to explain his or her actions.

However, sometimes even stronger action is required, and in this case the plaintiff will have to make a claim for forced sale. The result of this claim may be that the misbehaving unit owner will be forced by the court to sell the unit and leave the condominium permanently. Again, the decision to take this action must pass by 3/4 of the total votes and 3/4 of the total unit owners, and the offending unit owner must be given another chance to explain him/herself. This action is taken in only the most extreme cases and does not occur very often.

Regulations for Rebuilding

Also included in the 1983 revision of the law were articles regulating the rebuilding of condominiums. Rebuilding literally means when an existing condominium is torn down and a new one is built to replace it. The decision to rebuild a condominium must be passed by at least 4/5 of the total votes and 4/5 of the unit owners in a general association meeting. If the vote is successful, there are still other conditions that regulate rebuilding activities.

The first is that the reason for rebuilding must be that the existing condominium is falling into a state of dilapidation. The second condition is that the cost of simply making repairs, rather than rebuilding, would exceed the cost of the original condominium. Finally, if a condominium is torn down for the purpose of rebuilding, a new condominium must be built, not some other kind of building that might be more affordable. The exception to all of the above conditions is, if there is 100 percent agreement among the unit owners, they can do as they wish with the condominiums as it is legally their private property. The conditions were added to the law in order to protect the rights of those owners who may not wish to see the original condominium torn down.

Application to Housing Complexes

The laws governing condominiums in Japan theoretically apply only to condominiums with one building. However, they are also applied to condominiums with multiple buildings, and we will refer to these projects as housing complexes. A housing complex can be defined as a group of condominiums, a group of detached houses, or a group of condominiums and detached houses, all of which share common spaces among them. In this manner, Japanese law is similar to condominium laws in the United States in its flexible definition of the term "condominium." Yet, in Japanese law, the articles relating to bylaw violators and to rebuilding issues are only applicable to one-building condominiums and not to housing complexes.

Condominiums built in the same project and in the same time period should have only one Management Association and only one set of bylaws. The association performs the business of management for the entire housing complex. One association normally manages approximately three buildings and an average of 133.7 units. The problem with this law is that when common areas are shared by a number of Management Associations, meetings by representatives of umbrella associations are not approved. Thus, it is necessary to have a meeting of all unit owners. This system is quite cumbersome because it is not realistic to have that many unit owners meet together.

EXISTING CONDITIONS IN MANAGEMENT ORGANIZATIONS

As mentioned in an earlier section, the law states that there must be an organization of unit owners in each condominium. Actually, almost all condominiums do have bylaws, an administrator, and regular meetings, with the exception of very small condominium complexes. Most associations have six to 15 officers that are either elected or chosen in a general meeting. Most associations at least have a president, a vice-president, an auditor, and a financial director. Almost all officers are unit owners; however, sometimes a renter is selected for a position. Also, 80 percent of the officers serve a term of one year and then either serve another term or are replaced by a different unit owner. Finally, when large-scale repairs are required, most associations create a special committee and special officers to oversee the repairs.

There are three categories of meetings held by each association: the first is a general meeting for all unit owners, the second is a meeting of just the officers, and the third is for special committees. The general meeting is usually held once a year, either in April or May, and typically only 20 to 30 percent of the unit owners actually attend. In fact, my research shows that less than half of the unit owners show up at over 80 percent of all general meetings. The officers usually hold 10 to 15 meetings every year, except in smaller condominiums where about five officer meetings per year is adequate.

The workload for officers varies a great deal, depending on the type of management employed in the condominium. In the first management type, the Management Association turns all business over to an outside management contract company. This style is used most often in high-price, luxury condominiums or in resort condominiums. In the second type, the association turns over part of the business to a contract company, such as the paperwork and collecting management expenses from the unit owners, and the rest of the tasks go to individual specialist companies who handle jobs such as cleaning or equipment maintenance.

In the third type, the association hires an on-site manager and possibly other employees, and these people assist the association officers in the business of management. In the last type, the owners and renters conduct all management tasks by themselves, which usually occurs in condominiums with fewer units. According to a survey conducted in western Japan in 1979, the first and second management types were used by 73 percent of associations, while the third type was used by 11 percent, and the fourth type was used by 15 percent of all associations surveyed.

In the first and second management types, the initiative to conduct management business is most often held solely by the third-party contract company, and the unit owners are not involved at all. But in some condominiums, where the unit owners have more interest in management issues, the owners retain the decision-making powers and must direct the contract company before any actions will be taken. The latter two types are most often seen in condominiums with relatively few units, as well as in those complexes built by public developers. In general, most unit owners prefer that the initiative be left in their hands, but that they have the luxury of turning over responsibility for action into the hands of an outside company.

There are many reasons why the management type used in a condominium may change. Perhaps there are some troubles with the contract company so the association decides to find a new one and retain the initiative to make decisions regarding management. Or perhaps the original bylaws created by the developer turn out to be unsuitable for the condominium and the association needs to make appropriate changes to meet their particular needs. Or it may be that the association is tired of working with an outside company. It is crucial to maintain a comfortable living environment that the condominium have an appropriate and effective management system. See Table 11.2.

Working with Management Contract Companies

As mentioned above, many Management Associations hire third-party contract companies, but problems develop when the contract itself is not specific enough. This situation is exacerbated by the fact that these companies have often shown themselves as lacking in common sense and possessing questionable business ethics. For example, in spite of requests by the association to keep their money separate, some major contract companies pool all management expenses and repair reserve funds into their own accounts, even though these funds are the property of the Management Association. Another problem is that unit owners often lack experience and expertise in negotiating contracts and thus do not choose a suitable company. Also, the developer sometimes determines the management contract company at the time of construction; changing to another company later on can be difficult.

According to the survey conducted in my seminar in 1986, in which I researched 63 condominium associations in western Japan, there were many associations whose contracts with outside companies were too vague. Specifically, associations complained that the explanations regarding rate of payment to these outside companies were not satisfacto-rily clear, creating a great sense of discontent and uneasiness among the unit owners and associations. In this particular survey, 12 of the associations had changed contract companies at least once due to the belief that the company was charging them unreasonably high rates.

Disagreements over money is probably the most frequent cause of breakdowns in relationships between Management Associations and their contract companies. In particular, confusion about the administration of management funds can lead to a great deal of trouble. In Japan, funds can only be withdrawn from the bank with the appropriate passbook and seal, yet these two items are not always kept together.

Table 11.2.   *Preferences of Condominium Owners for Manage-
                     ment Types*

Trust all of management to the management contract company	26.7%
Trust the business to the contract company, and operation is performed by condominium owners.	51.6%
All management is performed by condominium owners.	10.3%
Any of them can be taken	11.3%

Source: Kinki Branch Housing Section, Architectural Institute of Japan,
"Study on Private Condominium Management," 1980.

According to the above survey, only 24 percent of the associations
had possession of both the passbook and the seal for the accounts where
their funds were kept.   However, 34 percent of either the on-site
managers or the management contract companies had possession of both
items. We can see that unit owners of the associations are often unaware
of exactly the state of their accounts.

Contents of Bylaws

As I mentioned previously, the bylaws are usually drafted by the
developer of the condominium.   However, since the 1983 revision of
condominium law, many Management Associations have changed their
bylaws to reflect the new regulations. Thus, most bylaws existing today
have been improved by the associations using them and are proving to be
much more effective. Table 11.3 shows the results of a 1988 survey
conducted by the Ministry of Construction regarding the origins of
bylaws. The bylaws for condominiums constructed by public developers
are usually created by the Management Association, but in privately
developed condominiums, the number of bylaws drawn up by management contract companies equalled approximately the number created by
associations.

Table 11.3. *Creation of Bylaws*

| | Organizational Source of Bylaws | | | |
	Management Association	Developer	Contract Company	Other or Unknown
Total	38.8%	25.8%	30.6%	4.8%
Projects built by public developers	81.9%	12.8%	0	5.3%
Projects built by private developers	34.5%	27.1%	33.7%	4.7%

Source: Ministry of Construction, Condominium Investigation, 1988.

Since the model bylaws for middle high-rise residential condominiums were created by the Ministry of Construction in 1983, the number of bylaws conforming to this model has increased steadily every year. The main items determined in the model bylaws are listed below:

1. Space of the exclusive section: The exclusive section shall be composed of the interior space of the unit, including the ceiling, walls, floors, but excluding the framing of the building. Walls or columns that are not part of, or connected to, the external walls are considered the property of the unit and thus can be remodelled or removed according to the desires of the owner. Owners are free to redecorate or repaint the interior if they choose. Regarding the entrance door, the lock and interior surface of the door are the property of the unit, but exterior surfaces remain the property of the common element. Finally, the window frames and window glass are also property of the common element, and not of the unit.
2. Common spaces: The share of common spaces assigned to a unit normally depends on the percentage of floor area located within the unit. Floor area is calculated by measuring the entire area of the unit.

In the case where a unit shares a party wall with another unit, area is measured from the center line of the wall and includes the thickness of the wall.

3. Acceptable uses of the unit: Units must normally be used for residence only and shall not be used for other purposes without express permission of the entire Management Association. The rights of private use of balconies and parking spaces, and any fees required for this private use, are determined in the bylaws. Rights of private use can be revoked if a unit owner lends or sells their unit without permission from the association.

4. Determining parking rights: In many condominiums there are fewer parking spaces than there are unit owners who wish to use one; thus there is almost always a shortage of available spaces. When a shortage occurs, there are two methods of determining which owners will receive a parking space. In the first method, occupants who wish to have a private parking space all draw lots once every year, so rights of private use change hands annually. In the second method, either a lottery system or the sequence of application determines the rights to a parking space, and there is turn-over only when a unit owner moves out or relinquishes his space voluntarily.

5. Management finances: The total annual expense for management, and the share to be paid by each unit owner, is determined in the bylaws. The bylaws also determine that a certain amount of money must be set aside in a reserve fund to pay for large-scale repairs. Finally, the budget, settlement of accounts, collection of management expenses, and the dates of the fiscal year are determined in the bylaws.

6. Management affairs: The bylaws state qualifications for membership in the Management Association and determine business to be performed by the association, election, or selection processes for officers, general meeting procedures, and the total number of votes based on unit areas.

Other Regulations Often Found in Bylaws

The Management Association determines bylaws to regulate issues not already included in the model bylaws. These regulations vary depending on the association; however, most typically create regulations for condominium use, car park use, meeting room use, and bicycle parking areas. These issues may be touched on in the model bylaws, but are described in more detail by each association.

The regulations pertaining to condominium use often include items that help promote community life. Some of these regulations apply to elevator safety, garbage disposal, emergency procedures, and restraints on possessing dangerous objects and keeping pets. Most of these things are based on common sense and help prevent unnecessary problems among the unit owners.

There are many things that detract from the quality of community life, such as noise, pet-related problems, graffiti, misuse of equipment, and disagreements over parking spaces. Because these problems occur naturally in a community living environment, quarrels often flare between neighbors and unit owners. Solutions are sometimes difficult, but mutual consideration from all the unit owners is the best way to promote good relations. Various community social events such as parties, bazaars, and sports outings tend to increase communication between unit owners and therefore limit misunderstandings among them. See Table 11.4.

Illegal Building Work

Illegal building work sometimes occurs in condominiums, and there are extreme cases that end up being settled in a court of law. In middle- and high-rise condominiums illegal building often takes the form of enclosing balconies with glass windows. Because these kinds of irregularities mar the overall appearance of the building, and because enclosed balconies eliminate a possible escape route in case of emergency, the Management Association usually asks the owner to remove the glass. However, many occupants do not comply with these requests because of the money they have invested in the remodelling and because they desire to keep the changes.

Problems relating to architectural control occur even more frequently in two- and three-story townhouses. Town houses usually have a private courtyard, and it is easy for unit owners to believe that they have the same rights to rebuild and remodel as would the owner of a detached house. There have been many cases where unit owners have remodelled rooflines or external walls because the developer or manager did not sufficiently explain the prohibitions against such work. Although the relative number of town houses in Japan is small, the number is increasing steadily, and it is gradually becoming common knowledge that town houses are legally more like condominium units than like detached

Table 11.4.   *Dissatisfaction Contents for Management*

Requested the contents of the persons (2,052 persons) who answered dissatisfaction for management condition.

Some residents are not cooperative	**46.7%**
The management contract company or the on-site manager is no good.	31.9%
Directors of association are not experienced	29.5%
Class of residents is different.	27.1%
Finance is poor.	23.3%
Management interests differ from owner interests.	22.6%

Source: Ministry of Construction, Condominium Investigation, 1988.

homes.   This issue shows once again just how important it is for developers to provide complete and understandable explanations to prospective buyers before a purchase is actually made.

Management Expenses

According to the 1988 survey by the Ministry of Construction, the average monthly management expense per unit is 10,000 yen (about $77). In addition to this, each unit owner contributes monthly to the association reserve fund by direct payment to the Management Association. This expense ranges between 1,000 and 7,000 yen per month ($7.70 to $54), depending on the association.   Generally, the sum of the management expense and the reserve fund payment is proportionate to the relative size of the unit.

The main sources of income for the Management Associations are the management expense and the reserve fund payment made by each unit over each month.   Besides these sums, the association gains interest on rental income and other miscellaneous income.   All by itself, rental income comprises approximately 13 percent of an association's total income. A little more than 80 percent of that rental income comes from car park usage fees. The associations may also gain income when they collect special assessments for periodic large-scale repairs.

According to my research, which spans a 10-year period, when a third-party management company is contracted to manage a middle- or high-rise condominium, approximately 80 percent of the total management expense is divided evenly between maintenance expenses and contract costs (see Table 11.5, column 1). The management costs for common spaces can be broken down into expenses for water, electricity, and gas that are used for maintaining these areas (see Table 11.5, column 1). Unlike in some other countries, the quantity of water used by each unit is measured by a meter, and the cost is charged to each unit individually. Therefore the cost of water used by each household is not included in the monthly management expense.

The contract cost is the fee paid to the management contract company. Approximately two-thirds of this fee pays the on-site manager's wages, and the remaining money is split between office expenses and profits. The operational expense of the association breaks down into printing expenses and the cost of miscellaneous consumption goods used by the association. The composition of payments for self-managing condominiums is shown in Table 11.5, column 2.

Large-Scale Repairs and Long-Term Repair Plans

Among the tasks performed by the Management Association, maintenance of the buildings is very important. In particular, large-scale repairs performed every few years are of chief importance because the cost of major repairs is so high. Some typical large-scale repair projects are painting the steel handrails, repainting of external walls, waterproofing the roof, and upgrading the plumbing system.

These tasks must be performed in a timely manner because repairs made too early waste money, but repairs made too late allow unnecessary dilapidation to occur. Painting of the steel handrails should take place every three to four years, while repainting of external walls and waterproofing of the roof needs to be done about every 10 years. The frequency of these repairs is different in each condominium depending on the structure and construction materials used in the buildings.

In many condominiums, a long-term work plan for large-scale repairs is created by the Management Association or by their management con-

Table 11.5. *Composition of Payment of Management Expense of Association*

	(1) Contract Company Type High Rise Condominium	(2) Self Management Type Condominium
Operating cost for common elements	14.0%	32.3%
Taxes, Insurance	2.0%	3.7%
Association Management Cost	1.8%	7.5%
Maintenance Expense	38.7%	49.8%
Contract Cost	42.3%	0.0%
Expense for Community Life	1.0%	5.1%

Source: Kajiura Seminar, Osaka City University, "Study on Management Expense of High and Middle Rise Condominium," 1988, Modern Housing Research and Promotion Fund.

tract company. One reason for this plan is to roughly estimate both the time involved and the amount of money that will need to be spent. Another reason is that the cost of repairs is usually quite high, so money must be collected into the reserve fund beforehand. The details of the time-frame and the budget for these repairs is usually determined in a general meeting of the association. Also, since the work is performed while residents are living in their units, the cooperation of the unit owners is absolutely essential. To assure this cooperation, thorough discussion and clear decisions should take place in a general meeting of the association.

For large-scale repair work, the officers of the Management Association must be concerned with making sure that the proposed repairs are suitable, that they are accompanied within a reasonable budget, and that they are finished in a timely manner. Sometimes the owners are dissatisfied either because they chose a less expensive building contractor and got poor quality results, or because they chose an expensive company and still got poor results.

In an effort to prevent these kinds of repair-related problems from occurring for Management Associations, the federation of associations created a specialized agency to help them out. It is called the "Mansion Doctor," and it provides the associations with generalized plans for repairs as well as estimates for reasonable costs of the repairs. It is a nonprofit organization, and it assists the Management Association as a technical advisor. It performs inspections of buildings for both defects in the building and for structural soundness. It creates work plans for major repairs, and it inspects repair work once it has been completed. all of these services are paid for by the association.

RECENT PROBLEMS WITH CONDOMINIUM MANAGEMENT

During the last 20 years, the problems relating to condominium management have steadily increased. Countermeasures have been taken, but many of the problems remain. One of the most problematic situations has been caused by soaring land prices in major metropolitan areas. Unethical buying and selling practices by real estate dealers have increased drastically in the last decade, especially in Tokyo or other major cities. Certain traders buy up available units in a number of condominiums, and then proceed to make it difficult for other residents to continue living there. These traders use unscrupulous tactics to force the occupants to sell, and little by little, they gain possession of the entire condominium. In extreme cases, the traders may illegally cut off electricity and water, creating completely unlivable situations. Lawsuits often result from these cases but are rarely successful for the tenants.

Once the trader gains control of the condominium, he sells the site for a high price to persons who use the site for another purpose, such as building an office complex. This phenomenon is referred to as "jiage," which means when one person or organization attempts to buy out individual unit owners in the hope of gaining possession of the whole site. Another factor that enables this to happen so frequently is that zoning in Japanese town planning is very unclear, and there are many sites that can be used for either commercial or residential use.

When it becomes evident that someone is trying to force jiage on their condominium, owners generally react in one of two ways. They either resist the pressures to sell for as long as they can, or they give in immediately in order to prevent further troubles for themselves. The latter scenario occurs most often in the relatively small condominiums with few units. Those who try to stay in their units soon find themselves faced with growing management problems. For example, when the owner who was responsible for elevator maintenance moves out, there is no one left to take care of it or handle repairs. Furthermore, any sabotage or interference on the part of the illegal traders greatly exacerbates the situation. The overall living conditions in the condominium are bound to deteriorate, and those owners who want to keep their homes have no effective recourse.

A second major problem with condominium management is caused by the dramatic increase in the number of rented units. Occupants of condominiums can be divided up into three categories: resident owners, absentee owners, and renters. My research shows that in most of the condominiums where rental units make up at least 20 percent of the total residents, there is a growing trend for the absentee owners to neglect to attend the general meetings. This makes it difficult to hold these meetings and conduct the necessary business. Furthermore, many absentee owners purchase their units only as an investment and do not have an understanding of or sufficient interest in the activities of the Management Association.

The renting of condominium units occurs in two different forms referred to as encroachment renting and block renting. In the first form, the condominium was originally inhabited only by unit owners, but over a number of years the number of renters gradually increases. These renters are often family members or acquaintances of the unit owner, and therefore usually have some knowledge of condominium life and management issues for that building. In this case, successful communication between the renters and the other occupants is likely. Also, the number of renters increases gradually, allowing new renters sufficient time to become familiar with life in the condominium. Block renting, on the other hand, occurs when units remain unsold in a new building, and renting is the only profitable option for the developer. Many more problems occur with this form of renting because the tenants do not have an adequate understanding for management of the condominiums. Also, because renters feel they have no solid relationship with the Management Association, they often are not inclined to cooperate with it.

In recent years, there has been an increase in difficulties due to non-residential use of some condominium units. If the bylaws prohibit non-residential use, it usually does not become a problem. However, if the bylaws do not specifically prohibit nonresidential use, it is likely to occur. When it does, the quality of life in the condominium will certainly decline. In addition, unusual residential use is occurring more frequently. Examples of this are when owners keep the unit as a storage area, or as a second home, or when the unit is left empty for extended periods of time. Whenever the unit is used for purposes other than normal, everyday residential life, communication between these unit owners and the rest of the condominium community often becomes strained.

Some Solutions for Recent Problems

In Japanese cities, condominiums will certainly only increase in number as the years go on and will become the best housing option for a greater number of people. Therefore, the urban Japanese living in condominiums must develop a comfortable way of life and social customs to support quality living environments in this rapidly growing housing choice. In order to do this, unit owners must learn to cooperate for the sake of creating and preserving harmony in their community. This can be very difficult, however, as living in such close proximity with one another can cause many disputes.

In my opinion, certain efforts are necessary to solve the management problems of condominiums, and these efforts must come from developers, public organizations, real estate traders, unit owners, and occupants. Specifically, developers must consider not only the construction and sale of condominium units, but also the quality of life for the future occupants and owners. They must take potential management problems into consideration from the very start of the project. Also, public organizations must be responsible for affording protection to the consumer and for providing comfortable housing environments to the citizens. The central government and local public organizations must convey to developers and to management contract companies that they share the responsibility for providing occupants with a comfortable housing environment. However, at this time, local public organizations are not actively creating these kinds of policies.

Also, it is important that management contract companies be brought up to a standardized level of technology and common sense business practices. Furthermore, employees of these companies must be adequately trained. In Japan, most on-site managers are retired persons and have not received sufficient training regarding management tactics, the legal situation of condominiums, or how to operate building equipment for electricity or water. Thus, most on-site managers do not have enough knowledge, skill, or experience to manage a condominium property. The government should create an organization to train on-site managers and to promote a positive image of on-site managing as a valuable profession in society.

In the 1980s the federation of Management Associations was created and now includes every region of Japan. The activities of this federation revolve around solving management problems from the viewpoint of the unit owners. The federation is composed of only the member Management Associations, and their individual members, and does not include companies that they do business with. This makes the federation quite different from its American counterpart, the Community Association Institute. Basically, the federation meetings serve as a forum for exchanging experiences in condominium management, and it publishes a newsletter for those people who cannot personally attend the meetings. It also offers frequent seminars on pertinent management topics, and larger conferences to discuss any differences the individual associations or unit owners are experiencing. Finally, it offers regular training sessions for all new officers of the individual associations. All of these activities are performed by volunteers, and the federation is financed mainly by membership fees.

Management Strategies

There is much discussion about whether management by contract companies or self-management by unit owners is more effective. There are many problems that make condominium management difficult, such as disinterested or apathetic unit owners, numerous renters, or too many absentee owners. There is some question as to whether or not unit owners can form an association and manage the condominium effectively. Some people feel that unit owners will always be amateurs and that condominium management should be handled only by professionals. On the other hand, we must realize that management problems cannot be solved by professionals, without the active participation or support of the unit owners.

In my opinion, it is important that management business be left up to the professionals in most cases. However, I believe that participation of residents is necessary in condominiums occupied mostly by families. In Japan today, this description fits most condominium complexes and will fit most of those built in the future as well. My reasons for believing that cooperation between occupants and management companies is vital are listed below.

The first reason is that citizens must continue their direct involvement in their communities in order to create and maintain desirable living conditions, for the present and for the future. From now on, common spaces within residence communities will increase steadily. Management of common spaces must reflect the needs and wants of all the residents who use the spaces. The most important element of a community is the people who live there, and thus a positive living environment is possible only with their active participation in self-government.

The second reason is that misunderstandings between unit managers and management companies happen all too easily, and the damage caused by these difficulties is immeasurable. Theoretically, occupants should be responsible for managing the condominium themselves; however, they often lack the time, the knowledge, or the technology to effectively perform the necessary tasks. Therefore, it is more practical and economical to leave the business of management to professionals. Yet the professionals must manage the condominium with the owners' particular needs in mind. As owners pay for this service, they tend to become more and more demanding without much consideration for the specialists they have hired.

This happens especially when the owners have little understanding for the practical difficulties involved in managing their condominium. Sometimes they ask the professional manager to solve problems that can really only be solved by the efforts of the owners themselves. The professional managers often become angry but do not express their dissatisfaction for fear of losing their jobs. However, their bad feelings towards the owners are apparent in the quality of work they do and sometimes the unfair amounts they charge for their services.

To improve current situations, occupants must take responsibility for some management duties, even if the burden seems extreme. In some cases, they should take responsibility for aspects of community life without asking for third-party assistance. If another occupant is using their parking space, or if a neighbor is habitually too loud, the occupant should handle it himself. Although the manager, or a third party, is often useful as an intermediator, independent action on the part of the occupant is most important.   Yet occupants typically will not understand the necessity or effectiveness of independent action if they have not had previous experience in dealing with management issues.   Owners who have been an officer in the Management Association, or who have actively participated in general meetings, are more likely to pursue independent solutions. Furthermore, because of this experience, they are less likely to cause problems for their condominium community.

Occupant participation in the association should theoretically take on two forms, both in the decision-making processes and in following through with the results of those decisions.   By attending the general meetings and taking the opportunity to express their opinions and exercise their votes, the unit owners satisfy the first part of their obligation.   The second part is satisfied only when they fulfill their responsibility for handling any assigned management tasks, or by voluntarily working at things that are not assigned but would benefit their community.   Some examples of this could be assisting in annual cleaning projects, or organizing social events for all the occupants, or contributing to the association newsletter.   Mostly, it is vital that occupants continuously give some of their own time and efforts to the management of their condominium.

It may be too much to expect all owners to participate that actively, but it is not too much for every unit owner and renter to at least be aware of and concerned about the current management issues in their condominium.   If they miss a general meeting, they should find out what issues were discussed and what decisions were reached.   Some people, such as the young and single, are perhaps better off living in condominiums where an outside management company handles most of the management tasks.   This is because their interest level and commitment to a community may be relatively low.   Other people, such as families with children, are better suited for life in self-managing condominiums as they are generally more involved in condominium community life.   These self-managing condominiums do not require that the unit owners become extensively involved in management tasks, rather that they are willing and able to participate in management and that they maintain a self-governing attitude.   It is best, therefore, that condominiums clearly offer either self-management or third-party management so that potential occupants can choose a living environment that best suits their lifestyles.

12

Condominium Regulation and Urban Renewal in Dutch Cities

Jan van Weesep

INTRODUCTION

Horizontal property titles (condominiums) have existed in Europe for centuries. During the Napoleonic conquests, the "Code Civil" established the legal foundation for the condominium in all countries under French control. As common ownership forms became more widespread, further regulation and standardization of title descriptions proved to be necessary to facilitate sales, mortgaging, insurance, and so on. During the Great Depression of the 1930s, certain drawbacks of the limited legal arrangements in the Civil Codes surfaced with a vengeance; particularly that the default of some owners could cause problems for all others in a complex.

Such problems can be prevented if the legal arrangements are more specific and sufficiently uniform (Van Weesep and Maas 1984). Therefore, many European countries adopted Horizontal Property Acts, including Belgium (1924), Italy (1934), France (1938), Germany (1951), and the Netherlands (1951). In the United States, the National Housing Act of 1963 prompted many states to adopt similar legislation (Van Weesep 1987a). Although these acts differ in many details, the general definitions of condominium are very similar; they always distinguish between ownership of separate parts and joint ownership of common elements.

In the Netherlands, where forms of common ownership have existed since the seventeenth century, condominiums did not become an important form of real property until the 1950s. Even then, new construction of complexes remained a relatively minor factor in the growth of the condominium housing sector. Instead, there was extensive conversion of existing property, especially in the big cities. By 1988, more than 25,000 condominium units in Amsterdam accounted for almost eight percent of the total housing stock. In Rotterdam, 57,000 condominium units made up 21 percent of the housing stock. In The Hague more than 90,000 condominium units were registered, accounting for almost 50 percent of the housing stock.

Other European countries experienced a similar increase in condominium conversions during the 1970s and 1980s (Hamnett and Randolph 1981), sparking off a passionate debate. In some countries, national governments or local administrations attempted to stem the tide because the conversions were perceived as a threat to housing policies intended to protect tenants (Van Weesep 1984). Other issues were also raised. In the United States, the development of new condominiums initially led to serious complaints regarding developer abuses such as approval of high-cost, long-term leases for recreational facilities between the developer and the condominium association during the initial period in which the developer controlled the association (HUD 1975). Later the displacement of the poor because of conversions emerged in the U.S. as a major issue (Lauber 1980; HUD 1980). In Britain, the main problem was the tense relationship between the buyers of "long leases" and the converters who, although being in the business for short-term profits, must retain long-term responsibility for management under British law (Hamnett and Randolph 1988). In the Netherlands, the poor functioning of the homeowner associations was identified as a problem, in addition to the general negative impact of the conversions on the housing opportunities of low-income groups (Van Weesep 1987b).

Conflicts between condominium associations as private legal entities with their own strategies and goals and the policy aims of public authorities are clearly at the heart of many issues. In order to control such conflicts, conversion restrictions have been enacted in many places. This has also been the case in the Netherlands. But the forces that drive the conversion are not easily neutralized, especially where the alternative is disinvestment and abandonment of derelict housing (Hamnett and Randolph 1988). This leads to the question of the role of the condominium in the context of urban renewal strategies: Does the presence of a large number of condominiums necessarily threaten the completion of urban renewal plans? Or are there ways in which condominium conversion can be used to help the improvement of the existing stock and the regeneration of older urban areas?

These questions form the core of the present discussion of the role of condominium conversion in the Netherlands. First, a brief overview is presented of existing legislation, especially with respect to conversion controls. Subsequently, some of the characteristics of the condominium stock in the Netherlands are sketched. This is followed by an outline of the major dimensions of Dutch urban renewal efforts. This includes a summary of the functioning of condominium associations with respect to maintenance and improvements, before turning to the discussion of the attitudes and strategies of public authorities with respect to condominium conversions in urban renewal areas.

CONDOMINIUM LEGISLATION IN THE NETHERLANDS

The Dutch Condominium Act of 1951 was a very limited law: it only prescribed the procedures to subdivide properties and defined the rights and obligations of the owners of condominium units. When the law was amended in 1972, some of the more pressing issues were addressed. This law finally required the establishment of a condominium association to promote the interests of the unit owners and to take on the responsibilities for the common elements. But a condominium is not nullified if the master deed fails to set up an association. At present, many condominium complexes are still without a formal association. In addition, in many smaller complexes the associations often do not function according to the letter of the law. This can have severe repercussions for maintenance and improvements as we shall see below, and in general, it can make the condominium unresponsive to public policy initiatives.

The rapid increase in the number of conversions that began at the end of the 1960s caused a prolonged discussion of the need for, and the ways through which the conversions could be controlled. The authorities foresaw that the buyers of units in the older parts of the cities would experience financial hardships because of high maintenance costs. In addition, they feared that their urban renewal efforts would be undercut by the resulting rapid degradation of the housing stock.

Eventually in 1975, the Housing Act was amended to allow municipal conversion controls. Once the municipality established such controls, a conversion permit was required before an existing building could be converted into a condominium. Local administrations could request restrictive powers but could only stop conversion on three grounds: they can withhold the permit if inspectors find violations of the building code, if the units are not fully equipped as independent dwellings, or if the building is situated in a declared urban renewal area. The restrictions could only be applied to properties built before 1945. Later, in 1986, the expected negative impact on housing policy was added as a ground to stop an intended conversion.

Fifteen cities were granted such powers; one of these is a small town with a negligible number of condominiums. This study is therefore limited to the 14 others (cf. Table 12.1). They include the four largest cities of the Netherlands (Amsterdam, The Hague, Rotterdam, and Utrecht), some of their older suburban towns (Rijswijk, Schiedam, Vlaardingen, Voorburg), some medium-sized cities in the urbanized western part of the country (Delft, Dordrecht, Leiden), and similar cities elsewhere in the country (Groningen, Nijmegen, Zwolle). The conclusions of the analysis are therefore not representative for all cities since it must be assumed that the composition of the housing stock in the 14 cities is different and that the housing issues they face are also not the same as elsewhere. If other cities had a similarly large condominium sector and similar housing problems, they would presumably also have applied for powers to curb further conversions.

CONDOMINIUMS IN DUTCH CITIES

The Condominium Sector in General

After the adoption of the Condominium Act in 1951, it took several years before the condominiums accounted for a significant share of the housing stock in the Netherlands. Cooperatives enjoyed a more advantageous tax treatment, and initially the banks proved to be reluctant to provide mortgage financing for condominiums (Beekhuis 1973). But by the end of the 1960s, the conversion of rental housing had become an established practice. They are now found throughout the Netherlands, albeit not evenly distributed. There is a clear concentration in the highly urbanized western part of the country, since they correspond closely to the distribution of the private rental sector. Also, the proportion of multi-family structures and the age of buildings are positively correlated to the prevalence of condominiums (Van Weesep et al. 1988). The big cities and some medium-sized cities have been the main stage for the conversion process because of the characteristics of their housing stock (Hoek-veld 1987).

Many properties converted to condominiums do not currently function as such, because for various reasons the sale of the units lags behind the title conversions. The (immediate) sale of the condominium units is not always the motive for the conversion. Frequently, large rental complexes are subdivided into separate management entities, for instance when they contain commercial premises and dwellings. Many institutional investors routinely convert the title of a rental complex into a condominium regime, to safeguard the eventual sale of units at the end of their operating period. But even if the direct sale of the units is intended, the actual transactions have to wait until the sitting tenants vacate the property, since they cannot be evicted upon the consummation of a sale. Yet the sales have gradually expanded the number of individually owned condominiums. Between 1978 and 1985, at least 140,000 condominium units were sold for direct occupancy (Van Weesep et al. 1988). With 640,000 single-family homes sold during the same period, condominiums increased the number of ownership homes on the market by one fifth.

The condominiums cover a wide range of physical housing types. Many consist of single, older buildings subdivided into a very small number of individually owned units. There are large new complexes consisting of hundreds of individually owned properties. There are also large older complexes, established when a landlord converted an entire block of rental property previously owned through one single deed. Of all the associations registered as nonprofit entities with the chambers of commerce, 14 percent consisted of two to four units and 12 percent of more than 50. The remainder covered the range between these extremes (Van Weesep et al. 1988). In the largest cities, the proportion of smaller complexes is higher than elsewhere.

The condominium sector is very diverse by price, as well. Exact prices are not meaningful since the value is recorded at the moment of sale, and increases since then render comparisons meaningless. But the sales price statistics make clear that from 60 to 80 percent of the condominiums are found in the inexpensive to moderate price range.

Finally, the housing market position of the buyers serves to differentiate the condominium sector. In this respect, there is a strong correlation with the price of the units. Various case studies in the big cities have shown that there are two broad categories. On the one hand, the condominium conversion has provided home ownership opportunities for high-income households. This was badly needed, since the (social) rental sector dominates the housing stock of the big cities, forcing many affluent people to move out to the suburbs. On the other hand, the many inexpensive condominiums provided direct access to housing for households with a low priority ranking on the waiting lists for rental housing. For them, the acquisition of a condominium is a negative choice, and this part of the condominium sector is thereby marginalized (Van Weesep 1984).

The Situation in the 14 Cities

The size of the condominium sector in the 14 cities ranges from significant to very large. In the municipalities of The Hague metropolitan region, the condominium sector covers close to 50 percent of the total housing stock (Table 12.1). In several cities of the Rotterdam agglomeration (Rotterdam, Schiedam, Vlaardingen) approximately a quarter of the housing stock consists of condominiums. In other cities like Groningen and Utrecht a similar share was registered. Lower percentages were encountered predominantly in smaller cities, but also in Amsterdam. In the latter city, the authorities have systematically discouraged the conversion process.

The Position of Condominiums in the Local Housing Market

The development of the condominium sector in the big cities largely dates back to the period before the introduction of conversion controls. The decrease of the number of conversions during the second half of the 1970s seems to be related to the fact that by then the most suitable properties were already converted, and also to a general decline in demand for owner-occupier housing after a sharp fall in prices in 1978. Conversion only continued in Amsterdam with its relatively small condominium sector. Here, most of the latest conversions are concentrated in the oldest parts of the city, where gentrification is occuring (Musterd and Van der Ven 1991). The decline has also been noted in the medium-sized cities, where the number of permit applications decreased to several dozen annually, almost all for small complexes (Dijkhuis-Potgieser 1985). New condominium complexes are still being built, but many are first used as rental housing.

The condominium sector in the 14 cities varies in structure. In Amsterdam, Rotterdam, and The Hague, the condominiums are concentrated in the older parts of the cities (cf., Table 12.1). In Amsterdam, Delft, Groningen, and Zwolle, there is a clear concentration in the historic core. In the medium-sized cities more than two-thirds of the condomin-

Table 12.1.   *The Number of Condominium Units in the 14*
Municipalities by Age of the Neighborhood
(percentages)

	< 1914	AGE 1914-1940	> 1940	N (=100%)	% of local housing stock
Amsterdam	53.9	24.3	21.7	25,485	7.8
Delft	13.0	24.8	62.2	5,411	14.8
Dordrecht	24.0	7.9	68.1	5,384	12.4
The Hague	37.8	43.3	18.9	92,126	47.3
Groningen	22.1	28.9	49.0	15,745	22.2
Leiden	32.9	8.4	58.5	6,285	15.4
Nijmegen	40.3	6.2	53.4	5,436	9.7
Rotterdam	20.2	45.8	34.1	56,766	21.3
Rijswijk	*	12.1	87.9	10,828	51.1
Schiedam	10.5	37.5	52.0	6,686	31.4
Utrecht	39.0	15.2	45.8	19,567	21.7
Vlaardingen	11.5	19.7	68.7	7,193	23.6
Voorburg	*	31.7	68.3	9,183	51.9
Zwolle	18.6	13.7	67.7	2,023	5.9

* included in 1914-1940 neighborhoods
Source: Land Register.

iums are found in the postwar areas, with the exception of Groningen and
Nijmegen. Still, the condominiums are only a minor fraction of the postwar housing stock. Some complexes were newly constructed, others are
converted rental complexes or cooperatives. Many of the new condominium complexes are still used as rental properties by institutional investors.
These differences are also reflected in the price levels of the condominiums. In the medium-sized cities, most condominiums are moderately
priced. In the big cities, however, the condominium sector is much more
polarized between expensive and very cheap units. The latter ones are
especially found in the urban renewal areas (Table 12.2).

Table 12.2.   *The Number of Condominium Complexes and the Number of Units in Urban Renewal Areas (percentages of total prewar condominium stock*)*

	Complexes	Units	Prewar condominium stock (N = 100%)	
	%	%	Complexes	Units.
Amsterdam	34.9	33.6	3,113	19,944
Delft	62.0	88.4	527	2,046
Dordrecht	49.1	65.3	216	1,717
The Hague	27.0	24.1	16,874	74,706
Groningen	97.8	104.6	2,286	8,032
Leiden	84.0	72.7	476	2,595
Nijmegen	66.9	89.1	287	2,534
Rotterdam	68.9	69.7	5,588	37,437
Rijswijk	100.0	100.0	328	1,311
Schiedam	66.1	57.2	613	3,212
Utrecht	95.7	93.4	2,980	10,604
Vlaardingen	110.0	136.8	309	2,250
Voorburg	100.0	100.0	736	2,914
Zwolle	137.8	54.6	37	1,197

*Where urban renewal areas are broadly defined, they may contain large tracts of postwar housing; shares may then be larger than 100 percent.
Source: Land Register.

Condominiums in Urban Renewal Areas

Given the large number of condominiums in urban renewal areas, where they can account for a significant proportion of the total housing stock, the way the condominium sector is dealt with is important for the urban renewal strategies of the municipalities under investigation. The introduction of conversion controls was partly motivated by the fear that the condominiums might impair the urban renewal programs of the cities. The large number of owner-occupiers would make the coordination of urban renewal more difficult since it multiplied the number of actors. To substantiate whether or not this fear was realistic, I shall first turn to the description of the urban renewal strategies and the record of the condominium associations.

URBAN RENEWAL STRATEGIES

Development of the Urban Renewal Model

Urban renewal, in the sense of a government-sponsored large scale renewal of existing urban areas, became a characteristic process in Dutch cities from the late 1960s. By that time, the postwar housing shortage was quickly being resolved and more attention was devoted to the improvement of dilapidated residential areas. Until then, there had not been an urban renewal policy; instead, there were slum clearance projects and public works to make room for central city functions, infrastructure, and other improvements (Van den Ham and Stouten 1988).

By the late 1960s, public-sector initiatives towards urban renewal changed. Entire neighborhoods were being tackled because of their poor quality as residential environments. This process was politicized when the population of the older neighborhoods resisted the large-scale demolition plans and objected to the resulting changes in the urban structure (De Kleijn 1986). No longer could the process of renewal be handled entirely by engineers and planners.

In the early 1970s, after a prolonged and often bitter political struggle, it became widely accepted that urban renewal had to serve the interests of the inhabitants of the neighborhoods where the activities took place; this became know as the "redevelopment for the locals" principle. Since then, the local population has come to play an important role in the process. Consequently, urban renewal became defined as a social process, a comprehensive approach to the renewal of communities, rather than focused on the renewal of buildings and infrastructure (Van den Ham and Stouten 1988).

As the renewal of the oldest, worst neighborhoods neared its completion, areas of more recent vintage became the predominant location of the urban renewal activities. Since the housing quality in these areas was better than in the older ones, renovation became the obvious strategy; this strategy can serve the goal of improving the housing stock for the benefit of the sitting tenants. At the same time, this implied that private landlords and homeowners had to become involved in the process, since it was not feasible to condemn their properties and demolish them. The outcome became increasingly defined by the result of negotiations among the owners and city officials.

Private Renovations and Improvements

The 1985 Urban and Village Renewal Act changed the rules of the urban renewal process (Yap 1985). The act is an expression of the ongoing decentralization process in the housing system, which entails the transfer of responsibilities from the central government to local authorities. The most important result of this for urban renewal was the abolition of some 20 subsidy programs through which the municipalities received special grants for such purposes as the purchase of private properties for demolition, for aid to private homeowners, etc. Instead, these special programs were combined into one single fund from which the cities receive a "block grant." The block grant must be spent on urban renewal, but the local authorities determine their own approach.

Urban renewal programs had neglected the approach of encouraging private landlords and homeowners to renovate and improve their properties. It was easier for the cities to concentrate on dilapidated areas where the properties could be purchased under the threat of condemnation and where large tracts could be amassed. Negotiations with individual owners about improvements took a great deal of time and demanded a highly tailored approach. But most of all, the approach to urban renewal through teams of municipal experts and residents did not allow for great flexibility in the negotiations over renovations with private parties.

When the condemnation approach could no longer be taken, the properties would either have to be purchased at market prices, or the stimulation of private renovations would have to be taken seriously. Large-scale purchase of properties proved to be too expensive. The acquisition of the property of homeowners especially had to be avoided, because the level of compensation would quickly deplete the urban renewal budgets. In rental property, given the widespread system of rent control, in many instances the most urgent question was what could be done to entice landlords to make investments if these could not be earned back through rent increases. Extra rent increases are only allowed if the quality of the property is significantly increased; this is, however, not the case when code violations are amended or other (expensive) maintenance is carried out. In order to bring owners to participate in renovation schemes a balanced approach of subsidies and building inspections for code violations was developed (Van den Ham and Stouten 1988).

The stimulation of private renovations is increasingly being incorporated in the overall strategy. This is reflected in the proportion of the total urban renewal budget that is allocated for improvement subsidies to private owners (Table 12.3). The differences among the 14 municipalities in our study are very large: from 1.3 percent of the total budget in the industrial city of Dordrecht to 100 percent in Rijswijk, a relatively wealthy suburban community of The Hague. Eight of the 15 municipalities spent over 7.5 percent on subsidies for private owners, and the cities that have made subsidies available to homeowners since 1970 are all represented among the top half of the municipalities. The recent decision reached by Voorburg and Rijswijk, and later by The Hague, to include such a subsidy program in the urban renewal strategy was inspired by their growing awareness of the size of their condominium sector.

The municipalities subsidize structural improvements rather than amenities that raise housing quality. It is generally assumed that the quality is improved anyway, if not by the owner then by the tenant. Various investigations among homeowners showed that most efforts are directed at the upgrading of amenities. By means of the subsidy program, various municipalities try to stimulate collective improvements; do-it-yourself was sometimes cause for deductions, and six municipalities limit the availability of subsidy to specified areas (Table 12.4). The investigations also showed that three cities required the subsidy to be (partly) repaid if the owner sold the dwelling within a period of five to 10 years, to avoid speculation. Amsterdam and Rotterdam make the subsidies available only to persons with a low or moderate income, while The Hague and Schiedam have chosen to make part of the subsidy available in the form of subsidized loans. Other experiments to stimulate concerted private renewal activities are being tested, such as (free) technical advice and assistance, and intensive inspections for code violations.

The Functioning of Condominium Associations

The condominium associations are responsible for maintenance and improvements of the common elements. As buildings age, more effort is required to keep them in good condition. Therefore the condominiums in the older areas of the cities demand more attention than those in the postwar areas. A series of case studies of condominium complexes in neighborhoods across the 14 cities has shown, however, that the buildings in the older areas are not given more care than the newer ones (Van

Table 12.3.   *Subsidies for Private Renovations and the Size of the Total Municipal Urban Renewal Budget, 1986 (thousands of guilders)*

	Amount available for private renovations	Total urban renewal budget	Share of subsidies for homeowners
Amsterdam	3,375	179,220	1.9%
Delft	1,265	13,863	9.1%
Dordrecht*	171	12,906	1.3%
The Hague	7,000	76,070	9.2%
Groningen	1,724	20,000	8.6%
Leiden	1,000	11,160	10.7%
Nijmegen*	1,675	8,034	20.9%
Rijswijk*	695	695	100.0%
Rotterdam	3,000	114,524	2.1%
Schiedam	800	16,608	4.8%
Utrecht	4,315	31,666	13.6%
Vlaardingen*	438	6,153	7.1%
Voorburg	300	1,648	18.2%
Zwolle*	652	4,903	13.3%

*Data for 1985.

Weesep 1986). Some owners declared that no work was necessary, but many reported that conflicts among owners and/or the lack of money was the reason that necessary work did not take place. Expenditures for work on the common elements (per owner) are much lower than the average cost of work on the individual units. Rarely are financial provisions made for necessary repairs. When work must be carried out, special assessments are common practice, and this hampers rational decision making in cases where social relations among the unit owners are not good. In several instances, owners reported having paid for urgent repairs of "their" common elements, without being able to collect from the others.

The studies demonstrate that the larger homogeneous complexes with formally run associations promote good maintenance. The same is true

Table 12.4. *Clauses of Municipal Subsidy Programs for Renovations by Homeowners*

	Collective action	Discount do-it-yourself	Delimited area	Anti-specu-lation	Income limita-tions	Credit program
Amsterdam	-	55 %	+	+	+	-
Delft	-	?	-	-	-	-
Dordrecht	-	?	-	-	-	-
The Hague	+	+	+	-	-	+
Groningen	+	?	-	-	-	-
Leiden	-	+	-	-	-	-
Nijmegen	+	50 %	+	+	-	-
Rotterdam	+	+	+	+	+	-
Rijswijk	+	+	-	-	-	-
Schiedam	+	+	+	-	-	+
Utrecht	-	55 %	+	-	-	-
Vlaardingen	-	?	-	-	-	-
Voorburg	+	+	-	-	-	-
Zwolle	-	60 %	-	-	-	-

- = not applicable or special requirements
+ = specified in the subsidy program
? = unknown

of the very informally run small associations, where the social relations among the owner-occupiers are good. But when the unit owners in the same complex differ in opinion about the necessity of work on the common elements, the most urgent problems may be taken care of, but in general, less work gets done. In fact, the way management decisions are arrived at can aggravate existing tensions among the unit owners. Differences of opinion on the need for work on the common elements were recorded between owner-occupiers and absentee owners, but also among resident owners. A well-functioning condominium association could help resolve such problems, but these are relatively rare. Especially at the lower end of the market, where the condominium complexes in urban renewal areas concentrate, tensions seem to rise over the issue of deferred maintenance. Few owner-occupiers were aware of their rights and obligations, and even fewer had attempted to use the legal instrument of the association bylaws to take care of necessary maintenance and repair work (Van Weesep et al. 1988).

In general, the increase of condominiums in an area does not automatically lead to improvements of the housing quality. Even though homeowners may be less sensitive to the economic aspects of investment in repairs and improvements, there are other bottlenecks. The often sluggish decision making within the condominium associations is a major obstacle, and this tends to slow the process of urban renewal. This has instilled a sense of urgency among the responsible officials, which makes them look for creative solutions, including, paradoxically, the promotion of condominium conversion on specific terms.

CONDOMINIUM CONVERSION TO THE RESCUE?

A critical gap in urban renewal programs has been adequate funding for rehabilitation subsidies. Here condominium conversion offers an opportunity to local authorities.

The common approach to urban renewal is to deal with single blocks at a time, which provides much more flexibility than when large tracts of land were consolidated in renewal projects. But flexibility does not guarantee success. Success also depends on the costs of the renovations for the owners. These costs are the most important bottleneck, and it determines to a large extent the speed of implementation of the process. Most inhabitants of the urban renewal areas—including the condominium unit owners—belong to low-income groups, and expensive proposals are generally rejected. The renovations, therefore, have to remain rather limited; in general, the total costs should remain below 30,000 to 40,000 guilders per unit. (In 1994 one U.S. dollar stood at just below two guilders.) After taking the subsidies into account, the owners still have to contribute from 10,000 to 20,000 guilders. Even such relatively small amounts can generally only be secured if the municipality sets up a loan (guarantee) program. If financial instruments are not available, the implementation has to be phased over a long period. In some cities, government agencies have helped to set up condominium associations, and in Utrecht a local government agency has purchased condominium units in various complexes in order to participate in the decision making about maintenance and improvements of the owners.

The financial bottlenecks impeding the renovation of rental housing led some municipalities to use the condominium conversion controls to generate funds to stimulate renewal. The value of a rental property is derived from the annual yield, which is generally much below the vacant possession value, the price a homeowner is willing to pay. This price is related to household income and to financing costs (Boddy 1980). Because of tax relief and favorable long-term financing conditions, an owner-occupier can afford to pay a higher price than a landlord, even one who intends to rent to a tenant with the same income as the potential owner (Nevitt 1966). In order to maximize capital gains, the owner of a multifamily property must convert it to condominiums. Since the time that the conversion permit has been required, the city holds the key to the profit potential of the conversions. This power implies that the conversion permit can become an element in the negotiations in the urban renewal process.

The owner of a rental property is offered a conversion permit, which guarantees a windfall profit; but to "earn" the permit, the owner has to invest a substantial part of the profits in the renovation of other local rental properties. With the help of the subsidy program, the renovation of the rental housing can then take place. The strategy becomes even more pervasive when the building inspector cannot only dangle the carrot of the permit and subsidy, but can also wield the stick of citations for code violations.

The strategy can help to improve the remaining rental stock, and the buildings to be converted benefit as well. The permit process requires that existing code violations in the converted housing be corrected before conversion takes place. Further improvements may be added by the new owners, and in some cities the new homeowners qualify for financial assistance. At least for the time being, the housing stock benefits from another round of investments. In the long run, however, upkeep is subject to the logic of the management of older rental property and the investment strategies of the homeowners in condominium units. (Few units are likely to be retained by the converting landlords, who are looking for capital gains, and few condominium units are bought by investors rather than owner-occupiers.) Since the financial position of the unit owners or lack of activity of the owners' associations are not conditions that are conducive to good maintenance practices over the long run, the conversion strategy, like any limited renovation program, will provide only temporary relief.

However effective such a "flexible" approach may be in bringing about (temporary) quality improvements in the older housing stock, the irony is that an instrument that was primarily designed to bring the conversion process under control happens to be effective for the improvement of the quality of the older existing stock, but only by actively promoting conversion!

CONCLUSIONS

From shortly after World War II, the growth of the condominium sector proceeded rapidly in the Netherlands. As the drawbacks became clear, the authorities responded with legislation. First, the procedures were standardized in the Condominium Act of 1951 to strengthen the position of the unit owners. Then in 1971, the management problems were addressed by requiring the foundation of a condominium association to take responsibility for the common elements and to provide a vehicle for the regulation of the relationships among the unit owners. When the negative effects of the conversions of older, dilapidated apartments for low-income buyers became apparent, the establishment of condominium regimes in older buildings was subjected to a permit requirement. This implied rigorous inspections by public officials of the quality of the buildings and their suitability for use as self-contained units.

At the same time, the problems caused by the condominium conversions for housing and urban renewal policies were addressed. Once it was clear that condominium owners were not able to maintain and improve their buildings in certain areas—because of their low incomes, or because of poorly functioning condominium associations— the authorities tried to stop conversions in designated urban renewal areas. The multiplication of owner-occupiers hindered the traditional approach to urban renewal—the acquisition of all the buildings in an area for demolition or renovation. The projected cost of this was far beyond the scope of the budgets earmarked for the programs. The wholesale conversion of buildings in urban renewal areas also introduced special interest groups in the area, which made the negotiations about the urban renewal strategies and goals more complex. Consequently the attitude of the authorities towards condominium conversion tended to become hostile, and their strategy was to stop the process, or at least to limit it as much as possible. This has been most clearly the case in Amsterdam, where the housing policy has been most strongly in support of social rental housing provision for the lowest income groups. The urban renewal model employed since the beginning of the 1970s is very much an expression of this.

Two contextual developments have changed the attitudes and strategies of the authorities since the early 1980s. As the negative effects of the concentration of low-income groups in the cities became clear, the housing authorities diminished their emphasis on social housing. They recognized that they needed to allow the middle- and higher-income groups to find housing in the cities to balance the population structure. Thus their negative opinion of the provision of owner-occupier hous- ing—and of more expensive housing in general—was softened. Condominiums were more welcome, since high-density residential development was often the only feasible option. Even in Amsterdam, condominium conversion is now accepted in various parts of the city.

The second development followed from the change in urban renewal strategies. As the accent shifted from demolition and new construction to renovations of existing buildings, private owners needed to be mobilized to support the urban renewal efforts. No longer could the cities afford to purchase the properties in urban renewal areas and to fund the intervention from public budgets. But given the various housing regulations, including rent control, it is difficult to entice private owners to invest in major repairs and improvements. Since direct subsidies are not large enough to compensate the owners for such uneconomical investments, some cities have discovered how they can entice them to make improvements in at least part of their rental properties. The funding mechanism is the windfall profit they can make by converting some of their holdings to condominiums. On the condition that they use part of the profits for investment in the remaining rental properties, the landlords receive the coveted conversion permits.

It is somewhat of a paradox that the mechanisms designed to limit the conversion of rental housing to condominiums, which ran counter to the goals of public housing policy, are now being used to bring the private owners in line with public policy. The public sector and the private sector have finally discovered some common ground with regard to condominium conversion in the Netherlands.

REFERENCES

Beekhuis, J. H. 1973. *Het appartementenrecht.* Deventer: Kluwer.

Boddy, M. 1980. *The Building Societies.* London: MacMillan.

De Kleijn, G. 1986. "The State of Urban Renewal." *The Netherlands Journal of Housing and Environmental Research* 1: 235-52.

Dijkhuis-Potgieser, H. I. E. 1985. *Ontwikkelingen op de woningmarkt 1985.* Gravenhage: Ministerie V.R.O.M.

Hamnett, C., and W. Randolph. 1981. "Flat Break-Ups." *Roof 1981* (May/June): 18-19, 24.

_____. 1988. *Cities, Housing and Profits: Flat Break-Up and the Decline of Private Renting.* London: Hutchinson.

Hoekveld, G. A. 1987. *Development of Post-War Built Residential Areas and the Functioning of Local Housing Markets in the Netherlands.* Steprorapport 69a. Utrecht: Geografisch Instituut.

HUD (U.S. Department of Housing and Urban Development). 1975. *HUD Condominium Cooperative Study.* Vol. 1, National Evaluation. Washington, D.C.: U.S. Government Printing Office.

_____. 1980. *The Conversion of Rental Housing to Condominiums and Cooperatives. A National Study of the Scope, Causes and Impacts.* Washington, D.C.: U.S. Department of HUD.

Lauber, D. 1980. "Condominium Conversions: The Number Prompts Controls to Protect the Poor and the Elderly." *Journal of Housing* 36: 201-09.

Musterd, S., and J. van der Ven. 1991. "Gentrification and Residential Revitalization in Amsterdam." In *Urban Housing for the Better-Off: Gentrification in Europe,* ed. J. van Weesep and S. Musterd. Utrecht: Stedelijke Netwerken.

Nevitt, A. 1966. *Housing, Taxation, and Subsidies, a Study of Housing in the United Kingdom.* London: Nelson.

Van den Ham, C., and P. Stouten. 1988. "Urban Renewal in Rotterdam: Changing Conditions and Perspectives." *The Netherlands Journal of Housing and Environmental Research* 3: 241-58.

Van Weesep, J. 1984. "Intervention in the Netherlands: Urban Housing Policy and Market Response." *Urban Affairs Quarterly* 19: 329-53.

_____. 1986. *Condominium: A New Housing Sector in the Netherlands.* Utrecht: Geografisch Instituut.

_____. 1987a. "The Creation of a New Housing Sector: Condominiums in the United States." *Housing Studies* 2: 122-33.

_____. 1987b. "Coping with the Condominium in the Netherlands." In *Housing and Neighborhoods, Theoretical and Empirical Contributions*, ed. W. van Vliet-, H. Choldin, W. Michelson, and D. Popenoe. Westport, Conn.: Greenwood.

_____, and M. W. A. Maas. 1984. "Housing Policy and Conversion to Condominiums in the Netherlands." *Environment and Planning A*, 16: 1149-61.

_____, K. J. v. G. Nielsen, S. Reith, and M. Wiegersma. 1988. "Appartementsrechten, het Gebruik van het Splitsingsregime." *Nederlandse Geografische Studies* 65. Amsterdam/Utrecht: K.N.A.G. /Geografisch Instituut.

Yap, H. S. 1985. "The New Urban and Village Renewal Act." *Tijdschrift voor Economische en Sociale Geografie* 76: 63-66.

VI. Conclusion

13

Public Life and Private Property in the Urban Community

Stephen E. Barton
Carol J. Silverman

PUBLIC AND PRIVATE LIFE

We tend, in the United States, to overlook social institutions and focus on physical structures or emotional states. The Garden City idea of Ebenezer Howard, for example, presented both a design for new cities and a call for public ownership of the land. But even after the work of the radical Regional Planning Association of America, the Garden City legacy in the United States was suburban Radburn and such ideas as superblocks that separate children's play areas from traffic.

Condominiums and planned developments are similarly thought of as physical structures or as "communities" by virtue of the mere fact that the residents are neighbors. Left opaque are their challenges to traditional notions of property ownership and intricate combinations of legal rights and obligations among co-owners. As we have seen, the resulting institutional structure of the common interest development generates a complex political and social life in which its residents participate, however unknowingly or unwillingly. The research on these developments suggests important lessons for our understanding of the institutions of government and private property and the relations between private and public life in modern societies. The research also points to social and political tensions that will continue to grow along with the number of homes in common interest developments.

We have argued that private life is the domain of deep personal emotional ties and, beyond that, of personal control and freedom from unchosen others. Private property ownership is commonly understood to create a legal wall, sheltering private life and freeing owners to act on their individual choices. When private property is collectively owned, however, the owners must jointly decide on its use and are interdependent, at least as far as that property is concerned.

Public life, we have argued, is the domain of interaction among members of a public, interdependent people who did not choose that association with each other and who must nonetheless cooperate and make decisions about things they may not agree on. Public life exists wherever involuntary interdependence exists, although it may be partially suppressed by some authoritarian force.

The necessity of public life is nowhere more evident than in the urban setting. There are those who have argued that there is nothing distinctive about the city—that it is simply a denser location for class conflict or market relations or a collection of urban villages. But there is a long line of thought, from Tönnies and Simmel on to the more recent work of the Loflands and Fischer that finds a distinctive quality to urban life—the pervasive presence of strangers. The presence of strangers makes distinctively visible the public nature of much of urban life. These strangers are not just people who are passing through, such as visitors or traders. They are fellow citizens, coworkers, and neighbors with whom we must share space and with whom we are necessarily interdependent in our joint use of shared space. They are strangers in that we do not know them personally. They are not part of our private life.

Normally the residential neighborhood is identified with private life, because it is the location of the home and because it shares the home's physical separation from the worlds of commerce and politics. Private life need not end with the enclosing walls of the house itself. Yards and decks that extend the private domain into the outdoors are very important to people, as are the entryways that mark transitions to the larger neighborhood. But while many people's private lives are contained within the neighborhood, they jointly occupy it and must somehow negotiate standards of behavior and maintain public order (Silverman 1983).

Public order is particularly important to neighborhood residents because of their expectations concerning privacy and the home. Neighbors, because they share boundaries with surrounding homes (including above and below if they are in an apartment building) pose the greatest threat to private life (Silverman 1983). The intrusions may not be deliberate: sound carries through walls, trees grow to block views, dogs or children unknowingly cross property lines. In other cases neighbors must somehow decide on the relative value and priority of, for example, one neighbor's added bedroom or the other neighbor's view of the bay.

Public life is a necessary, but quite difficult, part of living in a civilized society. People are interdependent, yet often disagree with each other. Indeed, in a free society it is inevitable that people will disagree with each other on some important things. As a result people must sustain their society by both cooperating with others who may see things differently from themselves and by being prepared to negotiate over their differences. The defining characteristics of public life are uncertainty over whether others will be in agreement and the need to be able to simultaneously cooperate and disagree.

It is not easy for people to live with uncertainty or with the potential for conflict with people who cannot be avoided. Jane Mansbridge, in *Beyond Adversary Democracy* (1980), has eloquently described the fear of conflict experienced by people in both a small New England town meeting and in small nonprofit organizations with participatory management. Disagreement, and even the possibility of disagreement, generate emotions, ranging from anger to fear of humiliation, which create problems for people who want to participate in public life. As individuals they must develop the ability to express themselves clearly despite their feelings, and as members of a community they hope to express disagreements without creating lasting rancor.

People are very aware of the harmful impacts that conflict can have on their day-to-day social relationships with neighbors or coworkers, whether the disagreement is in a formal decision-making process or simply in the informal negotiation of public life in its most local aspects. A San Francisco neighborhood leader defined a good neighbor as "somebody I can negotiate with about conflict over noise, space or whatever. That I can feel free to call up and I don't need to worry that it's going to escalate into something awful" (Barton 1985). While neighborhood conflicts rarely erupt into vandalism or violence, fear of "something awful" is pervasive, fueled by widespread knowledge of cases where something awful did in fact result from a neighbor conflict. Often the fear is so great that people avoid any direct contact with neighbors who do things they dislike (Baumgartner 1988; Sennet 1970; Silverman 1983).

To enable people to overcome the fear of conflict that pervades public life, people need the help of cultural traditions and institutions that enable them to understand public interaction with others and to safely participate in public life. In the line of thought that Robert Bellah and others call "civic republicanism," which runs from Aristotle to Jefferson to de Tocqueville and beyond, private property ownership is thought both to provide the resources to engage in public life and to protect private life from undue intrusions. In so doing, private property ownership supposedly creates a sense of personal responsibility that acts as a moderating and unifying force and enables property owners to engage successfully in public life.

It is partly for this reason that homeowners typically try to prevent the encroachments of higher density development that would bring renters, who do not own property, into their neighborhoods. Because they do not own, renters lack the leading societal symbol of personal responsibility. Homeowners believe that their shared interests as property owners mean that they can be relied on to follow societal norms of decent behavior and thus avoid conflict with one another (Perrin 1977). This exclusionary tendency within the civic republican tradition is a major difficulty in a heterogeneous, urbanized society.

The common interest development provides one means of organizing the relationship between private and public life in the neighborhood setting. Where residents of the traditional neighborhood must rely either on voluntary agreements or on local government, the common interest homeowners' association has a mixture of individual and collective private property rights designed to encompass many potentially difficult forms of interaction among neighbors. Before we examine the effectiveness of the common interest development in enabling people to deal with their interdependence, however, we need to explain property rights and look at a perspective that claims public life is virtually unnecessary.

PRIVATE PROPERTY AND THE EVASION OF PUBLIC LIFE

Property rights are a relation between people, establishing who has the legal right to use, control, and transfer scarce resources and determining the circumstances under which people may invoke the coercive powers of government to enforce these rights against claims by others. The process of establishing and defending the property right is public—without lawmaking and the courts there are no legal rights. The archetypical form of property, however, is private. Private property rights establish a boundary within which a private individual, association, or corporate person—the property owner—is free to act without hinderance from others in either their private or public roles. Within this boundary, individuals also are solely responsible for how they do or do not take care of the resources they control.

Property ownership involves bundles of rights and obligations that can be put together in many ways. A homeowner may be able to remodel or even tear down a house, while a few blocks a way, in a historic preservation district established by city ordinance, a similar house can be sold, rented, or remodeled inside but not changed on the outside. The owner of yet another house that is part of a common interest development may also be prevented from making exterior changes by conditions, covenants, and restrictions attached to the deed by a private developer. Another house may not be changed inside or outside, or even sold by the private, nonprofit preservation foundation that owns it.

Property rights are central to the social structure of modern societies, and particularly that of the United States. They are central to the economy—production and distribution will take place differently with different forms of property ownership, and widespread private property ownership is generally believed to result in a more efficient and productive economy. Property rights are central to politics—government action is continually required to establish any particular bundle of rights and obligations, and of course there are ongoing political struggles over the composition and distribution of those rights. And finally, property rights are central to American culture—valued, ironically, as the means by which private life is protected from intrusions by both government and the market economy.

There are major currents of thought that claim that altering property relations will enable society to eliminate the potential for legitimate conflict that creates the moral necessity for public life. Today, with the collapse of the Soviet Empire we have seen the collapse, in Europe at least, of one of those utopian visions—the idea that extensive government ownership of property would eliminate conflicting private interests based on private property ownership and replace them with a unifying public interest. Such a unified public interest would effectively eliminate the need for public life, other than to articulate the consensus. This effort to create consensus inevitably settled for the appearance of unity created through suppression of dissent, since differing interests and beliefs remain even if private property does not.

In the wake of that collapse, we are hearing with renewed vigor from proponents of the opposite utopian extreme—the idea that privatization of virtually all government functions will allow voluntary market transactions to satisfy the needs of private life and largely eliminate the need for public life. Government would be reduced to a caretaker role—the night-watchman state, whose function is the protection of private property rights.

There are two ways in which privatization could potentially eliminate the necessity of public life. Public life and collective decision making can certainly be eliminated by placing all of those people under one private authority structure in which they have no control or right to voice personal interests. This is the case, for example, within the private corporation, in which ownership is entirely separate from membership in the interdependent group of people that do the work of the corporation. There is an extensive literature on the corporation as a private government and the company town is a means of privatizing decision making on a territorial basis, but the private authoritarianism that is currently accepted in the workplace is not generally acceptable in the place of residence.

The ideal of a democratic republic of independent small property owners remains strong among proponents of private property-based political systems. In modern society this ideal is necessarily far removed from its preindustrial social base of farmers, craft workers, and merchants. Despite rhetoric about the continuing importance of small businesses, the ideal has not been adapted to the workplace conditions of industrialized societies, where work is typically under the control of the management of various sizes of corporations. Instead, the basis of the ideal has shifted from the workplace to the residence, and the main source of small property ownership is now homeownership (DeNeufville and Barton 1987; Perrin 1977).

Small property ownership by many people creates the need for some means of cooperation or coordination among them, since neighboring property owners, as they make use of their own property, often affect each others' property. Friedrich Hayek, author of the classic attack on planning in *The Road to Serfdom* (1944), created an exception for town planning in his subsequent *Constitution of Liberty* (1960) in order to deal with the interdependence of neighboring property owners. Land-use regulation, the most widespread form of local government planning in the United States, derives its broad political support from homeowners, the largest group of private property owners, who desire to control what their neighbors do with their property. If the irony of American socialism has been working-class hostility to government, then the irony of American capitalism is property owners' opposition to the free market, which they believe would result in unwanted changes in their neighborhoods unless carefully restrained.

Over the past two decades, however, conservative market-oriented policy institutes have promoted common interest homeowners' associations as a privatized vehicle for performing the functions of local government, including neighborhood protection through land-use regulation. (See, for example, Frazier 1980, 1989; Nelson 1989). Homeowners associations, in this view, provide a means of dealing with interdependence among property owners through private agreements, which remain entirely within the private sector. They thus offer the promise of a reduced role for government and an end to the conflict and tensions of political life.

There is a basic conceptual error in this free market utopia, however, as there is in the communist utopias. Both fail to distinguish between what we commonly call the public and private sectors, meaning government or nongovernment ownership of property, and the public and private domains of life. Just as the lack of private property ownership does not eliminate differences between private individuals, the lack of governmental decision making does not eliminate the need for and moral value of democratic choice among interdependent people. As we have seen, common interest developments have an abundance of public life, however awkwardly the residents may engage in it.

The libertarian, free-market perspective draws on a widely held belief that private property ownership does allow one to escape from interdependence with others. This is a very different perspective indeed from the role of private property ownership in the "civic republican" tradition, in which it was a tangible representation of both independent standing within the community and interdependence as a member of that community.

PRIVATE PROPERTY AND PUBLIC LIFE IN THE COMMON INTEREST DEVELOPMENT

The idea of the neighborhood as a basis for civic participation is a powerful one for people from a variety of intellectual and political persuasions. Within the current ecology of neighborhoods, coresidents are relatively homogeneous in terms of social class and political power. Unlike larger-scale political participation, in which appeals to unity and cooperation can mask profound social divisions and inequalities, neighborhood participation often does involve people who are relative equals. As coresidents, they are similarly affected by many actions of governments and private corporations and by the physical and social character of their residential space.

Morris Janowitz has argued that the "community of limited liability" is the normal form of voluntary neighborhood organization (1952, 1978). The community of limited liability is one among a "mosaic of overlapping boundaries" that allow people to decide between participation in "two or more competing communities" as "a voluntary choice among options rather than one prescribed on the basis of residence alone" (Suttles 1972, 59). In contrast, the common interest development has definite boundaries based on property lines, and its association membership is not voluntary but mandatory, though based on property ownership rather than residence. The common interest homeowners' association raises neighbors' interdependence from a fact of daily life to the level of formal organization and decision making. Our research shows the tension created by combining neighboring and political social relations into this form of organization.

Homeowners and condominium associations look a lot like neighborhood governments, rather than voluntary associations. They have the power to tax; they make and enforce rules; they own property; they provide public services, and they hold elections. This setting offers certain means to support public life. To begin with, there is the expectation of a homogeneous and relatively egalitarian community of private property owners, united in their belief in the value of private property ownership. This is not entirely true, of course. We have seen, from the California Common Interest Development Survey, that most of these homeowners' associations have a substantial minority of members who are absentee owners, with a corresponding number of residents who are not members. But it is rare that a great many units are held by one owner, so at least the association, if not the residents as a whole, is normally made up of people with relatively equal ownership interests.

Curtis Sproul has explained the mixed character of the common interest homeowners' association and shown that, while they have some of the characteristics of a local government, they are much more limited in scope. A major part of their function is the business of property management. Nonetheless, the property management function is not simply carried out to maximize profit. Rather it is carried out to meet the needs of the property owners, most of whom typically live in the development and are at least as concerned with the quality of life as with the eventual sales price or rental value of their home. This means that the association's objectives can only be decided on through discussion among the homeowners. As a result, the homeowners' association needs to meet basic democratic standards of openness, fairness, and responsiveness to its members.

The basic unity of an association of small property owners could be sufficient to enable people to participate in the decisions made by a homeowners' association. This participation would be made easier by the limited nature of association decision making, and it would also be strengthened by the exercise of free choice in the purchase of a home within the common interest development, which would screen out those who did not share similar values. An optimistic view of the common interest development, then, might be that it allows a relatively small and homogeneous group of people to deal with a very limited part of human interdependence in an accessible setting. In contrast, local government, which must deal with multiple and intransigent issues, can be overwhelming for people and thus discourages participation. But as Gregory Alexander's and our studies show, apathy and avoidance predominate instead, while frustration and occasional conflict lie just below the surface of the common interest community.

James Winokur has shown that the purchase decision rarely involves adequate understanding of the conditions that a common interest development places on residence. The model of the informed consumer choosing the mandatory homeowners' association and its detailed deed restrictions, the "servitude regime," fails to describe reality. The immediate reasons are buyers' normal lack of interest in standardized deed restrictions that vary little from one development to the next. The buyer is primarily concerned with the appearance and physical quality of their new home and neighborhood. If a mistake is made, however, it is not an easy matter to make a new choice, since it involves the very substantial financial and other costs of selling one's home and moving to a new neighborhood.

Winokur also suggests longer-range reasons for the inadequacy of the informed consumer choice model. People's ongoing personal development during the life cycle results in changing beliefs and desires that are hard to predict. From the standpoint of development of the whole person, then, the deliberative nature of a democratic process and the ability for a public to adapt their institutions are at least as important as the market's ability to aggregate current preferences. Like Sproul, Winokur finds the common interest association a potentially workable but flawed tool for collective decision making.

In common interest developments, at least part of what we usually think of as the "public sector" is privately owned, and politics takes place in a setting most closely identified with private life. The authors' case studies and personal interviews in California made it clear that the fact of private ownership in common interest communities had helped to obscure the interdependence among neighbors. Homeowners in common interest developments believed that the association was an extension of their ownership rights, giving them a right to certain services, among which was control over neighbors to prevent behaviors that might be harmful. Many residents did not see the association as creating reciprocal obligations along with rights. Instead, while they supported restrictions on their neighbors, they reacted with strong, negative emotions to apparent infringements on their own rights as private property owners. These residents treated the governing board of directors not as trustees of the public interest but as neighbors who had unfair powers over them. The reality of common interest communities is that common status as private property owners does not reduce and indeed intensifies conflicts within the community, as people assert their property rights against each other.

Robert Bellah and his associates, in *Habits of the Heart*, argued that the difficulty Americans have with public life stems from their supposed radical individualism and the lack of a language of civic commitment that can enable people to move beyond such individualism. Clearly, in common interest homeowners' associations privatization of the governing process reinforces individualistic and uncivic understandings of the situation. Like many proponents of privatization, owners in common interest developments often do not understand the difference between private ownership and private life. Indeed, they often seem to combine the negative aspects of both the civic and libertarian traditions, seeing property ownership as a basis for excluding renters from membership in their community, but seeing the community as something to be endured and avoided rather than valued.

Our findings of pervasive conflict and fear of conflict, accompanied by apathy and avoidance within the community, run counter to the normal picture of community organization. It is an almost universal assumption in the community organization literature that residents' sense of community will not only strengthen their ability to organize but also will strengthen their desire to control their own community (Boyte 1980). When common ownership of property strains residents' ability to cooperate and threatens the preservation of civility within the neighborhood, it seems that, instead, a strong sense of community could lead people to avoid taking actions to improve their own lives because this might result in conflicts among members of the community.

This is where we believe that Bellah and his associates are fundamentally wrong in their analysis of the lack of civic commitment in American society. It is true that many Americans lack a language of civic commitment and for this reason have difficulty understanding and valuing public life and are unlikely to support ideals of economic democracy that will create more of it. But public life is a difficult thing, and people can have a rich language of both civic and community life and still not want to expand the civic domain. In our studies of San Francisco Bay Area neighborhood leaders and residents, as well as of common interest homeowners' associations, we have found a wealth of examples of very rich civic language (Barton and Silverman 1987; Barton 1985; Silverman 1983). For these people the barriers to stronger support for collective ownership as a means to community control were not an inability to conceive of common civic commitment, but a very realistic understanding of the difficulties of public life.

Nor can American individualism be held responsible for the conflicts that exist in a wide range of other societies. Tsuneo Kajiura, in his description of the problems of condominiums in Japan, brings out many parallels, including widespread conflict between individual homeowners and the association. Similar problems show up in the Netherlands and in Israel, though Lazerwitz and Ginsberg suggest that in Israel they are reduced, not by a different culture but by lack of restrictive covenants to be enforced by the condominium management.

Changes in structure as well as understanding are essential to support public life. The case study by Heskin and Bandy shows what happens when individual profit motives, though not other individual sources of conflict, are removed from neighborhood governance. Intense conflicts do arise. In the case of conflicts over admission to the cooperative, equivalent conflicts scarcely even exist in condominiums, which rarely control sale of the units. In general, however, conflict resolution appears easier, because in a cooperative common ownership is more visible and understood, and in a limited-equity cooperative fears about property values are largely absent.

Jane Mansbridge argues that we can get "beyond adversary democracy" by creating political settings where people do not have vital interests at stake. The limited-equity cooperative removes one interest often considered vital, but certainly others necessarily remain. As neighbors and citizens people have what they perceive as vital interests at stake almost constantly in the ongoing and continuous work of keeping up the fabric of civility and cooperation. Financial investment may not be an issue, but the political struggle to define the content of residents' property rights, and with them neighborhood character, remains.

In the typical neighborhood ongoing conflict over the content of property rights, as the primary means to control neighborhood character, is fought out lot by lot, hearing after hearing, and election after election before the condominium or homeowners' association, the planning commission, or the city council. Often people from within the same neighborhood are on opposite sides, whether the issue is a tot lot, a subsidized housing project, expenditures for landscaping, or a treatment center for alcoholics. The neighbors involved can neither get "beyond" an adversarial situation nor accept a simple adversarial stance towards the other neighbors they must continue to live with. They need to sustain a public life that involves both cooperation and conflict.

While Heskin and Bandy's work is suggestive, it is not a sufficient basis to say that this progressive version of Jeffersonianism, removing economic gain from the place of residence or providing universal rights that broadly protect everyone's vital interests, is actually more successful in sustaining public life. We lack sufficient studies of conflict and conflict resolution in a variety of settings and among people with varied beliefs about property rights. While versions of Jeffersonian social theory are held by people throughout American society, it is remarkable how little empirical work has been done to verify aspects of the theory or to learn how to strengthen people's understanding of and ability to engage in public life.

Stanley Scott's argument with the large, exclusive planned development is that broader connections are needed between people throughout American society, a large minority of whom cannot afford to purchase their own homes, as well as between people within the same neighborhood. Scott's concern was that common interest developments would simply serve to create isolated and protected islands of higher-income homeowners, devoid of any concern for the institutions and quality of life in the rest of society. Certainly that has always been a tendency within American urban development, one that was at the very origin of the common interest development. Such economic segregation cannot provide the underpinnings for an adequate public life throughout American society, even if it were enough in certain neighborhoods. Our ironic conclusion, though, is that even the homogeneous neighborhood of private property owners is unable to avoid the necessity of public life and unlikely to provide sufficient understanding of public life that its residents will do well in meeting its challenges.

COMMON INTEREST DEVELOPMENTS AND THE PUBLIC INTEREST

The large increase in common interest developments is transforming the urban and suburban landscape in their social and political as well as physical dimensions. The consequences have not been sufficiently recognized. The dominant impulse among elected officials is to write such developments off as private—and not properly a subject for government concern. Yet, as we have argued, the common interest development is shaped in great detail by local and state government requirements. Inattention now will have consequences in the future as CIDs comprise ever-increasing percentages of residences in the United States.

These developments raise questions of equity. While services among neighborhoods have never been equal, tax dollars redistribute monies within a municipality, codes require minimum standards for construction of infrastructure, and municipal provision of services equalizes access. Common interest developments, in contrast, often provide their own services and infrastructure. More affluent developments are then able to subsidize much better provision. The less affluent ones, those least able to absorb the costs of major repairs, will be more likely to have lower quality streets, sewers, and the like. Furthermore, owners in common interest developments continue to pay local taxes, even as they provide their own services. This reduces their willingness to support local taxes and may even promote tax revolts.

As common interest developments foster inequities between neighborhoods, they foster increased dependence within the neighborhood. Members are financially dependent. When a owner is unable or unwilling to pay assessments, the remainder of the development must absorb the loss. Since defaults are more likely in lower-cost associations, people who have the least financial resources find themselves most affected by the misfortunes of their neighbors. Such developments also have the highest percentage of absentee owners. The combination of people who only have investment interests and people who cannot afford dues increases means that it is harder to get needed assessment increases through, affecting the finances and quality of life in the association for all.

However, the most insidious aspect of the common interest development is its potential effects on the political process in general. We are by no means prepared to say that the quality of public life in common interest developments is always inferior to public life in other settings. Indeed, we have good reason to think the quality of public life elsewhere is often very similar. Many small suburban towns seem little different from large homeowners' associations in the issues they deal with and in the way in which the councilmembers and citizens perceive the purposes of the city government. Thus the study of common interest developments may have implications for certain types of local governments as well.

Nonetheless, the common interest development differs from even a small town government in three significant ways. First, neighbors govern neighbors with no separation of powers between the people who make and enforce the laws and determine both guilt and punishment. In a common interest development the same person may write an architectural control, determine that a neighbor is violating it, and mete out the fine. In town government, that responsibility is split between the city council, the planning commission, the police, the public prosecutor, and the courts. Not only do boards have less legitimacy than their small town counterparts, this aforementioned absence of separation of powers leaves them open for both perceived and actual exercise of favoritism and abuse of powers. We have argued throughout this book that the absence of cultural understandings of shared property creates friction between board and membership. This friction is exacerbated by the unitary powers given the board.

Second, in a town representation is based on residence, not ownership. In common interest developments not only are residents who rent normally excluded from the governing process, but the entire governing process is based on private property ownership. The professionals who work for common interest developments do not see themselves as public servants but rather see the common interest development solely as a business that should be rationally managed. The management professionals who advise the associations' governing boards see the political aspects of the association as "people problems" that are an annoyance and impediment to getting the real work done. Differences among residents are perceived only as troublesome interference with the smooth operation of the association or, at best, as business for lawyers.

Finally, the governing board of common interest developments are quite literally the neighbors of the rest of the association. People cannot disagree and then physically separate to the extent that is possible in all except the very smallest towns. It is thus difficult to cool out differences through separation since people must see each other on a daily basis. "Just neighbors" are asked to take on governing responsibilities without a clear source of legitimacy. Their neighbors perceive their work as a process by which other people inappropriately interfere with individuals' rights to use property as desired.

None of this builds understanding of the necessity and legitimacy of public life. As a result of these differences from local government the common interest developments can fail to legitimize the political processes in the governing association and, by privatizing the process of adjudicating rights and responsibilities, the common interest development associations have the potential to further weaken people's understanding of public life. The necessity of public life in this "private" setting reveals the limits of privatization in local governance and underscores the importance of civic education and the development of civic institutions in these new settings where part of the public life of 30,000,000 Americans takes place.

REFERENCES

Barton, Stephen. 1985. *Property Rights and Democracy: The Beliefs of San Francisco Neighborhood Leaders and the American Liberal Tradition.* Berkeley, University of California Ph.D. dissertation.

_____, and Carol Silverman. 1987. *Common Interest Homeowners' Association Management Study.* Sacramento: California Department of Real Estate.

Baumgartner, M. P. 1988. *The Moral Order of a Suburb.* Oxford: Oxford University Press.

Bellah, Robert, Richard Madsen, William Sullivan, Ann Swidler, and Steven M. Tipton. 1985. *Habits of the Heart: Individualism and Commitment in American Life.* Berkeley: University of California Press.

Boyte, Harry C. 1980. *The Backyard Revolution: Understanding the New Citizens Movement.* Philadelphia: Temple University Press.

De Neufville, Judith I., and Stephen E. Barton. 1987. "Myths and the Definition of Policy Problems: An Exploration of Homeownership and Public-Private Partnerships." *Policy Sciences,* Vol. 20: 181-206.

Fischer, Claude. 1984. *The Urban Experience.* San Diego: Harcourt Brace Jovanovich.

Frazier, Mark. 1980. "Privatizing the City," *Policy Review* (Spring): 91-108.

_____. 1989. "Seeding Grass Roots Recovery: New Catalysts for Community Associations." In *Residential Community Associations: Private Governments in the Intergovernmental System?* Washington, D.C.: U.S. Advisory Commission on Intergovernmental Relations.

Hayek, Friedrich. 1944. *The Road to Serfdom.* London: Routledge & Sons.

_____. 1960. *The Constitution of Liberty.* Chicago: University of Chicago Press.

Janowitz, Morris. 1952. *The Community Press in an Urban Setting: The Social Elements of Urbanism.* Chicago: University of Chicago Press.

_____. 1978. *The Last Half-Century: Societal Change and Politics in America.* Chicago: University of Chicago Press.

Lane, Robert. 1962. *Political Ideology: Why the American Common Man Believes What He Does.* New York: The Free Press.

Mansbridge, Jane. 1980. *Beyond Adversary Democracy.* New York: Basic Books.

Nelson, Robert H.   1989.   "The Privatization of Local Government: From Zoning to RCAs."   In *Residential Community Associations: Private Governments in the Intergovernmental System?* Washington, D.C.: U.S. Advisory Commission on Intergovernmental Relations.

Perrin, Constance.   1977.   *Everything In Its Place: Social Order and Land Use in America.* Princeton, N.J.: Princeton University Press.

Sennet, Richard.   1970.   *The Uses of Disorder: Personal Identity and City Life.* New York: Random House.

Silverman, Carol.   1983.   *Neighbors and Neighbors: A Study in Negotiated Claim.* University of California Ph.D. dissertation, Berkeley.

Suttles, Gerald.   1972.   *The Social Construction of Communities.* Chicago: University of Chicago Press.

About the Authors

Gregory S. Alexander is Professor of Law at Cornell Law School. A former member of the law faculty at the University of Georgia, he has also taught at UCLA and the University of Virginia. He teaches and writes in the areas of property, American legal history and trusts and estates. He is the author of "Dilemmas of Group Autonomy: Residential Associations and Community," which appeared in the *Cornell Law Review* in 1990 and received the Community Associations Institute Foundation Research Award.

Dewey Bandy is an associate at the Center for Cooperatives at the University of California, Davis, where he coordinates programs in cooperative housing and rural development. He received a Ph.D. in urban planning from the University of California, Los Angeles. His primary interests are in the development of affordable cooperative housing and rural community development. He has conducted policy, sociological, and historical research on cooperatives and economic development.

Stephen E. Barton is a senior planner with the Community Development Department of the city of Berkeley. He has been a visiting lecturer in the Urban Studies Program at San Francisco State University and at the University of California, Berkeley, where he received his Ph.D. in city and regional planning. His primary interests are in urban policy, urban development, housing, and community organizations. He is the author of articles on tenant and neighborhood organizations, property rights, and urban policy. His *Common Interest Homeowners' Associations Management Study*, co-authored with Carol J. Silverman, won the Community Associations Institute (CAI) Foundation Research Award in 1987, and for the past five years he has been president of his condominium homeowners' association.

Yona Ginsberg received her M.A. in sociology at the Hebrew University of Jerusalem and her Ph.D. at Harvard. She is currently on the faculty of the sociology department at Bar-Ilan University, Israel. She is also a member of an interdisciplinary team preparing a master plan for the absorption and housing of over a million new immigrants for the Israeli government. Her research interests are urban sociology, housing problems, neighborhood and communities, gentrification and social policy. Many of her studies of condominiums have been sponsored by the Ministry of Construction and Housing of Israel.

Allan Heskin is a professor in the Urban Planning Program of the Graduate School of Architecture and Urban Planning at the University of California, Los Angeles. He is the author of the award winning book, *The Struggle for Community* (1991), which expands on the themes set forth in his chapter in this book. He is a 10-year resident of one of the cooperatives discussed in this chapter.

Tsuneo Kajiura is a professor in the Department of Housing and Design of the Faculty of Human Life Science at the Osaka City University. He received his Ph.D. in engineering from Kyoto University and is also a registered architect. He is also on the board of directors of the Apartment Maintenance Association and the West Japan Federation of Condominium Owners Associations. His areas of teaching include housing management, residential area planning, and house planning. His recent publications include *Condominium Management for Residents* (1988), and *New Town Development in Japan* (1984). He was awarded the Prize of the Architectural Institute of Japan for studies of condominium management in May 1994.

Bernard Lazerwitz is Professor Emeritus in the Department of Sociology at Bar-Ilan University, Israel. His current research interests deal with the characteristics and impact of North American migration to Israel; the influence of the Israeli condominium system upon social integration; and the sociological characteristics of denominational affiliations in the United States and Israel. He is currently writing a monograph on the denominational findings of the 1990 national survey of the American Jewish population and is a co-author of a book dealing with American migration to Australia and Israel.

Stanley Scott was a member of the administrative, editorial, and research staff of the Institute of Governmental Studies from 1947 until retirement in 1989. Over the years he wrote or co-authored a lengthy list of publications, including *Governing a Metropolitan Region: The San Francisco Bay Area* (1968) and *Governing California's Coast* (1975). In

development and the role of government, of which the *Public Affairs Report* article on local government and the homes association was one. After the Alaskan earthquake of 1964, and the San Fernando earthquake of 1971, his interests shifted to include seismic safety and public policy. He served for 18 years as a member of the California Seismic Safety Commission (1975-1993). His most recent publication on seismic policy is *California's Earthquake Safety Policy: A Twentieth Anniversary Perspective, 1969-1989* (1993). In retirement since 1989, he has continued a program of oral history interviews with older engineers, geologists, and other active participants in California's continuing effort to deal with the earthquake hazard.

Carol J. Silverman is Program Director at the Center for Self-Help Research in Berkeley, California, a collaborative research center between academics and leaders in the mental health self-help movement, which is concerned with self-help among the mentally disabled. She received her Ph.D. in sociology from the University of California, Berkeley, where she is also a visiting lecturer. Her research interests are in urban sociology, community and social networks, mental health and homelessness, research methodology, and social psychology. She has published articles on neighboring, community organization, and community associations. Her *Common Interest Homeowners' Associations Management Study*, co-authored with Stephen E. Barton, won the Community Associations Institute (CAI) Research Foundation Award in 1987.

Curtis C. Sproul is a partner in the Sacramento law firm of Weintraub Genshlea & Sproul. He received his A.B. degree from the University of California, Berkeley, in 1970 and his J.D. degree from Boalt Hall School of Law in 1973. He is currently a member of the State Bar Business Law Section Executive Committee and is a past chair of the Business Law Section Committee on Nonprofit Corporations and the State Bar Real Property Committee on Common Interest Developments. In 1984-85 he served as a member of the Legislative Task Force that drafted California's Davis-Stirling Common Interest Development Act. He is the co-author and editor of *The Law of Politics* (CEB 1977) and co-author of *Advising California Condominiums and Homeowners Associations* (CEB 1991) and *Advising California Nonprofit Corporations* (CEB 1984). He has written many articles on legal issues affecting common interest real estate developments, most recently "Common Interest Community

Associations and Their Management Structure," *California Real Property Journal* (1994).

Jan van Weesep is Professor of Urban Geography and Urban Policy at Utrecht University in the Netherlands. He is director of the urban research program of its Faculty of Geographical Sciences. His research interests cover the whole field of the geography of housing. For more than 10 years he has studied various aspects of condominium conversion in the Netherlands and the United States, beginning with his Ph.D. dissertation at Utrecht University on "Condominium: A New Housing Sector in the Netherlands." He was a European Research Fellow at Johns Hopkins University, where he worked on the topic of condominium conversions in the United States. He has published widely on urban development and urban social issues and is currently investigating gentrification in European cities. He recently co-edited *Government and Housing* (1990), *Urban Housing for the Better-Off: Gentrification in Europe* (1991), and *Residential Mobility and Social Change: Studies from Poland and the Netherlands* (1990).

James L. Winokur is Professor of Law at the University of Denver College of Law and special counsel with the Denver law firm of Holme Roberts & Owen. He is also a trustee of the national Community Associations Institute (CAI) and helped secure passage of the Colorado Common Interest Ownership Act of 1990. He graduated from the University of Pennsylvania Law School in 1969 after serving as editor of its *Law Review*. His current research focuses on private land-use restrictions and community associations. His article "The Mixed Blessings of Promissory Servitudes" in the *Wisconsin Law Review* won the CAI Research Foundation Award in 1989. He is the author of *American Property Law: Cases, History, Policy and Practice* (1982), and co-editor of a forthcoming volume on legal perspectives on community associations.